US Relations with Afghanistan and Pakistan
The Imperial Dimension

US Relations with Afghanistan and Pakistan
The Imperial Dimension

HAFEEZ MALIK

OXFORD
UNIVERSITY PRESS

OXFORD
UNIVERSITY PRESS

Great Clarendon Street, Oxford OX2 6DP

Oxford University Press is a department of the University of Oxford.
It furthers the University's objective of excellence in research, scholarship,
and education by publishing worldwide in

Oxford New York

Auckland Cape Town Dar es Salaam Hong Kong Karachi
Kuala Lumpur Madrid Melbourne Mexico City Nairobi
New Delhi Shanghai Taipei Toronto

with offices in

Argentina Austria Brazil Chile Czech Republic France Greece
Guatemala Hungary Italy Japan Poland Portugal Singapore
South Korea Switzerland Turkey Ukraine Vietnam

Oxford is a registered trade mark of Oxford University Press
in the UK and in certain other countries

ISBN 978-0-19-547523-4

Typeset in Times
Printed in Pakistan by
Pixel Grafix, Karachi.
Published by
Ameena Saiyid, Oxford University Press
No. 38, Sector 15, Korangi Industrial Area, PO Box 8214
Karachi-74900, Pakistan.

Dedicated with love to
my son Dean H. Malik,
his wife Jessica
and
their children
Maya, Adam and Sarah.

Contents

Preface

I

This is a multi-dimensional analysis of the United States' asymmetrical relations with Afghanistan and Pakistan since the rise and decline of the Taliban, and the ascendance of the Clinton and Bush administrations. This analysis includes in varying degrees, a discussion of the foreign policies of India and China and to a lesser extent Russia, as these impinge upon the development of relations between the United States, Afghanistan and Pakistan. Iran's role in South Asia is also considered.

The current phase of relations between these three states was spawned by the tragic events of 11 September 2001. The United States mainly held the Taliban and their collaborators of the Al-Qaeda movement led by Osama bin Laden responsible for this attack. I have not discussed the ideological aspects of Al-Qaeda in the analytical chapters, and the description of their ideology and structure is reserved for the concluding chapter which highlights in broad strokes the trajectories of their future developments.

While this study is the product of my many years of reflection and scholarship in world politics, it is not free from my personal orientation towards political realism, both as an academic of long standing and an erstwhile commentator for the Pakistani press in the late 1950s and early 1960s, when I was an accredited correspondent in the press corps of the White House in Washington, DC. This invaluable experience opened up the vistas of US power to my observation. I was able to observe especially how Presidents Dwight D. Eisenhower and John F. Kennedy made and executed foreign policies, and exercised the formidable power of the United States to contain the Soviet

Union, and curb the revolutionary zeal of the Peoples Republic of China. By 1956 the United States had replaced Britain and France as the reigning power in the Middle East, and it had extended its sway to the Far East, thereby becoming a guarantor of stability in Asia. Pakistan was roped into this new architectural design of security crafted by US power. Afghanistan chose to remain non-aligned, but moved close to the Soviet Union.

In dealing with United States power, I have accepted the view that the United States is not just the sole superpower in the hierarchy of states, but is in fact also an imperial system which practically regulates the affairs of the largest number of states in the world. However, I have maintained a distinction between the concepts of 'imperial system', and 'imperialistic policy of conquest'. The latter policy led the European powers in the eighteenth century to conquer weak states in order to exploit their natural resources and capture their economies where they could dump their surplus of goods, and invest their surplus capital. The 'imperial system' implies the role of a chief executive officer presiding over the management of the 'world corporation', with its designated board of directors, financial and political control, and maintenance of armed forces to keep refractory elements in control.

For the United States, the traditional areas of political-economic imperialism have been (a) Europe where NATO's enlargement after December 1991 established a new security framework; (b) the western hemisphere of 33 states stretching from Alaska to Argentina, where the initial steps were taken in December 1994 to create a free trade zone in the Americas (the inner core of this region was underlined by NAFTA linking the US, Canada and Mexico); and (c) the Middle East, where the success of the United States after Operation Desert Storm in 1990 internationalized Arab oil wells and consolidated the preeminence of Israel. The United States' security arrangement with Saudi Arabia, Egypt, the Gulf States and Israel became the linchpin of the region for American hegemony. (At times I have used hegemony as the near equivalent of 'imperial system' or simply the Latin term *imperium* and no pejorative connotation is implied or intended.)

In addition to the basic regional interest, the United States has also articulated, negatively as well as positively, its global role. In March 1992 a defense department planning document spelled out post-Cold War global strategy: 1) 'to prevent the reemergence of a new rival, either on the territory of the former Soviet Union, or elsewhere...,' 2) 'to prevent any hostile power from dominating a region whose resources would, under consolidated control, be sufficient to [its status] as a global power,' 3) to maintain the mechanism for deterring potential competitors from aspiring to a larger regional or global role.'

No clearer statement of the United States' option to play the roles of a regional and global leadership could have been made. This document and subsequent planning documents of the defense department singled out as potential threats, Japan in East Asia, India in the South, Germany in Europe and China at the global level. The European Union has not been mentioned in official documents either as a challenge or as a potential threat to US power, but knowledgeable non-official and influential members of the foreign policy community have certainly raised anxiety about the EU's potential challenge to the power of the United States. This issue, which is bound to be a matter of serious concern for the US establishment, has also been discussed in the concluding chapter.

Under the shadow of the United States, Russia's foreign policy since December 1991 has remained two-dimensional: irredentist and 'Soviet' oriented. Actually more sophisticated is the irredentist policy which draws the CIS countries to its fold in the name of historical determinism, economic interdependence, restoration of the single monetary system and collective security. In order to promote security of the CIS states under Russia's aegis, the Collective Security Treaty was signed in May 1992 in Tashkent. To restore and foster economic interdependence, an interstate Economic Committee was created in 1994, in which Russia possessed 50 per cent of the votes, Ukraine acquired

14 per cent, Belarus, Uzbekistan, and Kazakhstan received 5 per cent each, and Azerbaijan, Kyrgyzstan, Tajikistan and Georgia 3 per cent each.

However, after 9/11, Russia proposed to the United States that it would accept the United States' 'global leadership' if the US allowed Russia 'hegemonic responsibility for the former Soviet Union'. Offered from a position of weakness, this proposal 'was rejected by Washington, which was only prepared to discuss 'the rules of the road'. By 2005, according to one estimate, Russia started to act like the great power it was during the Tsarist period, it: 1) conducted its first-ever military exercises with China, and a smaller one with India; 2) welcomed Hamas leaders of Palestine to Moscow; and 3) squarely rejected the idea of imposing sanctions on Iran for its uranium-enrichment activities and decided that Russia would remain neutral should the United States decide to attack Iran. A Sino-Russian alliance at some point in the future cannot be completely ruled out.

Because of China's 'peaceful developmental policy', it has adopted a regional policy, and has laid no claims to global leadership. In February 1992 the National People's Congress issued a law on China's territorial waters and contiguous areas, and thus laid claim to 80 per cent of the South China Sea with a boundary that runs the length of Vietnam's coastline and then swings to waters off Malaysia, Brunei and the Philippines (nearly 90 per cent of Japan's crude oil imports traverse this area). China also declared unofficially the Spratly Islands a 'sacred and inviolable part of Chinese territory'.

In addition to China's regional interests in Southeast Asia, China has firmed up its economic and military relations with Pakistan, a state in South Asia. Also Pakistan is linked through the Karakoram Highway to China via Xinjiang, which is another assuring element to its security vis-à-vis India. China has also assured itself that Pakistan will remain benignly neutral toward China should there be a Chechnya-type movement for self-determination in landlocked Xinjiang, a Muslim-Turkic region likely to invoke Pakistan's sentiments of Islamic solidarity.

In early 2006, Pakistan signed thirteen agreements with China further strengthening the bonds of strategic partnership with China. Notable among these agreements were the defence and nuclear energy pacts in addition to a $350 million loan to buy Chinese goods. China also committed itself to upgrade the Karakoram Highway, which was badly damaged by the earthquakes in 2005. Other agreements covered expanding economic ties, cooperative endeavours in health, trade, meteorological research and help to Pakistan in providing vocational training. Pakistan also sought Chinese assistance in constructing a gas pipeline from the newly developing port of Gwadar in Balochistan province to western China. This facility could also provide China with a shorter and more economical route for its oil supplies from the gulf region.

India is determined to play a leading role in South Asia, especially in Sri Lanka, the Himalayan states of Nepal and Bhutan, Afghanistan and if possible Pakistan (Afghanistan was almost a Soviet and Indian 'ally' before 1979). If Russia managed to turn Tajikistan (a state which is very narrowly separated from Pakistan by the Wakhan Corridor of Afghanistan) into its protectorate, or India made Tajikistan into its surrogate, Pakistan's security would be in jeopardy.

However, the United States' current fascination with India is driven by its policy of strengthening India to be a potential counterweight to the rising power of China. In addition to the very sober calculation for this policy of the Bush administration, there are elements of fascination with the Indian political culture and its fairly impressive economic development: 1) India's middle class numbers 300 million, and it keeps growing annually; 2) its scientific engineering achievement is reflected in India's three hundred universities. India graduates more engineers in one southern state than the United States does as a whole country; 3) India has a large and developed financial sector, which is well-regulated and supervised; 4) its savings rates of 29 per cent of GDP are rising and are impressive; 5) Indian investment flows, a measure of confidence in its economy, run at about $10 billion a year. In 2006 they have been in excess of $1 billion a month; 6) India has become a big buyer of US aircrafts. In 2005–2006 India placed about $15 billion of orders for the purchase of Boeing aircrafts.

Last but not least is the US admiration for India's 'true and functioning democracy', which enabled India to forge 'a nation from extraordinary diversity'. The United States sees Indian democracy as 'an important bedrock' of its relationship with India. While in most countries President Bush's popularity hit rock bottom in 2005–2006, in India it remained considerably higher, and 71 per cent Indians approved of the United States. The US perceives to the credit of Indian democracy and its diversity the presence of 150 million Muslims, both Sunni and Shia, as 'non-radicalized and fully engaged in India's democracy'.

In 2006, the US signed 'a comprehensive open skies agreement' with India, the details of which are not fully known, but it was billed 'as the most liberal and open agreement in the world'. In June 2005, the US signed 'the new framework for US–India defence relationship' which included a programme 'for defense co-production and industrial participation in projects in India,' and established a 'new defense and procurement and production' programme under the supervision of the Indian Cabinet.

The Bush administration repeatedly emphasized that the US must 'look at India in a new light'. What is the new light? Clearly it is the rising power of China. From two different perspectives both China and the United States have urged Pakistan to normalize its relations with India, and resolve the Kashmir dispute by peaceful means. However, this dispute in the long run is very likely to damage Pakistan's national and economic development by engaging in a prolonged and unequal race with India for weapons and military preparedness—all in the name of Kashmir's self-determination.

In its current phase of relations US foreign policy toward India is driven by long term collaboration with India to enable it to be a counter-weight to the power of China. In its relations with Pakistan it is motivated by its determination to fight a protracted war against the al-Qaeda militants and the resurgent Taliban. Precisely for this reason Pakistan was declared a non-NATO ally, and it received $3.7 billion for counter-terrorism operations during January 2002–August 2005. In addition Pakistan expected to receive $900 million during 2006, and another $739 million in 2007. Moreover, Pakistan was paid $1.1 billion in 2005 from the United States for the logistical support it provided to US counter-terrorism operations, and its own military operations in Waziristan and other tribal areas.

By the end of 2007, Pakistan had received $10.5 billion; 60 per cent of the money was intended for the war on terror; 15 per cent or about $1.6 billion was for security assistance. Pakistan bought major weapons systems for this amount. Another 15 per cent was for budget support. About 10 per cent of US funds were for development and humanitarian assistance. (Craig Cohen, *A Perilous Course: US Strategy and Assistance to Pakistan* Washington, DC: CSIS, August 2007)

How long this type of relationship will last between the United States and Pakistan is very difficult to determine. However, the asymmetrical warfare in Afghanistan between the United States (and NATO forces) and the Taliban is expected to last between 5-10 years, which would keep the United States engaged with Pakistan.

II

In closing these introductory reflections it is my delightful obligation to express appreciation for the support of Villanova University which has not only been an intellectual haven for me, but it has also generously supported, for the last thirty years, the *Journal of South Asian and Middle Eastern Studies*, the Pakistan-American Foundation, and the American Institute of Pakistan Studies, which have also received generous support from the

Ministry of Education of the Government of Pakistan. I am equally indebted to Fr. Peter Donahue (President), Dr John R. Johannes (Vice President of Academic Affairs), and Fr. Kail C. Ellis (Dean of Arts and Sciences, and Founder-Director of the Center for Contemporary Arab and Islamic Studies) of Villanova University.

A colleague at Villanova University, my wife, Lynda P. Malik, a sociologist specializing on Islamic societies, was supportive and helpful in many ways. I have remained deeply appreciative of her endeavours in support of my scholarly activities. Among my friends, I single out Nadia Barsoum, who helped me in many ways to make this publication a successful enterprise. Some of my friends, both in the United States and abroad, have always been a source of encouragement and support: Muhammad Rafiq Tarar, my childhood friend, (who later became the President of Pakistan for three years), the late Yuri V. Gankovsky, Afak Haydar, Jack Schrems, Zaheer Chaudhry, Kamran Khan, Stanley Wolpert, the late M. Imtiaz Ali, Igor V. Khalevinsky, Vyacheslav Ya. Belokrinitsky, Anwar Aziz Chaudhry, the late Ralph Braibanti, Riaz Ahmad, Nasim Hassan, Sharif Faruq, Syed Jamil Shah, Sharif al-Mujahid, (Akhuna) Khalil Ilyas, Jawahirah and Rashid Makhdoomi, Aiyesha and Muhammad Latib, and the late Syed Abid Ali, and his devoted wife, Naznin Syed.

Special mention must be made of three very dear families— Sadaqat Gul and Waqar Asim Mansuri; Nasira and Javid Iqbal; and Nuria and Walid Iqbal, the latter graduated from the position of a 'nephew' to a dear friend. I value their friendship and cherish their affection. A dynamic educator in her own time, Amina (Begum) Majeed Malik, my aunt, was a source of inspiration, and was always admiringly supportive of my endeavours.

Dr Hafeez Malik
Professor of Political Science
Villanova University

1

Introduction

This is an analytical study of asymmetrical relations between the US, Afghanistan, and Pakistan which can be meaningfully understood only in the context of the imperial system which the US has maintained since 1945. The preeminence of the US in the global hierarchy of power was thrown into sharp relief when the Soviet Union collapsed in December 1991 under the weight of its own societal contradictions.

The exercise of power implies the ability to control the minds and actions of other nations and their leaders. In broad strokes, US relations with Afghanistan and Pakistan are described within this conceptual framework. While the thrust is primarily analytical, an attempt is also made to offer plausible policy options which a secondary regional power like Pakistan and a small state like Afghanistan could adapt to deal with the complexities of the global system which the US expected to lead during most of the twenty-first century.

I

If the true nature of imperialism as a policy is to overthrow the status quo and replace it with a new world order and to function as the primary guarantor of order for the international system, then to describe US policy as an imperial system is quite appropriate. This imperial system is not in pursuit of colonies or annexation of new lands to its existing territory. In the absence of any countervailing power the US is determined to remain a guarantor of international security, economic relations, and trade patterns between states.

In politics the US encourages the spread of democracy, regime change in dictatorial states, human rights, and the outlawing of genocide. Economic relations are also regulated by an international market which sets standards agreeable to the United States, urging governments to adopt policies and procedures for privatization, reductions in government subsidies, bank regulation (which ties the international banking system to that of the US) and encouraging foreign investments and a free flow of capital. Organized primarily by the US the World Trade Organization is a mechanism, under US supervision, for resolving trade disputes, and establishing 'fair' trade practices.

In contemplating these developments Richard Haass, a member of the US National Security Council, stated in 2000 that to be successful US policy would

> require that Americans reconceive their role from one of a traditional nation-state to an imperial power...To advocate an imperial foreign policy is to call for a foreign policy that attempts to organize the world along certain principles affecting relations between states and conditions within them. The US role would resemble 19th century Great Britain. Influence would reflect the appeal of American culture, the strength of the American economy and the attractiveness of the norms...

Haass published those views in the *Foreign Affairs* journal of September 1999, and publicly expressed them at the Atlanta Conference on 11 November 2000.[1] Four years later the well-known scholar Michael Ignatieff expressed the same opinion:

> America's empire is not like empires of times past, built on colonies, conquests and the white man's burden...The 21st century *imperium* is a new invention in the annals of political science, an empire lite, a global hegemony whose grace notes are free markets, human rights and democracy, enforced by the most awesome military power the world has ever known.[2]

The US has engaged in territorial expansion, by lease, by purchase, or by conquest. In less than a century and a quarter the US developed from thirteen coastal Atlantic states into a continental state with possessions in the far Pacific. The Louisiana Purchase in 1803 was followed by further acquisitions in 1845 (the annexation of Texas), in 1846 (the occupation of Oregon), the conquest of upper California, Nevada, Arizona, New Mexico in 1848, the Gadsen Purchase in 1853, and the purchase of Alaska in 1867. In 1898, the US annexed Hawaii (after arranging the abdication of Hawaiian sovereign, Queen Liliuokalani), and demanded the Philippines from Spain. President William McKinley (1896–1900) had an overnight epiphany to justify this territorial acquisition. He said:

> I walked the floor of the White House night after night until midnight; and I am not ashamed to tell you, gentlemen, that I went down on my knees and prayed Almighty God for light and guidance more that one night. And one night late it came to me this way – I don't know how it was, but it came:
> (1) That we could not turn them over to France or Germany – our commercial rivals in the Orient – that would be bad business and discreditable; [*economic nationalism*]
> (2) That we could not leave them to themselves – they were unfit for self-government – and they would soon have anarchy and misrule worse than Spain's was; [*racial superiority*]
> (3) That there was nothing left for us to do but take them all, and to educate the Filipinos, and uplift and civilize and Christianize them as our fellow-men for whom Christ also died. [*Altruism, the 'white man's burden' and missionary zeal. The Filipinos, by the way, were already Christians, Roman Catholics, with the exception of a small number of Muslim tribesmen.*]
> And then I went to bed, and went to sleep, and slept soundly.[3]

The purchase of Alaska from Russia in 1897 was a most fascinating tale of geostrategic considerations and good economics. That vast north-west corner of North America cost the US two cents an acre and totalled $7.2 million. To Russia the region had become an economic liability, and it was too far from the Russian heartland to be militarily defensible. Since Russia made the offer, Alaska as an American colony would be a buffer between Russian Siberia and British Canada. Three respected historians of the US David Burner, Virginia Bernhard and Stanley I. Kutler in their well-known study of American history stated that 'William Seward [Secretary of State], with the annexation of all Canada also in mind, quickly accepted'[4] the Russian offer and Russia formally transferred the territory.

By the nineteenth century the US had established itself as the pre-eminent power in the Americas, claiming to be the guardian and protector of all Latin American states. This role had been made explicit by the proclamation of the Monroe Doctrine in 1823, which the Secretary of State Hughes claimed was 'a policy of national self-defence'. The idea was reiterated by President Monroe in his message to Congress on 21 December 1823: 'We should consider any attempt on their [the European powers'] part to extend their system to any portion of this hemisphere as dangerous to our peace and safety'.[5]

The Monroe Doctrine contained a pledge and a warning: a pledge not to interfere with the existing European colonies in America; a warning that the US would resist with force of arms any attempt to gain new colonies in America, or to re-conquer the independent Latin American states. Between 1823 and 1898 there were breaches of the Monroe Doctrine on both sides, but the firm attitude of the US prevailed and the Latin American states were kept within the sphere of influence of the United States. In this period the US also employed methods similar to those of classical imperialism, reflecting prior European and Roman techniques.

Several illustrations may be offered: First, the Venezuela Boundary Affair of 1895, which developed out of a frontier dispute between Venezuela and British Guiana. Britain refused arbitration to settle this dispute. US Secretary of State Olney sent a note to London, which only an 'Emperor' would have drafted. The note warned that any extension of Guiana frontier would be a violation of the Monroe Doctrine, and that 'today the United

States is practically sovereign on this continent, and its fiat is law upon the subjects to which it confines its interposition'.[6]

This dispatch has been called the Olney Doctrine.

The British Foreign Secretary politely attempted to controvert this imperial dispatch; in retaliation US President Cleveland sent a special message of threat which could hardly be described as veiled. Britain retreated and accepted arbitration.

Further illustrations are the Lodge Resolution passed by the US Senate (but not approved by President Taft) in 1912, and President Theodore Roosevelt's famous declaration in 1904. The Lodge Resolution declared that the US could not permit the lease or concession of strategic harbours in America to foreign corporations. Roosevelt declared:

Chronic wrong doing, or an impotence which results in general loosening of the ties of civilized society, may in America, as elsewhere, ultimately require intervention by some civilized nation, and in the western hemisphere the adherence of the United States to the Monroe Doctrine may force the United States, however reluctantly, in flagrant cases of wrongdoing or impotence, to the exercise of an international police power.[7]

In the 1920s Professor Thomas Moon, a Columbia University specialist in international politics, in contemplating the territorial expansion of the American 'colonial empire' stated that it contained 'over 700,000 square miles in area with a population of almost 13,000,000 and a commerce of almost $700,000,000'. He estimated that 'it ranks ninth in area and seventh in population, but fifth in commerce', and illustrated these estimates in the following table:

Table 1: 'The Colonial Empire of the United States'

	Area (Square miles)	Population	Commerce + (dollars)
I. OUTLYING TERRITORIES			
Alaska	590,884	60,000	88,905,000
Hawaii	6,449	307,000	188,541,000
II. DEPENDENCIES			
Philippine Islands	115,026	11,076,000	243,356,000
Puerto Rico	3,435	1,347,000	172,478,000
Virgin Islands*	132	26,000	2,559,000*
Samoa*	58	8,000	294,000*
Guam	210	13,000	967,000
Wake and Midway Islands	29	X	X
III. LEASED TERRITORY			
Panama Canal Zone, Guantanamo, Fonesca Bay, Corn Island			
	527	27,000	
Total possessions	716,750	12,864,000	697,100,000
IV. NOMINALLY INDEPENDENT DEPENDENCIES			
Cuba	44,164	3,369,000	724,595,000
Haiti	11,072	2,045,000	28,872,000
Dominican Republic	19,325	897,000	51,843,000
Panama	33,667	443,000	16,250,000
Nicaragua	49,200	638,000	21,797,000
Liberia	36,834	1,500,000	2,528,000*
Total nominally independent dependencies	194,262	8,892,000	845,885,000
Grand total	911,012	21,756,000	1,542,985,000

*1923
**1924, *Commerce Year Book*

Source: Parker Thomas Moon, *Imperialism and World Politics* (New York: The Macmillan Company, 1937), p. 524.

For the fourth category of states, which Professor Moon described as 'nominally independent dependencies', he offered the following explanation:

But if Canada is part of the British Empire, and if Egypt and Iraq are under British control, then by the same standards Cuba, Haiti, the Dominican Republic, Panama, and Nicaragua are to be reckoned as falling in some degree under control of the United States, for they are subject to military intervention, which

Canada is not; their foreign affairs are to some extent submitted to American guidance, or at least to American veto; their economic life is in considerable measure under American supervision; and they are protected against non-American encroachment quite as genuinely as any French or British protectorate. Liberia may perhaps be added to the list, without serious dispute...we obtain a grand total that will put the United States colonial empire in sixth place for area, and for population and in second place for commercial value.[8]

'For a non-aggressive nation', Professor Moon asserted, 'the United States has done remarkably well, as compared with rivals candidly intent on imperial expansion. Only Great Britain has done better.'

II

The US won a military victory over Spain and expelled it from Cuba and Puerto Rico in 1898. The US also acquired control of the Panama Canal in 1903. These acquisitions gave the US unprecedented power in the Caribbean, while the Open Door policy of 1899 and the Root-Takahira Agreement of 1906 guaranteed US access to China. As the nineteenth century ended, Americans now joined the great imperial powers of Europe which had established a Eurocentric balance of power. This balance of power, which had developed at the end of Napoleonic wars, was dominated by five major powers (Great Britain, France, Russia, Austria and Prussia) and four secondary states (or empires) including Portugal, Spain, Holland and Sweden.

Established in 1815, this balance of power lasted until 1939, when Prussia (as a new German state) destroyed it by in a sense defeating France and Britain. Almost immediately after the Second World War, Britain and France lost their empires and fell to the status of secondary states in Europe. The real victors were the Soviet Union and the United States of America.

This new bi-polar system of power functioned fairly successfully until December 1991, when the Soviet Union collapsed. Almost immediately President George H. W. Bush proclaimed the dawn of a new unipolar world order. With the help of the US the European Community and other transnational institutions such as multinational corporations, the World Trade Organization, the International Monetary Fund, and the World Bank, this new world order would shape the new diplomatic system and when the chips fell, the military power of the US and NATO. These institutions are the instruments of the *pax Americana*, which functions fairly effectively under US leadership.

The history of ancient Rome revealed that imperial systems or policies always need an ideology. In the words of Professor Hans J. Morgenthau 'the dynamic quality of imperialism requires dynamic ideologies'.[9] No European state could ever forget that its model, the Roman Empire, had been founded as much upon glory as upon *pietas* – honour, piety and arms, which were inseparable. In Europe as in the US the conquest of weak people or states was explained as 'the white man's burden', 'the national mission', 'the sacred trust', 'the Christian duty'. In the US it was the 'manifest destiny', 'national honour', 'economic nationalism', and 'racial superiority' which were invoked to justify territorial acquisition. Moreover the US developed a distinct political culture, which is noted for American exceptionalism—the belief that the US is not just different from, but is better than other states. The exceptionalist view of America as of any other country, includes the notion of democracy's superiority, the penchant for political moralism, and the urge to justify political agenda and actions in moral terms and to judge other states' policies against American normative values. Especially since 1945, human rights have been the centrepiece of US foreign policy toward those states which are deemed to be in a challenging mode. In addition to these values US political culture spawned the belief in *laissez-faire* capitalism, free trade, and last but not least, messianism, that is the irresistible urge to mould the world in the American image[10] and to spread American cultural values, even if they subverted the cultures of other nations.

Since 1945 US foreign policy has been based on an amalgam of normative values and pragmaticism, but whenever there has been a clash between the national interest and moral values, the pragmatic approach has prevailed. In the light of this historic tension one should examine Professor Michael J. Sullivan III's thesis that the 'primary strategic goal of the United States since 1945 has been to supplant the major imperial powers of the pre-World War II era—United Kingdom, France, Germany and Japan—as the sole economic hegemon of the global capitalist system'.[11] A well-known foreign policy scholar at the Council of Foreign Relations, Walter Russell Mead, stated the same proposition as an elegantly defensive and unavoidable option for the US:

> In the 20th century, as the British system of empire and commerce weakened and fell, US foreign policy makers faced three possible choices; prop up the British Empire, ignore the problem and let the rest of the world go about its business, or replace Britain and take on the dirty job of enforcing a world order...the United States tried all three, ultimately taking Britain's place as the gyroscope of world order.[12]

From 1945 to 1999 Sullivan examined thirty cases of US's interventions in Latin America and the Caribbean, East Asia, the Middle East, and southern Europe. Some interventions are well known, and some less:

30 Cases Divided by Familiarity

Famous (Familiar Cases)	Obscure (Less Familiar Cases)
1. Greece – 1947-49	1. Italy – 1948 election rigging
2. Iran – 1953 CIA Coup	2. Philippines – 1946-53 counterinsurgency
3. Guatemala – 1954 government overthrow	3. Congo – 1961-65 civil war
4. Lebanon – 1958 military intervention	4. British Guiana – 1961-65 independence delay
5. South Vietnam – 1961-65 aid, coup, deceit	5. Laos – 1961-73 secret war
6. Cuba – 1961 Bay of Pigs invasion	6. Brazil – 1964 coup
7. Dominican Republic – 1965 military intervention	7. Indonesia – 1965-66 year of living dangerously
8. Cambodia – 1970 incursion	8. Kurdistan – 1971-75 missionary work
9. Chile – 1973 overthrow of the government	9. Angola – 1975 civil war
10. Nicaragua – 1981-88 contra war	10. Australia – 1975 parliament government ouster
11. Grenada – 1983 rescue of students	11. East Timor – 1975 genocide
12 Panama – 1989 drug lord capture	12 El Salvador – 1979-92 counterinsurgency
13. Iraq – 1991 liberation of Kuwait	13. Afghanistan – 1981-1988 support for *jihad*
14 Haiti – 1994 reinstall democratic government	14 Libya – 1981-86 bombings
15. Yugoslavia – 1995 Bosnia and 1999 Kosovo	15. Somalia – 1992-94 nation building

Sullivan *American Adventurism Abroad* p. 3.

The following table explains the imperial powers replaced, and the causal factors for the regime changes.

	a. Strategic (ex-colonial power replaced)	b. Economic (capitalism>democracy; non-democratic political form promoted)
1. Greece 1947-49	UK	Monarchists and fascists supported along with democrats; but only military in 1967-74
2. Italy 1948	Germany; (+UK, SU, '43)	1-CDP Party dominant government, 1948-93
3. Philippines 1946-53	–	CIA-influenced elections, 1953-62; Marcos dictatorship, 1972-86
4. Iran 1953	UK, Russia	Absolute monarchy of Shah Mohammed Reza Pahlavi, 1953-79
5. Guatemala 1954	–	Military dictators, 1959-85; Dulles law firm & United Fruit Co. key actors in 1954 coup
6. Lebanon 1958	France (+UK in. Suez)	Ethnic-based managed democracy keeps capitalism in Christian control for 17 more years
7. Congo 1961-65	Belgium	Mobutu military dictatorship, 1965-97, yields klepto-capitalism
8. Cuba 1961	(defends Vs. USSR)	n.a. (US unsuccessful)
9. British Guiana 1961-66	UK	Ethnic-minority 1-party dominant government, 1966-92
10. Laos 1961-73	France	Troika neutralist government has few democrats
11. South Vietnam 1961-65	France	Diem and later military dictators (Ky, Thieu) protect (primarily French) capital, 1954-75
12. Brazil 1964	–	Military dictatorships, 1965-85; capitalist 'economic miracle'
13. Dominican Republic	–	Civil war to restore crony capitalist Balaguer, 22 of next 30 years (over elected social democrat Bosch)
14. Indonesia 1965	Netherlands	Suharto military dictatorship, 1966-98; crony capitalism
15. Cambodia 1970	France	Lon Nol military dictatorship, 1970-75; provokes civil war that brings Khmer Rouge genocide

16. Kurdistan 1971-75	UK, Russia (see #4)	Shah of Iran, civil war in Iraq, preferred over self-determination (democracy) for Kurds
17. Chile 1973	–	Pinochet military dictatorship, 1973-89; alleged 'economic miracle'
18. Angola 1975	Portugal	Civil war, from November 1975 independence until November 2001 death of Savimbi
19. Australia 1975	UK	Elected government ousted, parliamentary democracy undermined, for US 'security' interests
20. East Timor 1975	Portugal	Indonesian 'colony' preferred over self-determination (democracy) for Timorese
21. El-Salvador 1979-1991	–	'progressive' juntas and 'demonstration-elections' democracy
22. Nicaragua 1981-88	–	Civil war 1981-88; subversion of 1984 election
23. Grenada 1983	UK	n.a. (quick, one year, transition to democracy)
24. Libya 1981, 1986	Italy, UK, USSR	n.a. (US unsuccessful)
25. Afghanistan 1980-88	Russia, UK	Civil war visited upon pre-industrial economy, 1980-88
26. Panama 1989	–	n.a. (democracy restored after drug thug Noriega tolerated, 1981-89)
27. Iraq 1991	UK	Kuwait monarchy upheld for Western capitalism
28. Somalia 1992-94	UK, Italy; USSR	n.a. (US unsuccessful; civil war not ended in pre-industrial economy)
29. Haiti 1994	–	Aristide's full term cut to make way for pliant Preval
30. Yugoslavia 1995, 1999	USSR/Russia	Ethnically partitioned, one-party nationalist governments welcoming capitalist reconstruction

– = not applicable (W. Hemisphere, Philippine Islands
n.a. = not applicable (n=5: Cuba, Grenada, Libya, Panama, Somalia)

Sullivan *American Adventurism Abroad* p. 5.

To this analysis of invasions, interventions, and regime changes since World War II, might be added the invasions of Afghanistan and Iraq for the purpose of regime change. The Al Qaeda-inspired terrorist attacks on the Pentagon and World Trade Centre on 11 September 2001 have spawned a new culture of fear in the US which led to an invasion of Afghanistan. The Taliban regime's close alliance with Al Qaeda's leader, Osama bin Laden, was well known, and needed no elaborate description. However, this culture of fear also means that in the US international problems are inflated, a self-righteous moralistic approach has taken hold of the policymakers, and new challenges are transformed into existential issues of survival. There is

> no corner of the known world where [America] is not alleged to be in danger or under attack. If the interests are not [American], they are those of [America's] allies; and if [America] has no allies, then allies are to be invented. When it is utterly impossible to contrive such an interest—why, then it is the national honor that has been insulted. The fight is always invested with an aura of legality. [America] is always being attacked by evil minded people, always fighting for peace. The whole world is pervaded by a host of enemies, and it is manifestly [America's] duty to guard against their indubitably aggressive designs.[13]

While this description of US relations with other powers is quite appropriate to contemporary conditions, I have utilized Joseph Schumpeter's language (for the description of Roman policies) with some tense and name changes to highlight the general orientation of US foreign policy. And it is against this orientation that one can understand US relations with Afghanistan and Pakistan. However, for a meaningful analysis, the role of two great Asian powers—China and India—cannot be ignored. The United States' grand strategy for Asia for the foreseeable future will revolve around China and India, with Pakistan and Afghanistan roped in to support US's policies.

The US establishment finds that armed conflicts such as those which are a matter of choice like Iraq, or those which are thrust upon the US like Afghanistan, are quite affordable as measured by their percentage of the gross domestic product as well as for their portion of the federal budget. There is no other country which can make the affordability claim for war.

Military expenditures in the US are rising in absolute terms and as a proportion of total economic activity as measured by the GDP. Total Department of Defence expenditures grew from $281 billion in the fiscal year 2000 to $436 billion in the fiscal year 2004. The national defence portion of the GDP rose from 3.8 per cent in the calendar year 2000 to 4.4 per cent in 2004. The conduct of war invariably exerts pressures on the military budget, as was the case during the Gulf, Korean, and Vietnam wars, and especially during World War I and World War II. When World War II was at its peak, military outlays equalled about 35 per cent of GDP, during the Korean War approximately 15 per cent, Vietnam War 10 per cent, and the Gulf War 6 per cent. In 2005 the ratio was 4.4 per cent.

For an economy of the United States' size, 4.4 per cent of the national output is by no means an unacceptable burden, especially when it provides employment to 1,500,000 men and women in the US armed services.[14]

III

Two hundred years ago Napoleon in a flash of intuition made a prediction about China: 'There lies a sleeping giant. Let him sleep; for when he wakes he will move the world.' Today the giant lion is asleep no more, and that is a source of anxiety for the United States.

I attended a seminar in June 2006 at the National Defence University, a Joint Chiefs of Staff-sponsored institution that includes the Industrial College of the Armed Forces and the National War College. Other participants included military officers above the rank of colonel, employees of several US intelligence agencies, private think tanks, and some faculty members like myself. This very well-informed group of participants unanimously agreed with an assessment of the Department of Defence that 'China's rapid rise as a regional political and economic power with global aspirations is an important element in today's strategic environment—one that has significant implications for the region and the world'.[15]

Central to the discussions was a very sharply articulated question: would China be a responsible stakeholder in the international political and economic system which the United States had established since 1945 or would it create a countervailing force to US power? No definitive answer could be given, but scholars have advanced arguments to support both positive and negative probabilities.

While the US has pursued a policy of engagement with China, the real policy appears to reflect a hedging strategy, just in case it confronts a negative scenario in dealing with China in the medium-term future. The US government's suspicion of Chinese intentions is reflected in its claim that China's military budget is not transparent. In 2006 China announced that it would increase its publicly disclosed military budget by 14.7 per cent, to approximately $35 billion. According to the US Department of Defence 'the officially published figures substantially under reported actual expenditures'. In reality the US maintains China's spending 'amounts to between $70 billion and $106 billion in 2006—two to three times the announced budget'.[16]

China's economy has been boosted by $50 billion a year in foreign direct investment (FDI), receiving $622.3 billion as of the end of 2005. During the last twenty years its economy has grown at the rate of 8.6 per cent, while in the future it is expected to grow at a reduced rate of 5.8 per cent. Comparatively, in 2025 Russia's GDP is projected to be $1.5 trillion, Japan's $6.3 trillion, and the US $22.3 trillion. China's military industrial base also benefits from FDI and joint ventures in the civilian sector.

China's spectacular economic development and lack of transparency in the budget for military allocations fuel the fires of suspicion in the US. In addition China's global activism is truly impressive. Four specific motivations were identified in the seminar as key drivers of increased Chinese global activism: 1) securing inputs for the economy; 2) protecting against a potential US containment strategy; 3) expanding Chinese political influence; and 4) pursuing Chinese commercial interests.[17]

1. SECURING INPUTS FOR THE ECONOMY

China's urgent need is to secure access to energy for continued economic growth. The International Energy Agency projects Chinese oil imports to rise from the current level of 6.37 million barrels per day (bpd) to roughly 14 million bpd by 2030. By 2030 China will depend on imported oil for approximately 75 per cent of its total demand with supplies coming from the Middle East. Demand for natural gas is also projected to increase dramatically, while coal will remain China's primary source; (the accompanying graph illustrates China's thirst for oil, and its efforts to produce it abroad).

A Growing Thirst for Oil

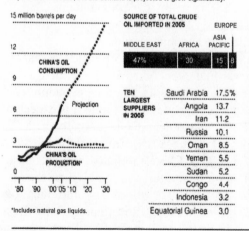

As China's economy has grown, the nation has been unable to meet its demand for oil domestically. The country's production capacity is not expected to increase, but the demand is projected to grow significantly.

To meet its growing need, China has been acquiring interests in exploration and production abroad.

15 million barrels per day

12

CHINA'S OIL CONSUMPTION

9

Projection

6

3

CHINA'S OIL PRODUCTION*

0

'80 '90 '00 '05 '10 '20 '30

*Includes natural gas liquids.

SOURCE OF TOTAL CRUDE OIL IMPORTED IN 2005

MIDDLE EAST	AFRICA	ASIA PACIFIC	EUROPE
47%	30	15	8

TEN LARGEST SUPPLIERS IN 2005		
Saudi Arabia	17.5%
Angola	13.7
Iran	11.2
Russia	10.1
Oman	8.5
Yemen	5.5
Sudan	5.2
Congo	4.4
Indonesia	3.2
Equatorial Guinea	3.0

MAJOR NEW OIL DEALS ABROAD

Iran in November of 2004, the Chinese oil company Sinopec negotiated a $70 billion deal for a 51% stake in Iran's Yadavaran oil field, which is eventually projected to produce about 300,000 barriers of oil per day.

Kazakhstan China National Petroleum Corporation bought Petrokazakhstan, a Canadian-run company that was the former Soviet Union's largest independent oil company last year. The company has also built a pipeline that will take the oil to the Chinese border.

Russia Last month, China and Russia announced a plan for two pipelines which could start supplying China in five years.

Sources: Energy Information Administration, Energy Intelligence Group   The New York Times, 19 April 2006

China's energy needs generate reciprocal suspicions. China suspects that the US and other western states which dominate the world economy could use their economic power to deny China access to energy and other raw materials. The US suspects that China is intruding into areas which were until recently within its economic and political orbit. A case in point is Saudi Arabia. Relations between China and Saudi Arabia became friendly in January 2006 when King Abdullah visited Beijing, and in April, President Hu Jintao made his first state visit to Saudi Arabia. Two years earlier the two countries had agreed to hold more regular political consultations.

In 2005 Saudi Aramco signed a $3.6 billion deal with Exxon Mobil and Sinopec for a joint oil refining and chemicals venture in South Fujian province and explored the possibility of a joint venture with Sinopec regarding investment in a plant in the northern Chinese port city of Qingdao. Saudi oil sales to China in 2005 account for almost 17 per cent of China's oil imports, while trade between the two countries exceeded $15 billion, having grown from almost zero to an average of 41 per cent a year since 1999.

American anxieties were further deepened in 2005, when China National Offshore Oil Corporation made an unsolicited $18.5 billion bid for Unocol, which had agreed to be sold to Chevron for $16.4 billion. To gain political acceptance for the largest acquisition of an American energy corporation, China suggested a national security review by the US government. Even this gesture did not soften opposition to the Chinese bid in Congress. Prudently China withdrew its bid, but US concern about China's rising economic clout has not abated, especially when the US trade deficit with China soared to $202 billion in 2005, up 25 per cent from the year before. In 2005 China also started to manufacture automobiles, following Japan and South Korea as a global competitor in one of the cornerstones of an industrial economy.[18]

The Chinese and US economies have become considerably interdependent, lessening to some degree US incentives to employ the policy of containment against China. China's foreign exchange reserves in 2005 were nearly $750 billion and heading for one trillion dollars—mostly in US treasury notes. Professor Paul Klugman commented that the US 'has developed an addiction to Chinese dollar purchases, and will suffer painful symptoms when they come to an end'.[19]

2. PREEMPTING A POSSIBLE CONTAINMENT STRATEGY

China's second motivation is identified as the plan to deny the US the ability to contain it. This may be described as the preemptive counter-containment strategy. Already some Chinese elites see the US practicing a 'strategy of 'soft' containment.'

Whether it is soft or becoming hard, it explains the current US policy towards Pakistan and India, where India is to be 'groomed' as a countervailing force against China in Asia and a fighter against Islamic fundamentalism and terror in the Middle East. Pakistan is expected to settle its problems with India, settle the Kashmir problem on its own, and join the balance of power system designed to contain China.

To entice India to play this new role the US repudiated its own nuclear policy of non-proliferation, and invited India to join the ranks of China, France, Russia, Britain, and the US as a legitimate nuclear power. President Bush refused to accord the same treatment to Pakistan. This was the President's major accomplishment when he visited India in March 2006, but it became a sore point for Pakistan, which insisted upon parity in her relationship with India and the US. When the new US-India nuclear deal was debated in the 50-member International Relations Committee of the House of Representatives on 5 June 2006 the co-chair of the Indian caucus in the House, Gary Ackerman, responded to Pakistan: 'If you want to be treated like India, be like India'. Congressman Dan Burton, a traditional supporter of Pakistan, commented that the nuclear deal with

India 'has a lot of merit and that India would be a greater ally of the United States and a good partner down the road'.[20]

Ashton B. Carter, former Assistant Secretary of Defence in the Clinton Administration and currently a faculty member at Harvard University, states that

> under the terms of the deal the United States commits to behave, and urge other states to behave, as if India were a nuclear weapons state under the NPT, even though India has not signed the treaty and will not be required to do so...Washington has also undertaken to stop denying civil nuclear technology to India and has determined to require India to apply the safeguards of the International Atomic Energy Agency (IAEA) only to nuclear facilities it designates as being for purely civil purposes. India is now authorized to import uranium, the lack of which had long stalled the progress of its nuclear program.[21]

Undoubtedly Indian diplomacy has succeeded brilliantly. India has supported the US on missile defence and, the International Criminal Court, facilitated US operations against Afghanistan in 2002, and voted in 2005 and 2006 with the US against Iran at the IAEA. When Pakistan proposed China as an observer in (2005) in South Asian Associates for Regional Cooperation, India skilfully brought in Japan, South Korea, and above all the United States.

Despite these diplomatic games an ultimate question about India's role as a player for the US against China remains to be answered. By the middle of the twenty-first century Indian diplomacy may opt for the role of a *balancer* between the three major powers, China, Russia, and the US and Pakistan would side with the power which would contain India.

In Afghanistan the US and its allies remain committed for at least five years under the terms of the Afghanistan Compact signed in London on 31 January 2006. The blueprint requires the restoration of the country's security, the building of a functioning economy, countering the rapidly expanding narcotics trade, and crushing the Taliban's resurgence in the battlefield. Along with its goals of strengthening democracy the Afghan Compact aims to eliminate illegal armed groups by 2007 and to construct an Afghan national army of 70,000 troops by 2010. NATO is expected to be deployed in Southern Afghanistan, enabling the US to reduce its troops by 2,500 to 16,500.[22] Afghanistan is expected to remain under the United States' umbrella of protection for at least ten years. This might facilitate the installation of US intelligence-gathering stations closer to the Chinese province of Xingjiang.

China is sensitive to these potentially 'dangerous' developments and has taken steps to thwart the harmful impact of the 'soft' containment policy of the United States.

CHINA'S COUNTER CONTAINMENT EFFORTS

China's counter containment efforts are focused on Eurasia, including Russia, India, Pakistan, and possibly Iran.

Soon after the collapse of the Soviet Union, Russia started to express diplomatic support for a multi-polar international system which could be a countervailing force against the United States', global pre-eminence. In December 1998 the Russian foreign minister, academician Yevgeny Primakov, proposed the concept of a strategic triangle to include Russia, China, and India, when he visited New Delhi. The proposal was not for a military alliance, but for a political structure to bring the three great Eurasian states together in an *entente cordiale*. Indian response was lukewarm, but the idea did not die.

Actually Sino-Russian relations have continued to improve since 1989, when President Gorbachev visited China and achieved considerable agreement on all disputed territories along the old Soviet-Chinese border. In 1996 and 1999 the two countries signed border agreements and the border areas were demilitarized. The extensive border agreement signed by China, Russia, and the successor Central Asian States of Kazakhstan, Kyrgyzstan, and Tajikistan launched the Shanghai Cooperation Organization (SCO). Five years after its founding as an obscure and very regional organization with a nondescript name, it has started to attract international attention as a means of balancing US power.

President Vladimir V. Putin of Russia visited China in July 2000, and then again in June 2006 to attend the annual meeting of the SCO. In the first meeting the two countries claimed to have developed 'a common position on the global security balance', and issued a ringing denunciation of the US for seeking 'unilateral military and security advantages with a missile defence plan that would violate the 1972 Antiballistic Missile Treaty'. Finally the Chinese President Jiang Zemin added that 'the two countries would push forward a global multi-polar process and establish a new political and economic order'.[23]

The SCO has admitted India, Iran, and Pakistan into its deliberations as observers, but the last two seek to join the group as full members. Pakistan, a longstanding ally of the United States whose strategic ties with China continue to strengthen, has proposed the construction of an energy corridor across its territory that would connect China and the Middle East. A contact group was created to explore the possibility of observer status for Afghanistan, whose President Hamid Karzai was invited to the 2006 meeting as a special guest.

Despite the SCO's declaration that it is geared to generate economic collaboration among its member states, the Russian and Chinese leaders at their meeting in June 2005 asked the US to withdraw its troops from Central Asia. This request revealed the trappings of a military alliance. If Iran is accorded full membership to the SCO no amount of argument will convince the United States that it is only an economic club.

CHINA'S RELATIONS WITH INDIA

Since 1962 when China inflicted a humiliating defeat on India in their border war, relations between the two states have never been cordial. When India tested its nuclear bomb in 1998 the potential military and security threat that China posed to India was given as a justification. The 2006 Indo-US deal on nuclear energy was viewed very negatively in China, since it was projected in the US as an attempt to rope in India in the hope of containing China. Also, Sino-Japanese ties have continued their downward spiral, while India and Japan have grown closer. Japan has started to flex its military muscles in the region. The Japanese navy has grown into a force of considerable reach, and the country recently launched its own spy satellites.

Against this background China decided to improve its relations with India, while it continued its 'all weather' friendship with Pakistan. Naturally India would balance its relations with China, Japan, and the US. India and China signed a Memorandum of Understanding on 30 May 2006 in Beijing, which called for the establishment of a mechanism to ensure frequent exchanges between leaders of the defence ministries and the armed forces in addition to developing an annual calendar for holding regular joint military exercises and training programmes. India also announced that a broad agreement had been reached on 'the political parameters and guiding principles for the talks on the border disputes'[24] between the two countries.

Clearly, India is uniquely suited to play the role of a classic balancer.

To compliment these initiatives China has undertaken an impressive programme to modernize its armed forces. While the war-fighting capacity of the People's Liberation Army (PLA) has increased in the last decade, its ultimate objective is to achieve 'strategic deterrence', which is defined by China's *The Science of Military Strategy* as

> the more powerful the war fighting capability, the more effective the deterrence...War fighting is generally used only when deterrence fails and there is no alternative. Strategic deterrence is also a means for attaining the political objective. Without resolute determination and firm volition, deterrence is feeble.[25]

A respected specialist on the Chinese military, Dennis J. Blasko, asserted in a seminar paper that the PLA's force structure is consistent with the needs of *deterrence*, *retaliation*, if attacked, and *defence* of China's sovereignty. However, the PLA is not trained, organized, and equipped to organize the type 'of joint operations the US military has executed on multiple occasions since 1991'.[26] The situation would certainly be different ten years from now. The Secretary of Defence's annual report on the *Military Power of the People's Republic of China (2006)* made this assessment:

> Today, China's ability to sustain military power at a distance is limited. However as the *2006 Quadrennial Defence Review Report* notes China has the greatest potential to compete militarily with the United States and field disruptive military technologies that could over time offset traditional US military advantages.[27]

Perhaps the Chinese navy has developed the capability to offset some of the US military advantages in the Taiwan Straits. A decade ago the US military ridiculed the idea of a Chinese attack against Taiwan 'as a 100-mile infantry swim'. In 1996 when China fired a warning missile against Taiwan, President Clinton responded by sending a carrier battle group to a position near Taiwan. Then China could do nothing about it. Today (2006) specialists say it can. China could now defeat Taiwan before American forces could arrive on the scene.[28]

China has, however, a long way to go before it could deploy space-based weapons, nor has Russia the ability to match the technological advance of the US in outer space. At the UN Conference on Disarmament in June 2006, Russia and China proposed to start negotiations on the prevention of an arms race in outer space. In 2006 the US is expected to issue a new space policy, underscoring the Pentagon's determination to protect its existing space assets and maintain dominance of outer space. A 1967 UN treaty bans weapons of mass destruction from space, but suspicions exist that the US might withdraw from that treaty, just as it withdrew from the 1972 Anti-Ballistic Missile Treaty so that it could start deploying a missile defence shield.[29] When the US announced its decision India readily supported it.

3. EXPLORING CHINESE POLITICAL INFLUENCE

The expansion of Chinese global influence is due to a range of factors, including soft power—China's ability to influence by persuasion rather than coercion. China uses soft power by a variety of means, including culture, diplomacy, participation in multinational organizations, business deals, and economic aid and loans. China's non-value-laden approach to diplomatic relations, it is widely believed in the US is designed to push Japan, Taiwan, and even the US incrementally out of her regional sphere of influence. China has also focused its attention on states whose relations with the US have soured.

China is allocating substantial resources to promote the Chinese language and culture. Foreign student enrollment in Chinese universities has increased from 85,000 in 2002 to 110,000 in 2004. About 75 per cent of foreign students are from Asian countries. Since 2004 more than twenty universities have begun to admit students from India and Pakistan. For hundreds of aspiring Indian and Pakistani medical students who were unable to get admission to universities in their own countries, China has become their Mecca for medical education.[30] The Chinese government provides some students with scholarships and financial assistance as well as the opportunity to obtain a valuable education in medicine.

China has also established Confucius Institutes—Chinese language schools—in some Asian universities, and has provided Chinese language teachers. China's embrace of free trade and promotion of the idea that it will become a source of foreign direct investment also bolsters its image.[31]

4. PURSUING COMMERCIAL INTERESTS

China's commercial interests are also an important rationale for its global involvement. China's exports are booming, but about 60 per cent of them are produced by foreign-funded enterprises based in China.[32] In order to seek technology China has signed technology sharing agreements with more than fifty countries, including Russia, Israel, and major western European countries.

China has been described as 'an avid practitioner of commercial diplomacy', whose trade, outbound foreign investment, and foreign aid are important tools. Chinese imports are fuelling growth through Asia and other regions of the world. In 2003 China became the largest export market for Japan, South Korea, and Taiwan. In the early 1990s she sent purchasing delegations to buy billions of dollars worth of US goods to influence key Congressional votes, when the most-favoured nation status was about to be debated in Congress. This tactic was repeated in April 2006, when the Chinese President Hu Jintao visited Washington and stopped over in Seattle, where Chinese companies signed $16 billion worth of contracts.

Development assistance is an important part of China's foreign policy. Her external assistance (in US millions) for 2002 was $602.77; for 2003 it was $630.36; and for 2004 it was $731.20.[33] China does not attach conditions to its economic aid like the US and the World Bank, and does not impose human rights conditions and anti-corruption measures, which become instruments of intervention of all kinds in the internal affairs of the recipients.

China has succeeded in establishing strategic partnerships with major countries – Brazil (1993), Russia (1996), France (1997), Saudi Arabia (1999), Iran (2000), ASEAN (2003), the European Union (2003), India (2003), the United Kingdom (2004), and Germany (2004). A strategic partnership is defined as a political declaration of mutual importance and goodwill. The content can vary from a quasi-alliance (like some aspects of the Sino-Russian strategic partnership) to a vague political declaration (like the partnership with India).

Finally I revert to the basic question: would China be a stakeholder in the US created international order or challenge it with an alternative system? My review projects the view that in structuring the architecture of an alternative system, China will not challenge US power until the middle of the twenty-first century. Until then Chinese policy will remain relatively peaceful. This time frame is postulated by Zheng Bijian, a well-known and respected strategic thinker, who was for some years a Deputy to President Hu Jintao of China.

Zheng crafted the view of a 'peaceful rise' of China, as China confronts: 1) resource shortages, 2) pollution, 3) corruption, 4) the need for a rule of law, and 5) uneven socio-economic development. Internationally China faces established western powers — most notably the US — which have their own economic and political interests which are not necessarily in harmony with Chinese concerns. Zheng estimates that 'China will basically realize modernization in the mid twenty first century, reaching the level of a moderately developed country'.[34]

In other words internal development imperatives mandate a peaceful period of at least forty-five years. Who knows what the Chinese policy will be after nearly half a century? Intentions change with the development of resources. Moreover China retains a deep psychic scar from western invasions, spheres of influence, and 1,000 unequal treaties, agreements and conventions which were imposed upon it between 1842 and 1943. According to another Chinese scholar, Dong Wang, contemporary 'Chinese nationalism is reflected in the various representations of the unequal treaties that display a triple concern for the linked themes of internal unification, international position, and a common Chinese culture'.[35] Would sentiments inspired by nationalism, of evening scores with the west, take over the foreign policy-making process before the forty-five years period is over? Who really knows. Naturally these dark areas of uncertainty inspire the US's soft containment policy.

IV

Clearly China is a strategic rival in the making to US power in Asia. While its policy of 'peaceful development' is underway, it presents an opportunity to some Asian states of an alternative to

US power. The US power continues to envelop 193 sovereign and independent states of the world in a circle of a diplomatic system. Within this invisible circle is a pyramid of power, which ranks these states according to their capacity to play the diplomatic role. Obviously the states' capacity is determined in the light of their geography, demographic strength, educational and industrial capacity – and finally their military capability.

In my view the independent states of the world can be divided into four vertical categories (shown in the following diagram): 1) super or imperial power 2) major regional powers 3) secondary regional powers and 4) inactive states. In my estimation, eighteen states possess varying degrees of leverage in world diplomacy. The rest simply follow the lead of the major powers, especially that of the US.

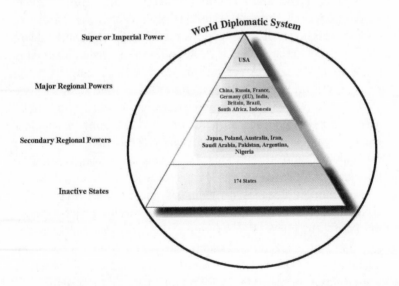

- ° UN Member States = 193
- ° Influential States = 18
- ° Inactive States = 175

Here an attempt is made to analyze US relations with a secondary regional state like Pakistan, and a small power like Afghanistan— which has survived as a 'failed' state since 1979. A profile of interaction between Afghanistan and Pakistan is also presented since it affects their relations with the US.

In the current phase of its relations with Pakistan, US determination to defeat the terrorists has motivated it to declare Pakistan a non-NATO ally. Actually the US-Pakistan subsidiary alliance is also described as a 'strategic partnership', implying a relationship which is presumed to survive the Bush Administration. In reality it is a marriage of convenience dependent upon the 'mercy' of terrorists.

In its global calculation the US is seeking as discussed above, a durable strategic partnership with India. This US-India relationship promises to be enduring, reflecting a basic convergence of national interests to establishing an Asian counterweight to the rising power of China. When President Bush visited India in March 2006 he let the Pakistan leadership know that when the American orchestra was playing its Asian tunes, Pakistan would be expected to play second fiddle.

Strategic ties with the United States would ensure that India achieves its aspirations as a major power, ending its nuclear isolation and yielding it the legitimacy it has long sought as a nuclear weapon state (This last aspiration was denied to Pakistan.) Under the terms of agreement the US will end a moratorium of decades on sales of nuclear fuel and reactor components, and India will separate its civilian and military nuclear programmes, and open the civilian facilities to international inspections. Despite Pakistan's demands for equal nuclear status with India, President Bush stated bluntly when he visited Pakistan on 4 March 2006 that 'India and Pakistan could not be compared to each other'. Then he added: 'so as we proceed, our strategy will take in effect those well-known differences'.[36]

For more than two decades Afghanistan was plagued by natural and man-made disasters, ranging from drought to earthquakes, protracted Soviet intervention, civil war among ethnic and ideological groups, cultural, educational, and political oppression by the Taliban. More than one-third of Afghanistan's population was displaced. Tragically women suffered the most. Steeped in the tribal conservative values of the Afghan Pashtuns, the Taliban denied millions of girls and women their basic human rights of education, and the opportunity to earn their living. Afghanistan is in consequence the fourth most under-developed country in the world—71 per cent of adults are illiterate, one in four children die before the age of 5 and fully half of the population remains without reliable sources of food or water. In this social and cultural backwardness Islamic fundamentalist mullahs have a field day in converting the uneducated people to their ideological causes.

Afghanistan, a fragile state under international 'protection' since the removal of the Taliban in 2001, started to relapse into violence and chaos in 2005, has really no foreign policy, properly speaking, and does not have much to negotiate about other than to complain about its own insecurity. As recently as 12 July 2006 Afghanistan's Minister of Defence, Abdul Rahim Wardak, complained loudly that the planned 70,000-member Afghan army could not secure the country without at least 150,000—200,000 troops, which 'should also be well-trained and equipped, with mobility and firepower and logistical and training institutions'.[37] Such a modern military force cannot be created even in twenty years, given Afghanistan's very low level of education and technical expertise. Assisted by its allies, the US expected a national Afghan army of 70,000 troops to be available by 2010.

No wonder that American media proclaimed in June 2006 that a 'revived Taliban are waging full-blown insurgency'[38] in Afghanistan. This insurgency is underway in three regions: 1) Southern Afghanistan 2) areas in and around Kabul and 3) the tribal areas of Pakistan. This time the insurgents are the Taliban, the cadres of Al Qaeda, and former Prime Minister Gulbaddin

Hekmatyar's Mujahideen,[39] who had fought against the Soviets.

Southern Afghanistan: The United States has 25,000 troops in Afghanistan but transferred control of some areas in the south to NATO forces, especially the British. NATO increased the number of troops in the region from an average of about 3,000 in recent years to about 6,000. However, in addition to the Taliban forces the Al Qaeda suicide bombers have started to terrorize the region. Despite its evident military superiority the US-led alliance has not been able to root out the insurgency. The insurgents have closed down some 200 schools through threats and burnings, and killed dozens of government officials, tribal elders and civilians during 2005-6. In Kandahar commerce declined sharply in 2006.[40] Afghan elders and notable influential individuals in the area, distrustful of the Karzai government in Kabul that they say is 'corrupt and exploitative, are sympathetic to the Taliban'.

What explains the resurgence and some of the popularity of the Taliban is the fact that the past four years of US assistance and the state building programme have had little impact in the rural areas of the south. Speaking at the US Institute of Peace in Washington DC in May 2006 Alex Their, Senior Advisor in the Rule of Law programme stated:

> Many Afghans have become skeptical about the central government and perceive it to be a client of the international community. Corruption is rife among local government officials. Justice Sector reform has been a glaring failure. The Supreme Court is corrupt, personalized and erratic.[41]

In a more charitable style Lt. General Karl Eikenbery, Commander of the US-led alliance, delivered this judgment on the Karzai government's performance: 'The best strategy when we have a problem is to hold a mirror to yourself. It means building a government, getting a clean government that is not corrupt, stopping poppy cultivation, building the Afghan national army and national police.'[42]

The weak institutions of the state have enabled the Taliban to fill the vacuum of power in southern Afghanistan. The United Nations' recent report about the status of security (as of 20 June 2006) indicated that 'a third of the country' was unsafe for the UN operations, while NATO increased the number of troops in the southern provinces to 10,000 from 4,000 during 2005. Also, the report identified eight danger zones in the south as medium risk (unstable areas), high risk (volatile areas), and extreme risk (hostile areas): 1) Kabul was described as volatile since riots erupted in May 2006; 2) Kandahar, Helmand, Uruzgan, Farah ad Zabul—provinces with the most intense fighting and highest numbers of attacks and deaths; 3) Wardak and Logar, known for suicide attacks and *shabnamas* (night letters) warning residents to leave; 4) Taliban Northern Command and Southern Command, leading operations in the north and in the south. During 2004-5 the UN agencies operated freely over 60-70 per cent of south Afghanistan; in 2006 they can work freely in six of the region's fifty districts.

The United Nations' report also identified four additional sources of resistance to the Karzai government and NATO forces. They acted in loose coordination from different parts of Afghanistan, and some were linked to drug trafficking: 1) Taliban Northern Command/Southern Command; 2)Wana Shura, tribal fighters operating out of the North and South Waziristan region of Pakistan; 3) Jalal-ud Din Haqqani, who was identified as an 'Afghan nationalist,' loosely affiliated with the Taliban; 4) Gulbuddin Hikmatyar, aligned with the Taliban operating in the south.[43]

The Taliban have succeeded in creating an alternative state infrastructure including courts, and people resort to them to resolve local conflicts. This worsening security situation brought President Bush, Secretary of Defence Donald Rumsfeld, and Secretary of State Condoleeza Rice in a quick succession to Afghanistan to strengthen President Karzai, who has been weakened considerably by the Taliban's surge in the south and by riots of June 2006 in Kabul.

Early in March 2006 Karzai blamed Pakistan for all of the security problems destabilizing his government. He alleged that the Taliban leader Mullah Muhammad Omar and Osama bin Laden were operating in Pakistan's Tribal Areas and in Balochistan. Using a less elegant phrase, President Pervez Musharraf lashed out at Karzai for 'bad-mouthing Pakistan'; but the reality did not vanish in the thin air. In July Pakistan's police arrested a noted commander and forty-two local leaders of the Taliban movement in Quetta. Also 140 Afghan nationals were arrested as 'illegal residents,' violence erupted in southern Afghanistan, and Taliban forces overran Afghan policemen in the Helmand town of Garmser, near the Pakistan border. In eastern Afghanistan US-led troops killed several suspected Al Qaeda fighters, including Arab and Chechen militants.[44]

Despite the change in government policy, much of the Pakistani public, especially in Balochistan and the North West Frontier Province sympathizes with the Taliban and the remnants of the Al Qaeda movement. This broad sympathy turns the tribal areas – especially North and South Waziristan into sanctuaries for the anti-Karzai forces led by the revived Taliban. Al Qaeda flourished in both Waziristans during the war against the Soviet Union. Some of the Arab fighters married Afghan girls and raised their families in this region. This ideological and physical fusion integrated the foreign fighters with the local Pashtun society, which made it practically impossible for Pakistan to conduct a census of the local and foreign population.

American specialists on the prevailing violence in Afghanistan have identified three sites within Pakistan where the Taliban leaders and Gulbaddin Hikmatyar are safely ensconced: 1) Quetta and Balochistan are the sanctuary for 'two leadership cells', including the senior commanders of Mullah Muhammad Omar. From Quetta they are supposed to direct military operations in the south-central Afghan provinces of Helmand, Kandahar, Uruzgan, and Zabul. 2) Out of Miran Shah, the capital of North Waziristan, the Taliban commander Jalal-ud-Din Haqqani and his sons operate. They conduct operations in Kabul, and the eastern Afghanistan regions of Khost, Logar, Paktia, and Paktika. 3) In Peshawar and the Bajur Agency are located various headquarters of Hikmatyar, who runs operations in the Afghan provinces of Kapisa, Kunar, Laghman, Nangarhar and Nuristan.[45]

The Taliban have focused their military operations in the rural areas, the way the Mujahideen had done against the Soviet forces. In the villages they expect to wear down the Karzai government, while the mullahs denounce him as a foreign puppet. Once the Taliban have acquired a secure leadership base in the remote parts of Afghanistan, the second civil war is intended to ignite, where the Taliban will once again confront the Northern Alliance and the Karzai forces, which are now being supported by the US-led coalition under NATO.

Pakistan deployed in 2005-6 70,000 of its troops to stem the tide of guerilla activity in Afghanistan through Waziristan, and lost a large number of its soldiers in combat with the Al Qaeda and Taliban forces. Finally the government of Pakistan resorted to the traditional technique for conflict resolution between the government and the autonomous tribes. A traditional Jirga consisting of forty-five members was formed, drawn primarily from North and South Waziristan with three representatives from the remaining five tribal agencies. It met in Peshawar in July 2006 with the provincial governor to establish its operational framework, and make clearly understood its mandate of establishing peace in the tribal region and stopping the infiltration of Taliban fighters into Afghanistan. The militants had already announced a month-long conditional ceasefire on 25 June. They also demanded: 1) the withdrawal of regular Pakistani troops from their current positions; 2) dismantling of the checkpoints; 3) the release of captured militants; 4) the government of Pakistan would restore all the privileges and rights of the tribes, open closed markets, restore jobs, and pay back the withheld salaries of the tribal employees.

As a gesture of goodwill the Pakistan government freed all the imprisoned fighters.[46] In a major policy concession it allowed the foreign militants (who are supposed to be Al Qaeda) to stay in the tribal areas on guarantees from the local tribesmen that they would fully obey the law of the land. Previously Pakistan had insisted that the foreign militants must either leave the tribal area or have themselves registered with the local authorities.[47] In his visit to Washington in September 2006 General Musharraf assured President Bush that his agreement with the tribal leaders had 'three bottom lines'. He said one was 'no Al Qaeda activities in our tribal agencies or across the border in Afghanistan.' The second was 'no Taliban activity' in the same areas. And the third was 'no Talibanization,' which he described as 'obscurantist thoughts or way of life.'[48]

Whether the Jirga system, operating on the traditional system of collective responsibility, will eliminate the Taliban and their sympathizers' activities remains to be seen! But one cannot be very optimistic. Meanwhile relations between Afghanistan and Pakistan continued to sour as President Karzai continued to woo India. In April 2006 he visited India and proposed a 'Tri-polar structure of cooperation' between India, Pakistan and Afghanistan, as his country was 'more south-Asian than central-Asian'. India reciprocated with a generous offer of $575 million for Afghanistan's reconstruction, as against Pakistan's $275 million. Back in Kabul, Karzai refuelled his row with Pakistan by repeating his calls for it to stop cross-border raids 'the same way it did during [the] Afghan elections'.[49]

Diplomatically Pakistan retaliated by vetoing Afghanistan's entry into the South Asian Free Trade Agreement (SAFTA). Afghanistan had become a member of the South Asian Association for Regional Cooperation (SAARC) in July 2006. Pakistani officials also let it be known that since 'the regime in Kabul was toeing the line of New Delhi and involved in all activities which are detrimental to Pakistan's interests', Pakistan would oppose Afghanistan's inclusion in SAFTA. Moreover, trade between the SAARC countries and India required the transit of goods through Pakistan's territory, 'which is against the economic interests of Islamabad'.[50]

To coordinate its operations with Afghanistan and Pakistan the US military has established the Tripartite Commission, which was called to an urgent eighteenth meeting in Kabul in August 2006. The delegates discussed future operations and steps to improve the security environment along the border area and conduct coordinated controls on 'their respective sides of the border simultaneously'.[51] Pakistan's delegate, a vice-chairman of the army staff, met President Karzai and offered him renewed assurances of cooperation on 'many strategic issues'.

However, the survival of the Karzai government cannot be guaranteed by Pakistan's cooperation alone. Karzai's success has been undermined by his 'failure to attend to a range of problems'–widespread corruption, causing the loss of public confidence, the perception of growing insecurity, which is affecting the psyche of the Afghan people, and his own mismanagement of the internal administration. Three million Afghans of a population of roughly 30 million still depend on food aid, and hundreds of Afghans apply daily to find work in Iran or Pakistan. 'Poverty and joblessness are among the factors pushing people into the arms of the Taliban'.[52]

Yet the US policy in Afghanistan is anchored in the leadership of President Karzai, just as US determination to fight terror relies heavily upon the resourcefulness of President Musharraf, who is also a uniformed general, and Chief of Pakistan Army's Staff. However, there are more generals in the Pakistan Army than there are American generals in the US Army.[53] Replacement of one general by another would not be a serious problem for the US. Despite this possibility there are some sound geopolitical realities which ensure a broadly based relationship between Pakistan and the United States, which could last for at least ten more years:

I. One basic reason for US-Pakistan relations is the need to fight terrorism, which first emanated from Afghanistan during the Taliban's rule. Precisely for this political imperative the US Commission recommended 'the difficult long-term commitment to the future of Pakistan', and to sustain 'the current scale of aid to Pakistan'.[54]

Pakistan has received US economic assistance worth $700 million annually. Two-way trade approached $5 billion in 2005-2006. In 2005 private US investment amounted to $369 million, while US government assistance to education in Pakistan came to $100 million annually.

II. Pakistan's strategic location once again highlights its importance to the US. Currently, the US is competing with Russia and China to obtain a substantial share of the energy resources in the Central Asian States. The US has already acquired a foothold in Kyrgyzstan and Kazakhstan, and would be keen to extending its influence beyond these two states. It has recently encouraged interest in the $7 billion Turkmenistan, Afghanistan and Pakistan Pipeline (TAP). The Asian Development Bank (ADB) is supposed to have developed a general framework, and interstate agreements to include India in the project.

The revisions in the framework agreement would allow the ADB to include the extension of the TAP pipeline to India in the pre-feasibility study, including routes, pipeline capacity, design, and security arrangements. However, this ambitious project confronts several major bottlenecks, including: 1) non-confirmation of uncommitted gas volume by Turkmenistan regarding the Daulatabad gas field, 2) lack of clarity about the price of the gas to be demanded by Turkmenistan, and 3) the lack of security in Afghanistan. Clearly the success of the project would depend upon the sustained support of the US.

III.   Since US relations with Iran are deteriorating over Iran's plan for uranium enrichment, the US would need Pakistan's assistance in any future crisis with Iran.

IV.   The US objective in pacifying the tribal areas on the Afghan-Pakistan border is obviously a part of the war on terror. This has proved to be a daunting task which might need several more years of jointly conducted war along the borders with Afghanistan.

V. Last but not least, the US is fearful of Pakistan's nuclear weapons falling into the hands of Al Qaeda terrorists who might use them against the US and its allies. The US will want to remain engaged with the Pakistani Army, which is responsible for the safety of these weapons. Indeed this will be a considerably drawn out process.

Several negative factors also exist, irritating relations between Pakistan and the US. Pakistan feels strongly the shifting of the balance of power in South Asia in favour of India, which is now the favourite of the US as reflected in the recent nuclear deal. Pakistan's ambassador to Washington, General Jahangir Karamat, publicly protested that 'instead of a country-specific deal on a subject as critical as nuclear technology, these should be packaged for both India and Pakistan.'[55]

Another irritant is Pakistan's down-graded status as an 'ally' of the United States. Officially 'the underpinnings of the US de-hyphenated policy in South Asia' is resented, and the US tilt toward India would erode 'the minimum deterrence' policy toward India.

NOTES

1. Richard N. Haass, 'What to Do with American Primacy', *Foreign Affairs* (September 1999), <http://www.brookings.edu/views/articles/haass/20001111.htm>; 'Imperial America', paper delivered at the Atlanta Conference, 11 November 2000, <http://www.brookings.edu/views/Articles/Haass/2000imperial.htm>.

2. Michael Ignatieff, 'The Burden', *The New York Times Magazine*, 5 January 2003.

3. C.S. Olcott, *Life of William McKinley*, Vol. II, p. 109; also see Parker Thomas Moon, *Imperialism and World Politics* (New York: The Macmillan Company, 1937), pp. 394-5.

4. David Burner, Virginia Bernhard and Stanley I. Kutler, *Firsthand America: A History of the United States,* Vol. II (New York: Brandywine Press, 4th Edition, 1996), p. 659.

5. W. R. Shepherd, 'The Monroe Doctrine Reconsidered', *Political Science Quarterly* (March 1924).

6. In this vein the whole dispatch makes fascinating reading, *US Foreign Relations* (Washington DC: US Government, 1895), Part I, pp. 545-5.

7. *US Foreign Relations* (Washington DC: US Government, 1905), p. XXXIV.

8. Parker Thomas Moon, *Imperialism and World Politics* (New York: The Macmillan Company, 1937), pp. 524-5.

9. Hans J. Morgenthau, *Politics Among Nations* (New York: Alfred A. Knopf, 1963), p. 92.

10. John R. Rourke, Ralph G. Carter, and Mark A. Boyer, *Making American Foreign Policy* (Guilford, CT: Dushkin Publishing Group, 1994), pp. 27-79.

11. Michael J. Sullivan III, *American Adventurism Abroad* (Westport: Praeger, 2004), p. 2. For the expression of this view also see Tony Gilbert and Pierre Joris, *Global Interference: The Consistent Pattern of American Foreign Policy* (London: Liberation Press, 1981), p. 7; Robert W. Tucker and David C. Hendrickson, *The Imperial Temptation: The New World Order and America's Purpose* (New York: Council of Foreign Relations, 1992), p. 2-6.

12. Walter Russell Mead, *Power, Terror, Peace and War* (New York: Alfred A. Knopf, 2004), p. 46-53.

13. Joseph Schumpeter, *Imperialism and Social Classes: Two Essays*, trans. Heinz Nerden (New York: Meridian Books, The World Publishing Company, 1955), p. 51.

14. For this thesis, see a very insightful analysis by Murray L. Weidenbaum, 'Why War is Affordable: The Military's Role in the US Economy', in *American Government 6/07* (Dubuque: The McGraw Hill Co., 2001), pp. 216-8.

15. 'Military Power of the People's Republic of China 2006,' (Washington DC: Department of Defence, 2006), p. 1 of the Executive Summary. Under the rules of the seminar, I am unable to attribute any statement to the speakers, except the written material which was available.

16. Ibid., p. 20.

17. Phillip C. Saunders, *China's Global Activism: Strategy, Drivers, and Tools* (Washington DC: National Defence University, June 2006), p. 7.

18. *Wall Street Journal*, 20 April 2006; *The New York Times*, 28 June 2005.

19. Paul Klugman, 'The Chinese Connection', *The New York Times*, 20 May 2005.

20. Gary Ackerman, 'If You Want to be Treated Like India, Be Like India', *The Hindu*, 6 June 2006.

21. Ashton B. Carter, 'America's New Partner', *Foreign Affairs* (July-August, 2006), p. 36.

22. Alan Cowell, '60 Nations Set 5-Year Goals to Aid Afghanistan', *The New York Times*, 1 February 2006.

23. Craig S. Smith, 'Russia and China Unite in Criticism of US Antimissile Plan', *The New York Times*, 19 July 2000.

24. Pallavi Aiyer, 'A Quick Step Forward in Sino-Indian Ties', *The Hindu*, 30 May 2006; also his 'Extensive Consensus on Defence Cooperation with China', *The Hindu*, 31 May 2006; 'China India Defence Accord', *Dawn*, 31 May 2006.

25. *The Science of Military Strategy*, pp. 215-228 in Dennis J. Blasko, 'Observations on Military Modernization and International Influence—An

Alternative View', (Washington DC: National Defence University Seminar, June 2006), p. 8.

26. Ibid., p. 9.

27. Secretary of Defence, *Military Power of the People's Republic of China, 2006* (Washington DC: 2006), p. 1.

28. Jim Yardley, Thom Shankar, 'Chinese Navy Buildup Gives Pentagon New Worries', *The New York Times*, 8 April 2005.

29. 'China, Russia Warn Against Deploying Space Weapons', *The News*, 9 June 2006.

30. Saunders, op. cit., p. 19; Pallavi Aiyar, 'Made in China—Indian Doctors', *The Hindu*, 17 May 2006.

31. Joshua Kurlantzick, 'China's Charm: Implications of Chinese Soft Power', *Policy Brief* (Washington DC: Carnegie Endowment, June 2006), p. 3

32. Odel Shenkas, 'Learning from China's Export Boom', *Business Week*, 19 January 2006.

33. 'The Dragon Tucks In', *The Economist*, 30 June 2005; Saunders, op. cit., p. 14.

34. Zheng Bijian, *Speeches of Zheng Bijian: China's Peaceful Rise, 1997-2005* (Washington DC: Brookings, 2005), pp. IX, 26.

35. Dong Wang, *China's Unequal Treaties* (Lanham, MD: Lexington Books, 2005).

36. *The New York Times*, 5 March 2006.

37. 'Gloomy Assessment by Afghan Defence Minister', *The New York Times*, 13 July 2006.

38. Paul Wiseman, 'Revived Taliban Waging Full-Blown Insurgency', *USA Today*, 20 June 2006.

39. For Hekmatyar's current 'alliance' with the Taliban see an informative study by Ishtiaq Ahmad, *Gulbaddin Hekmatyar* (Islamabad: Pan graphic Press, 2004), pp. 89-127.

40. *The New York Times*, 2 March 2006.

41. 'Afghanistan in the Crosshairs', *Peace Watch* (Washington DC: US Institute of Peace, April-May, 2006), p. 5.

42. Carlotta Gall, 'Taliban Rebels Still Menacing Afghan South', *The New York Times*, 2 March 2006.

43. Carlotta Gall, 'After Afghan Battle, A Harder Fight for Peace', *The New York Times*, 3 October 2006.

44. 'Taliban Take Control of Two Towns', *Dawn*, 18 July 2006.

45. Robert D. Kaplan, 'The Taliban's Silent Partner', *The New York Times*, 20 July 2006.

46. 'Jirga Peace Drive Begins Today', *Dawn*, 19 July 2006.

47. 'Breakthrough in Waziristan', *Dawn*, 23 August 2006.

48. David Sanger, 'Musharraf Defends Deal Made with Tribal Leaders', *The New York Times*, 23 September 2006.

49. 'Afghanistan Fuels Terror Row with Pakistan', *The News*, 8 March 2006.
50. 'Pakistan Decided Not to Include Afghanistan in SAFTA', *The News*, 31 July 2006.
51. 'Joint Patrol Along Afghan Border', *Dawn*, 24 August 2006.
52. This is the keen observation of a veteran American correspondent, Carlotta Gall of *The New York Times*, 23 August 2006.
53. This observation is based upon a study issued by the Carnegie Endowment for International Peace in Washington DC in 2006. The author of this study, Frédéric Grare (who has worked as a Counselor for Cooperation and Culture at the Embassy of France in Islamabad), provided the following data in February 2006 about American and Pakistani generals:
    Pakistani Army 550,000
    Generals in Pakistan 770-940 (including Brigadiers)
    US Army 502,000
    Generals in the US 881
    Frédéric Grare, 'Pakistan: The Myth of an Islamic Peril', *Policy Brief*, (Washington DC: Carnegie Endowment for International Peace, February 2006, No. 45), p. 6.
54. *The 9/11 Report*, p. 528.
55. Muralidhar Reddy, 'Islamabad Will Not Accept Discriminatory Treatment', *The Hindu*, 20 March 2006.

2

The Emergence of American *Imperium*

I

A relatively young country in the family of nations, the United States became the main power in a unipolar world after December 1991, when the Soviet Union collapsed under the weight of its own contradictions. This new Rome no longer had a Carthage to contend with. President Bush heralded a new dawn of *imperium*, when he stated that a new world order has started. Even at the peak of its expansion, the Roman Empire, Edward Gibbon estimated, 'was about 2,000 miles in breadth...that it extended in length more than 3,000 miles from the Western Ocean to the Euphrates.'[1]

Compared to the US's expansion, Rome was merely a major state with a good sized territory. Rome could never match the American military and economic power. No wonder Henry Kissinger declared in 2001 that the United States has achieved 'preeminence not enjoyed by even the greatest empires of the past.'[2]

Indeed the US shares some of the virtues of an empire with Rome. In 1776 the founding Fathers of the Republic, drawing upon the British historical experience, called it the wisdom of ages, drafted the Constitution which has survived more than 200 years with only 26 amendments. Most of the countries in Europe and Asia and elsewhere have suffered through violent revolutions, and coups d'état, without achieving political stability. The edifice of Rome was also structured by laws, and was adorned by arts which enabled the provincials as well as the citizens to 'enjoy the religion of their ancestors'.[3]

One reason for the strength of the US is that it has become an unusually open meritocracy. Secretaries of State Colin Powell, Henry Kissinger and Madeleine Albright, the former National Security Advisor and current Secretary of State Condoleezza Rice, and the Commander-in Chief of the Central Command General John Abized are prime examples of the scions of former slaves, scorned political refugees and Arab immigrants. The academic, artistic, medical and business communities have offered lucrative opportunities to a substantial number of talented men and women who come from foreign lands. It helps that in the US the state is secular—committed to remain neutral in matters of religion which guarantees the freedom of worship to all religious denominations.

The fact that the US rules the new world order does not mean that it rose up spontaneously out of the historical process and that its statesmen stumbled into an empire which they did not plan or foresee. Successful empires have never functioned in a political or economic vacuum or absent mindedness. Abraham Lincoln described America's founding 'as acquired in the world's last, best hope'. Throughout American history, its leaders have had messianic goals, justifying territorial and political expansion. Walter McDougall in his critically acclaimed book, *Freedom Just Around the Corner: A new American History, 1585-1828*, proposed that 'America is a priesthood of believers in a civil religion, master builders, revolutionaries devoted to creative destruction, a jealous people whose pursuit of happiness will not be interfered with, and hustling self-reinventors.'[4]

Professor Hans Morgenthau, a political refugee from Nazi Germany and a majestic exponent of political realism, cautioned empire builders that 'political realism refuses to identify the moral aspirations of a particular nation with the moral laws that govern the universe', and called it 'the blasphemous conviction that God is always on one side, and that what one wills oneself cannot fail to be willed by God also.'[5] Against these words of wisdom, let us read what President George W. Bush said in the context 'liberty' in 2002: 'his values were God-given values.

These aren't US created values'. Especially since December 1991 US foreign policy has been dedicated to remaking the world in its own image –'an evangelical project that contrasts with understandings of 'liberty' elsewhere in the world.'

II

THE PARAPHERNALIA OF US IMPERIALISM

Since its establishment in 1776 the United States has steadily acquired all the assets of a modern empire, including: 1) extensive contiguous and non-contiguous territories, 2) a remarkably well-developed economy and educated population, 3) highly developed scientific and industrial enterprises, and financial institutions that impact the economies of foreign states, and 4) military command structures to guarantee security.

GEOGRAPHY

The US contains four different kinds of territories: 1) the continental United States, 2) the non-contiguous states of Alaska and Hawaii, 3) the dependent commonwealth of Puerto Rico, and 4) literally dozens of island dependencies of substantial size. The US dependencies or territories are:

1) American Samoa
2) Guam, the southern most and largest of the Mariana Islands, located around 2,170 lm (1,300 miles) west of Honolulu, Hawaii
3) The Virgin Islands, 68 islands located 64 km (40 miles) east of Puerto Rico
4) The Marshall Islands
5) The Federated States of Micronesia
6) The Northern Mariana Islands, 16 islands located around 5,635 km (3,381 miles) west-southwest of Honolulu, Hawaii

7) Palau also known as Belau, some 200 islands in an archipelago that stretches for 650 km (390miles) located 7,150 km (4,290 miles) southwest of Hawaii and 1,160 km (696 miles) south of Guam (It became an independent country in October of 1994.)

8) Baker Island, a small uninhabited island located in the North Pacific Ocean around halfway between Hawaii and Australia, a mostly flat sandy coral island

9) Jarvis Island, a small uninhabited island located in the South Pacific Ocean around 2,090 km (1,254 miles) south of Hawaii

10) Johnston Atoll, a small uninhabited island located in the North Pacific Ocean around 1,328 km (797 miles) southwest of Hawaii – the islands have a maximum elevation of 4 meters (13 feet) and are a former nuclear weapons test site

11) Midway Islands, a group of islands located some 2,350 km (1,410 miles) northwest of Honolulu, Hawaii

From 18 July 1947 until 1 October 1994, the US administered the Trust Territory of the Pacific Islands. It entered into a political relationship with all four political units: the Northern Mariana Islands is a commonwealth in political union with the US (effective 3 November 1986); Palau concluded a Compact of Free Association with the US (effective 1 October 1994); the Federated States of Micronesia signed a Compact of Free Association with the US (effective 3 November 1986); the Republic of the Marshall Islands signed a Compact of Free Association with the US (effective 21 October 1986).[6]

The nineteenth century saw the largest territorial expansion of the United States. To many it seemed inevitable that the lands to the west of the Mississippi -- claimed by Mexico, England and a substantial number of Native American nations – should eventually be settled by Americans of European decent. In 1845 John O'Sullivan, editor of the influential *Democratic Review*, coined the phrase 'Manifest Destiny' to describe this mission of the United States, stretching from the Atlantic to the Pacific. The anti-slavery activists, whose perception of US federalism was threatened by the South, were opposed to expansion. They feared that it would upset the delicate balance of power between North and South. Once the Oregon territorial boundary was settled by a treaty with Britain, territorial conflict centered on Texas. A number of Americans declared their independence from Mexico in Texas in 1836 and expressed their desire to be annexed by the Unites States. They had their ambitions satisfied when Texas was annexed to the United States in 1845. To the Republic of Mexico this entire enterprise was an expression of imperial aggrandizement.

War broke out between the United States and Mexico in 1846; American armies occupied San Francisco, Santa Fe and the city of Monterey. By the end of 1847 the US had occupied the capital, Mexico City. The defeated Mexican government had no choice but to cede almost half of its northern territories—some 850,000 square miles—to the United States. The treaty of Guadalupe Hidalgo added the vast territories of New Mexico and California to the United States.

Actually by the nineteenth century the United States had become so powerful that in 1823, President James Monroe had issued a declaration, generally known as the Monroe Doctrine, which forbade additional European colonization in the western hemisphere. However, the United States acquired additional territories either through conquest, purchase or arranging coups d'état in foreign lands. In 1867 the United States bought Alaska from Russia at the rate of two cents an acre, amounting to $7.2 million, and paid $25 million to Denmark to purchase sovereignty over the Virgin Islands. The expulsion of Spain from Cuba and Puerto Rico in 1898 as well as the acquisition of the Panama Canal in 1903 gave the United States unprecedented power in the Caribbean. A coup d'état against Queen Liliuokalani of Hawaii lead to the islands' annexation in 1898.

In less than a century and a quarter the United States had developed from thirteen states strung along a narrow Atlantic coastline into a great world power with possessions in the far Pacific.

ECONOMY AND POPULATION

The US has the largest and most technologically powerful economy in the world with a per capita GDP of $37,800. In this market-oriented economy, private individuals and business firms make most of the decisions, and the federal and state governments buy necessary goods and services predominantly in the private marketplace. US business firms enjoy considerably greater flexibility than their counterparts in Western Europe, Japan, China, and Russia in decisions to expand capital plant, lay off surplus workers and develop new products. US firms are at the forefront of technological advances, especially in the areas of computer science, medical, aerospace, and military equipment. The years 1994-2000 saw substantial increases in real output, low inflation rates, and a drop in unemployment to below 5 per cent. The year 2001 saw the end of boom psychology and performance.

The response to the terrorist attack of 11 September 2001 demonstrated the remarkable resilience of the economy. A moderate recovery took place in 2002 with the GDP growth rate rising 2.4 per cent. A major problem in the first half of 2002 was a sharp decline in the stock market, spawned in part by the exposure of scandalous accounting practices, corruption and the swindling of enormous sums of money in some well-known major corporations. The invasion of Iraq in March 2003 by the US, and the so-called 'coalition of the willing' shifted enormous amounts of resources to the military. In 2002 US revenue was estimated to be $1.945 trillion, while its expenditures were $2.052 trillion.

According to one estimate: 'long-term problems [of the US economy] include inadequate investment in economic infrastructure, rapidly rising medical and pension costs of an aging population, sizable trade and budget deficits and stagnation of family income in the lower economic groups.'[7] In 2004 approximately 12 per cent of the population lived below the poverty line.[8]

In July 2004 the US population was 293,027,571 million, which makes the US the world's third largest country by population after China and India, and by size after Russia and Canada. Ethnically, the white population is 77.1 per cent of the total, black 12.9 per cent, Asian 4.2 per cent, Native American and Alaskan natives 1.5 per cent, native Hawaiian and other Pacific Islander 0.3 per cent and other 4 per cent. The US Census Bureau considers Hispanic to mean a person of Latin American descent (including persons of Cuban, Mexican or Puerto Rican origin). They may be of any race or ethnic group—white, black or Asian.

Religiously, Protestants account for 56 per cent, Roman Catholic 28 per cent, Jewish 2 per cent, other 4 per cent, none 10 per cent. These estimates were made in 1989. Since then the Muslims have increased considerably, amounting to about 6 million. Among them Pakistani-Americans were estimated at 500,000—700,000. After the 11 September tragedy an unknown number of those Pakistanis who had entered the country without proper visas were deported. While Pakistanis have been treated with some degree of suspicion, none were accused of involvement in the tragedy of 11 September. As recently as 1980 there were only 387,000 Indian Americans in the United States, but by 1997 this figure had more than tripled to 1,215,000. Now the Indian American community constitutes the third largest Asian-American population in the US, surpassed only by Chinese and Filipino Americans. Thus the Pakistani American community is only about one-tenth of the size of the Indian American community.[9]

Practically every ethnic community in the US has established interest groups or lobbies to protect its interests through the electoral process and to promote the strategic or economic interests of the parent countries. A directory of political advocacy groups, prepared by California State University at Chico, has listed 329 organizations under 43 broad categories, including gay, lesbian and bisexual groups and Arab American and Jewish organizations. The following table lists the number of major ethnic advocacy groups:

MAJOR ETHNIC ADVOCACY GROUPS

Jewish	Christian Protestant	Catholic	Arab-American	International Affairs	American-Islamic	Indian
10	12	3	4	23	1	1

Source: Kathi Carlisle, *Political Advocacy Groups: Alphabetic List*, (Chico: 18 May 2004)

Some are more successful than others. Israeli and Indian lobbies are the most well-organized and well-funded, and are most effective in influencing the House of Representatives, the Senate, and the Executive Branch of the US government. Pro-Israeli lobbies have converted the lobbying process into a fine art, and Indians hope to match them in the near future.

All Jewish organizations are committed 'to safeguard the welfare and security of the Jews in the United States, and throughout the world...and maintain ironclad relations between the US Congress and Israel.'[10] Indeed US policy towards the Middle East remains heavily skewed in favour of Israel.

Very successful and prosperous, the Jewish community is well organized and is a role model to other communities in the processes of integration and self-preservation. 'Jewish culture is no longer apart from but is, instead, a part of broader [American] culture.'[11] Being an integral part of the American power structure, the Jewish community is in a position to reward 'friends' – those who would enter into cooperative partnership—and punish 'enemies', who would want to harm its existential interests.

In addition to the interest groups there are 128 registered lobbying firms in Washington DC who are always prepared to take foreign governments as clients for a substantial fee. In 1999 these firms reported at least $1 million in income. Lobbyists have to file semi-annual reports with the Secretary of the Senate and the Clerk of the House of Representatives, the lobbyists identifying their clients, the lobbyists working for each client, and the amount of income they receive. Companies, unions, and foreign governments spent $1.45 billion on lobbying in 1999. Practically all Pakistani governments engaged lobbyists in Washington to plead their case with the US lawmakers.

The education level in the US population has reached an all-time high, according to Census 2000. Of the 182.2 million people aged 25 and over on 1 April 2000, 80 per cent had a high school diploma or more and 24 per cent had completed at least a Bachelors degree. Education has been included in the US Census questionnaire since 1840, when information was collected on the literacy of the population aged 20 years and over. In 1990 and 2000 the question was updated to reflect current interest in both the level of school completed and the types of degrees (if any) people had received. The census 2000 question allowed respondents to choose from a list of sixteen educational levels, ranging from no schooling completed to professional or doctoral degrees. The following figure shows the results:

FIGURE I

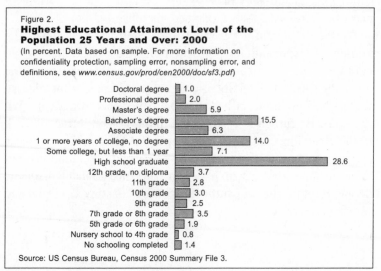

Figure 2.
Highest Educational Attainment Level of the Population 25 Years and Over: 2000
(In percent. Data based on sample. For more information on confidentiality protection, sampling error, nonsampling error, and definitions, see www.census.gov/prod/cen2000/doc/sf3.pdf)

Level	Percent
Doctoral degree	1.0
Professional degree	2.0
Master's degree	5.9
Bachelor's degree	15.5
Associate degree	6.3
1 or more years of college, no degree	14.0
Some college, but less than 1 year	7.1
High school graduate	28.6
12th grade, no diploma	3.7
11th grade	2.8
10th grade	3.0
9th grade	2.5
7th grade or 8th grade	3.5
5th grade or 6th grade	1.9
Nursery school to 4th grade	0.8
No schooling completed	1.4

Source: US Census Bureau, Census 2000 Summary File 3.

Source: US Census Bureau, 2000, http://www.census.gov/prod/2003pubs/c2kbr-24.pdf

Very few countries can match the educational attainments of the American population which is exceptionally patriotic. Since economic opportunities are available to the enterprising layers of the middle class, which is the largest in the population, Americans zealously safeguard their way of life. Indeed the upper classes are the backbone of the economic structure. An attack the magnitude of 11 September was perceived to be an existential threat to the national way of life. The American population can be roused into an intense nationalism when it is provoked or threatened.

CIVIL RELIGION

Despite the established policy of secularism, which obligates the lawmakers and the Executive to separate state from any religious denomination, American patriotism has spawned a 'civil religion'. In 1922, G.K. Chesterton described the United States as 'a nation with the soul of a church.' All US dollar bills contain the motto—'In God We Trust'. The Congress and the Supreme Court pray at the start of sessions. 'America the Beautiful', a patriotic song, asks that 'God shed his grace on thee'.

By the 1914 and 1939 the United States had assumed the burden of exporting its political faith. Some scholars wrote books on 'the American civil religion', and 'the religion of the flag'. By 1969 a University of California at Berkeley sociologist, Robert N. Bellah, described what he called the 'American civil religion'. He turned to history and found he could trace it back to the Founding Fathers of the Republic. They had preached a civil faith meant not to replace Bible-based denominations, but rather to stand above them in benign tolerance so that a disparate people might unite and fulfil the glorious destiny God planned for them.[12]

FINANCIAL INSTITUTIONS

Modern international economic relations are largely determined by the World Bank, the International Monetary Fund, and the World Trade Organization. The first two were created under US leadership in 1945 and have remained under it. This was a historical development as the European states had been ruined by World War II and their economies were in desperate need of help. Only the US was in a position to do so as it remained untouched by the war's destruction. Its economy was the strongest and most prosperous.

With the exception of the Soviet Union, no US ally wanted to overwhelm Germany and Japan with reparation debts. American diplomacy faced a dilemma: how to enable its former allies and enemies to continue their imports of US goods and services without German reparations. To solve this problem the US enlightened policy of national interest took the initiative in creating the International Monetary Fund, and the World Bank to supplement German reparations. Also the US made substantial grants through the UN Relief and Rehabilitation Administration during 1946-48, and through the Marshall Plan during 1948-51. Even during the war, the American leadership had recognized that given America's economic supremacy, 'a more open international economy would not threaten the US economy, but would link the economic activity of other countries into a satellite relationship with the United States.'[13]

In 1944 the IMF and the World Bank were established in Bretton Woods, New Hampshire as permanent debt-management consortia based in Washington DC where they have remained to this day. The National Advisory Council (NAC) on international monetary and financial problems was created within the US government to oversee the operations of both institutes. The US Executive Directors of the Bank and the IMF were directly responsible to the NAC for their votes in the organizations. US government control was ensured by the US Executive Director, who had 40 per cent of the votes on all matters.

The lending activities were designed to finance large-scale exports of capital, goods, and engineering services from the US, and later from other developing nations, without actually financing the development of those sectors in the emerging countries, especially agriculture, which might displace US exports.

During 1946-52 the World Bank's prime objective was to help in the reconstruction of Europe. From 1952 onward the Bank's lending activities expanded and were concentrated in the less developed countries financing some $9.8 billion of all exports from the industrial nations to these countries. About one-third of these exports were from the US. During 1960-69 Bank operations contributed an average $240 million annually to the US balance of payment on current account. This added up to $2.6 billion net inflow since the Bank's establishment.

The total US public and private investments in the Bank, approximating $2,443 million at the end of 1969, was an excellent investment as aggregate return exceeded 100 per cent from the Bank's inception through to 1969.[14]

A study conducted by the US Government Accounting Office concluded that during 1966-70 the World Bank took in more funds from twenty of its less developed member countries than it disbursed. Its collection of interest and principal from countries exceeded the new loans extended to them. For the seventy-two less developed countries taken as a whole, 'the Bank distributed an average $535 million a year. But repayments of principal and interest averaged $427 million, leaving an average net transfer of only $108 million.'[15] The Bank is not exactly an instrument of US generosity. It serves its economic interests, and keeps a large number of less developed states beholden to American *imperium*.

The Bank makes loans by borrowing in the open market at commercial rates, supplying these funds to borrowing countries with 1 per cent to 1 ½ per cent premium as compensation for risk. Its loans have been mainly for electrical power, transportation, irrigation, and road construction. Pakistan was a major beneficiary in the 1950s and 1960s when it divided the Indus River system with India. The Bank provided funds to build a network of canals to divide water between India and Pakistan.

During the 1980s and 1990s the Bank had to face macro-economic and debt rescheduling issues as the less developed countries found themselves unable to pay back the loans; later in this period, social and environmental issues assumed centre stage. More recently an increasingly vocal American and international civil society has accused the Bank of widening the gap between rich and poor, and between developed and impoverished countries. The Bank is now a big complex, encompassing five closely associated development institutions.

Structurally the IMF is similarly dominated by the US. The Board of Governors, the highest decision-making body, consists of a governor and an alternate governor for each member country. Actually several less developed countries are represented by one regional delegate. The governors normally meet once a year, the actual management of its affairs remains vested in the Executive Board. Altogether 184 members participate in the Board of Governors; each country's vote varies from the lowest of 0.01 to the highest of 6.1. The US possesses a commanding 17.14 per cent of the total votes. In 2004 the poorest countries owed a total debt of about $200 billion to the World Bank, the IMF, and to the private sector of prosperous western countries. Pakistan owed $33.54 billion combined to these creditors in 2003.

FOREIGN AID AS AN INSTRUMENT OF US DIPLOMACY

In addition to the World Bank and the IMF annual economic aid to more than 100 countries in the world is an effective instrument of the US *imperium*. (See Table I)

TABLE I

FY 2005 USAID COUNTRY ALLOCATION SUMMARY— ACTUAL APPROPRIATION

Regions	Number of States	Total Aid (Dollars Thousands)
I. Africa, including regional initiatives	35	1,897,441
II. Asia and Near East		
1. Near East	7	1,286,180
2. Asia	16	1,459,190
3. Asia/Near East regional issues i.e. women's issues, regional democracy and security		151,647
III. Europe and Eurasia		
1. Europe	14	428,893
2. Eurasia, Russian and Central Asian States	14	577,176
IV. Latin America and Caribbean, including regional initiatives	17	681,614
TOTAL	112	

Source: USAID, <http://www.usaid.gov/policy/budget/cbj2004/summary_tables_table4.pdf>.

The total amount is by no means very large. Yet foreign aid is not particularly popular with the average American citizen. The American public tends to look upon it as a distribution of economic resources 'doled out' to ungrateful foreigners. In popular perception poverty in foreign countries is spawned by corrupt political leaders, general lethargy of an indifferent population, addiction to religious dogmas, and the absence of work ethics. There may be a grain of truth in all of these perceptions, but the rationale for the economic aid is explained by the US government.

Officially, the policy of economic aid is explained as 'the single largest counter to the adversaries of freedom'. Who are the enemies of freedom? In the Cold War period (1947-December 1991) the mortal enemy was the Soviet Union and the ideology of communism. The Soviet Union presented a paradigm of rapid industrial and economic development and the promise of leap-frogging the capitalistic mode of economy from feudal backwardness and stagnation. Accelerated economic development and equality were presented to the Third World as a possibility through the replication of the totalitarian Soviet model. While the Soviet Union succeeded in establishing a military balance of power to counterbalance US influence, the ideology of communism presented a serious challenge to US corporate capitalism.

The US presented the package of freedom, which emphasized multi-party democracy and included: 1) the right to private ownership, 2) rule of law based upon human rights, 3) free international trade and 4) the freedom to invest capital to generate economic development. In the climate of the Cold War foreign economic assistance was projected as an act of benevolence to 'maintain foreign countries' independence'.[16] However, during the late 1980s the lawmakers were openly stating that 'foreign assistance is a valuable foreign policy tool in terms of promoting US security interests and its economic interests.'[17] Still the American public has very little understanding of the aid programme 'as an instrument of foreign policy, used to advance the US interests'.[18]

After the Cold War the enemies of freedom are perceived to be the Islamic fundamentalists—militant extremists, led by Osama bin Laden, who have launched the terror movement against the US. Since the 11 September tragedy the focus of foreign aid has shifted to promoting democracy in the Arab and Islamic world, and improving education in private religious schools and government-maintained schools by eliminating those subjects that might promote religious intolerance and hatred for non-Muslims. Funds are allocated to deal with the status and rights of women in Muslim states. President George W. Bush reflects in his statements a determination to democratize the Arab and Islamic states in order to 'force them to be free' from the shackles of absolute monarchies, secular political and military dictatorships. In his perception the lack of democracy and freedom has spawned the 'Islamic terror'.

THE WORLD TRADE ORGANIZATION

After World War II the US also emerged as the dominant trading nation. For more than half a century it employed the United Nations as the forum to create a world in its own image. The US manoeuvered with its allies to forge global accords about human rights, nuclear tests, selective promotion of democracy, and a fair market economy that Washington insisted the world mirror in its own values. After the collapse of the Soviet Union US diplomacy started to use a new institution that most Americans and other people had scarcely heard of—the World Trade Organization (WTO). It had its debut on January 1995. In April 2003 its membership had increased to 145 countries as against the UN Membership of 191 countries. Pakistan joined the WTO in January 1995.

In addition to the World Bank and the IMF, the Bretton System created under the leadership of the US in 1945 also envisaged the General Agreement on Tariffs and Trade, known as GATT. It was created to establish fair trade for a stable world economy. The GATT had a *de facto* role as an international organization before the creation of the WTO. It completed eight rounds of multilateral trade negotiations. The Uruguay Round— the Eight Round—concluded with the signing of the Final Act on 15 April 1994 in Marrakech, and produced the WTO.[19]

The WTO operates a system of trade rules, including: 1) the member states must not discriminate between their trading partners, and should not discriminate between their own and foreign products, services materials, 2) trade must flow as freely as possible; barriers concerning custom duties (or tariffs) and measures such as import bans or quotas that restrict quantities selectively must come down, 3) the business environment must be stable and predictable; with stability and predictability, foreign investment is encouraged, jobs are created, and consumers can reap the benefits of competition, 4) competition and productivity should be encouraged by discouraging unfair practices such as export subsidies and dumping products at below cost to gain market share.[20]

Critics contend the WTO's policies tend to perpetuate existing patterns of comparative advantage—and disadvantage—among nations.[21] However, in 1997 the United States' trade representative to the WTO, Charlene Barshefsky, shed voluminous light on the political as well as trade aspects of the US grand design. 'The United States has effectively exported the American values of free competition, fair rules and effective enforcement', she declared. She continued: 'In fact, exporting American values, and turning America's passion for deregulation into a tool of foreign policy is what the new agreement is all about.' The reference to the new agreement was the US approval of a huge accord to open the world's highly protected telecommunications markets to American-style competition.

The agreement for the first time empowered the WTO to go inside the borders of the seventy countries that signed it to review how quickly and effectively they were deregulating a key part of their economies. At the same time, however, the US was using the WTO as a tool to force political change in China. China's admission was blocked from 1997 to December 2001. Meanwhile the US required that China must move to stop protecting many of its key industries, and its huge subsidies to state-owned enterprises that employ almost half of the working population. In public the US declared that China must join the WTO on 'commercially acceptable terms', like every other country. The same set of agreements was applied to Russia's possible admission.

The agenda behind this 'commercial condition' was purely political. The liberal view on China, that advocates the policy of engagement is that accelerated internal economic changes would weaken the Communist Party's hold over the country's rapidly growing economy. That in turn could threaten the Party's hold on power. Barshevsky's predecessor, Mickey Kantor, commented on this policy: 'This is what we've meant for four years when we declared that trade and economics are no longer a separate sphere from the rest of American foreign policy.'[22]

Less developed countries see the US approach as economic imperialism, as they assert that the WTO is dominated by the United States. Oddly enough the exact opposite of this complaint is heard from the American public; they feel that the US does not have sufficient clout in the WTO.

MILITARY ESTABLISHMENT

The United States' national security, trade, and stability interests encompass all four populated continents of the earth and extend to the known and yet to be discovered limits of outer space. If any major power challenged the supremacy of the US, it would be construed as a potential adversary and confronted accordingly.

To deal with its almost unlimited earthly range of national interest, the US established five Combatant Commands (Central Command [CENTCOM], European Command [EUCOM], Northern Command [NORTHCOM], Pacific Command [PACOM], and Southern Command [SOUTHCOM]) to police instability in 197 countries and territories encompassing all the four continents and the world's oceans and seas. (See Map I and Figure II) On 6 February 2007 President Bush established the sixth command for Africa which would become operational by 30 September 2008.

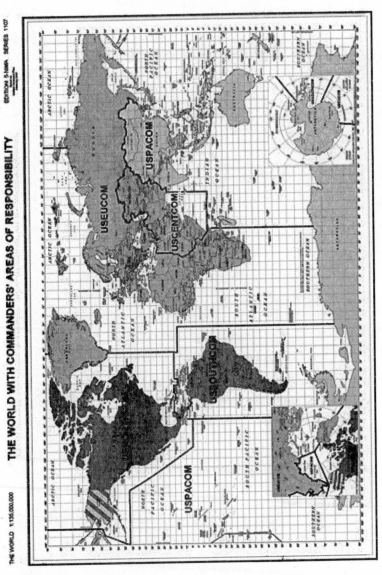

MAP I
Source: United States Department of Defence,
<http://www.defencelink.mil/specials/unifiedcommand/images/areaof_
responsibility.jpg>.

FIGURE II

Combatant Commands

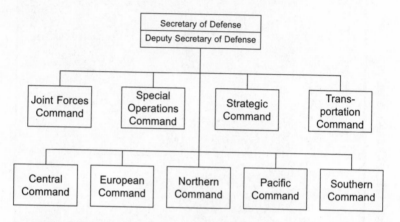

Source: United States Department of Defence,
<http://www.defencelink.mil/odam/omp/pubs/GuideBook/Pdf/Cmds.PDF>.

FIVE US COMBATANT COMMANDS

In addition to these Combatant Commands, there are four additional commands devoted to specific tasks of planning, supporting, and supervising the five area commands. They are: 1) Joint Forces Command 2) Special Operations Command 3) Strategic Command and 4) Transportation Command. All of these commands together present the picture of a global *imperium* unmatched by any great empire in the world's history. (See Table II)

TABLE II

United States Combatant Commands and Their Area of Responsibility		
Command	Area of Responsibility (AOR)	Size of AOR
(I) US Northern Command NORTHCOM	US, Canada, Mexico, parts of the Caribbean, and the contiguous waters in the Atlantic and Pacific Oceans	
(II) US Pacific Command PACOM	43 countries, 20 territories and possessions and 10 US territories	Covers 105 million square miles; traverses 16 time zones.
	Includes the world's largest armed forces: a) China, b) Russia, c) India, d) North Korea, e) South Korea	35 per cent of US trade is within this region.
	Five of the seven worldwide US mutual defence treaties: 1) US Philippines Defence Treaty, 1952 2) ANZUS-Australian-New Zealand-US Treaty, 1952	
(III) US European Command EUCOM	(1) 91 countries and territories (2) extends from the North Cape of Norway, through the waters of the Baltic and Mediterranean Seas, most of Europe, parts of the Middle East to the Cape of Good Hope in South Africa	Covers 21 million square miles.
(IV) US Southern Command SOUTHCOM	32 countries (14 Central and South American and 13 in the Caribbean)	Covers about 145 million square miles. The region represents about one-sixth of the landmass of the world.
(V) US Central Command CENTCOM	25 nations, ranging from Egypt in the west to Pakistan in the east	Covers more than 3,600 miles east to west, and 4,600 miles north to south. Includes mountain ranges with elevations exceeding 24,000 feet.
Total Coverage	197 Countries and Territories	

Source: US Department of Defence, *Defence Link-Unified Command Plan* (Washington DC, September 2004).

Even when relations between Pakistan and the US were very strained, the fact that Pakistan had been placed, without its consent, under the guardianship or ward of CENTCOM meant that it could enjoy the blessings of the US international security umbrella that guaranteed the status quo in South Asia—that is so long as Pakistan did not participate in any anti-US enterprises.

Before the 11 September tragedy, CENTCOM believed that instability in the South and Central Asian sub-region, especially in Pakistan and Afghanistan, created instability and uncertainty that extended far beyond the Central region. Continued instability in Afghanistan inhibited efforts to open traditional trade routes, and thereby limited the Central Asian states' economic options and stymied their access to the warm water ports on the Arabian Sea. In the early stages of Taliban rule, CENTCOM viewed them as providers of 'some stability to portions of Afghanistan', but as time went on it realized that they had only 'further aggravated political upheaval and armed conflict in and around the Kabul area escalating the ongoing civil war.' CENTCOM has viewed the Indo-Pakistan dispute over Kashmir as a conflict over 'border demarcation and water rights' that ignited 'historical animosity'.[23] In CENTCOM's perception, this Indo-Pakistan mistrust has continually 'undermined efforts to promote non-proliferation and threatened world security.'[24] When Iran's military capability exceeded the level that was required for self-defence, CENTCOM became alarmed because it viewed Iran as having the potential to disturb the status quo in the Persian Gulf. To curb Iran's development, the Clinton Administration enacted sanctions prohibiting trade and investment with it.

US military preparedness and its power projection at the global level is ensured by its rich and productive US economy, which can afford to allocate resources to the armed forces which far exceed the budgetary allocations of all other major powers. The US defence budget in 1996—266 billion, almost exactly equalled the combined total of the next six largest defence budgets, those of Russia, China, Japan, France, Britain, and

Germany. By 1999, its defence budget of $283 billion exceeded the combined total of the next seven largest—those six states plus Italy. By 2000, its defence budget of $295 billion exceeded the combined total of the next nine largest—the aforementioned seven states plus Saudi Arabia and India.[25] The increases projected after the 11 September 2001 terrorist attacks promised to widen the gap even more. In 2002 its defence budget increased to $300 billion, compared to:

Rank	Country	Military expenditures - dollar figure	Date of Information
1	United States	$ 518,100,000,000	2005 est.
2	China	$ 81,470,000,000	2005 est.
3	France	$ 45,000,000,000	2005
4	Japan	$ 44,310,000,000	2005 est.
5	United Kingdom	$ 42,836,500,000	2005 est.
6	Germany	$ 35,063,000,000	2003
7	Italy	$ 28,182,800,000	2003
8	Korea, South	$ 21,050,000,000	2005 est.
9	India	$ 19,040,000,000	2005 est.
10	Saudi Arabia	$ 18,000,000,000	2005 est.

Source: United States Central Intelligence Agency, *The World Fact Book*, 2005, <https://www.cia.gov/cia/publications/factbook/rankorder/2067rank.html> (18 September 2006).

In 2004 the US military budget exceeded $425 billion, which included the extremely high expense of the US War in Iraq.

III

THE NATURE OF AN EMPIRE

American public opinion is reluctant to accept the United States as an empire. Karl Marx identified modern imperialism as the product of capitalism, and Lenin added that when the monopoly stage of capitalism came into existence capitalism and imperialism became synonymous – in essence one and the same thing. In the past, imperialism was a mark of national glory. With the Marxist-Leninist description of imperialism as another name for the economic and political exploitation of poor and weak nations, imperialism in the American public opinion and elsewhere in the world acquired an obviously odious connotation.

After the collapse of the Soviet Union American political leaders and scholars shed their reluctance. Some, including Robert Kagan (Senior Associate at the Carnegie Endowment for International Peace), Jean Bethke Elshtain, Professor of Social and Political Ethics, and Niall Ferguson, Professor of History, began to urge the US to accept responsibility as the guardian of European security, and international order.[26] Michael Hardt and Antonio Negri, made a subtle distinction between traditional imperialist policies, and the United States' imperial role. 'Imperialism's project', in their definition is always to 'spread its power linearly in closed spaces, and invade, destroy and subsume subject countries within its sovereignty.' The American imperial role, on the other hand, is designed 'through the global expansion of the internal US Constitutional Project', which is imperial and not imperialist.

Hardt and Negri have identified three stages of imperial command of the US: inclusive, differential, and managerial. In the first stage all are 'welcomed within its boundaries, regardless of race, creed, color, gender and sexual orientation.' As the Statue of Liberty says: 'Give me your poor, your hungry, your downtrodden masses.' The second stage involves 'the affirmation of differences accepted within the imperial realm.' The third period is the moment of imperial control, which must be followed by the management of these differences in a general structure of command.[27]

In examining the foreign policies of Presidents George H.W. Bush, Bill Clinton, and George W. Bush during his first year in office, Andrew Bacevich demonstrated in his study, *American Empire*, that since the end of the Cold War the US has 'adhered to a well-defined grand strategy', which involved expanding 'an

American *imperium*'. Basic to this strategy is a commitment to 'global openness—removing barriers that inhibit the movement of goods, capital, ideas and people.' The grand objective is 'the creation of an open and integrated international order based upon the principles of democratic capitalism, with the United States as the ultimate guarantor of order and enforcer of norms.'[28]

Bush and Clinton subscribed to the consensus defining US foreign policy in the global age. This consensus, Bacevich maintained, constituted the substructure of post-Cold War US foreign policy, and contained the following imperatives:

(1) First was the imperative of America's mission as the vanguard of history, transforming the global order, and in doing so, perpetuating its own dominance.

(2) Second was the imperative of openness and integration, given impetus by globalization but guided by the United States.

(3) Third was the imperative of American global leadership expressed by maintaining US preeminence in each of the world's strategically significant regions.

(4) Fourth was the imperative of military supremacy, maintained in perpetuity and projected globally.[29]

A conservative cheerleader of American power, Charles Krauthammer, asserted that 'this American Republic has acquired the largest seeming empire in the history of the world – acquired it in a fit of absent-mindedness greater even than Britain's. And it was not just absent-mindedness; it was sheer inadvertence.' He added that unlike Rome, Britain, France, and Spain, and other classical empires of modern times the US 'do not hunger for territory'. If not, then what kind of an empire is it? He defined the American empire as 'a commercial republic that, by pure accident of history, has been designated custodian of international system.'[30]

Tackling the imperial issues, Zbigniew Brzezinski (President Jimmy Carter's National Security Advisor) did not mince words. In his book *The Grand Chessboard: American Primacy and its*

Geostrategic Imperatives, he forthrightly states that 'the three grand imperatives of imperial geostrategy are to prevent collusion, and maintain security dependence among the vassals, to keep tributaries pliant and protected, and to keep the barbarians from coming together.'[31] In November 2000 Richard Haass, a member of the National Security Council under President Bush I, delivered a paper in Atlanta on Imperial America. In order to achieve its objective of global preeminence, he asserted that it would be necessary for Americans to 're-conceive their role from a traditional nation-state to an imperial power.' He avoided the term 'imperialist' in describing America's role, preferring 'imperial'. Since the former is associated with 'exploitation, normally for commercial ends', and territorial control. Yet his intent was clear: 'To advocate an imperial policy is to call for a foreign policy that attempts to organize the world along principles affecting relations between states and conditions within them'. Haass asserted that US policy, like British policy in the nineteenth century, would follow 'the principles of extending control informally if possible and formally if necessary... coercion and the use of force would normally be a last resort'.[32]

Some well-known retired US generals also offered their view of American *imperium*. General Anthony Zinni, who retired in 2000 as Commander-in Chief of the Central Command, called the US 'an empire of influence', instead of 'an empire of conquest, occupation or colonies'. Metaphorically, he described the US as an 800-pound gorilla among nations, which defends itself, then

> protects its interests, maintains stability, and keeps itself on top by gradually taking over greater control (direct and indirect) beyond its immediate borders. It begins to impose its will by direct force unilaterally. Because it has the power to change distasteful situations or governments on its own, it asserts that power. The gorilla metamorphoses into an octopus, with ever-stretching tentacles. It becomes an empire.[33]

It is indeed a graphic description of the American *imperium*.

A former Director of the National Security Agency (1985-1988) Lt. General William E. Odom, and his co-author, Robert Dujarric, confidently asserte that 'empire' need 'not necessarily connote negative connotations.' The US, in their presentation, is an empire of willing members. They believe that 'countries struggle to become members; they do not have to fight to get out. None has left voluntarily, although a few have downgraded their military relations'. In their eyes the US is an ideological empire, not a territorial one; a wealth generating empire, not a wealth squandering one; and that 'countries struggle to join it, not to counterbalance it'.[34]

Odom and Dujjaric believe that the American empire 'is a sui generis regime type: unipolar, based on ideology, rather than territorial control, voluntary in membership, and economically advantageous to all countries within it.' They listed several organizations which are part of the US imperial system, including the US, the World Bank, the IMF, the WTO, and the International Court of Justice. In addition to these organizations, they added a table of 41 countries of North America, Europe, Asia-Pacific and the Middle East occupying different statuses in the American Empire.

ECONOMIC, MILITARY, AND POLITICAL MEMBERSHIP STATUS IN THE AMERICAN EMPIRE

Country	GDP in Billion US $	Military Ally	Constitutional Breakthrough
North America			
1. U.S.A.	$10,894		Yes
2. Canada	760	NATO	Yes
3. Mexico	664	No	No
Europe			
4. Belgium	266	NATO	Yes
5. Czech Republic	85	NATO	Uncertain
6. Denmark	190	NATO	Yes
7. France	1,531	NATO	Yes

Country	GDP in Billion US $	Military Ally	Constitutional Breakthrough
8. Germany	2,145	NATO	Yes[a]
9. Greece	146	NATO	Uncertain
10. Hungary	64	NATO	Uncertain
11. Iceland	9	NATO	Yes
12. Italy	1,278	NATO	Yes
13. Luxembourg	24	NATO	Yes
14. Netherlands	456	NATO	Yes
15. Norway	188	NATO	Yes
16. Poland	196	NATO	Uncertain
17. Portugal	130	NATO	Yes
18. Spain	710	NATO	Yes
19. Turkey	185	NATO	Uncertain
20. United Kingdom	1,646	NATO	Yes
21. Austria	218	Neutral	Yes
22. Finland	138	Neutral	Yes
23. Ireland	132	Neutral	Yes
24. Sweden	244	Neutral	Yes
25. Switzerland	285	Neutral	Yes
26. Bulgaria	17	NATO in 2004	No
27. Estonia	7	NATO in 2004	Uncertain
28. Latvia	9	NATO in 2004	No
29. Lithuania	13	NATO in 2004	Uncertain
30. Romania	47	NATO in 2004	No
31. Slovakia	25	NATO in 2004	No
32. Slovenia	23	NATO in 2004	Uncertain
Asia-Pacific			
33. Australia	436	ANZUS	Yes
34. Japan	4,229	Bilateral	Yes
35. New Zealand	62	ANZUS[b]	Yes
36. Philippines	83	Bilateral	Uncertain
37. Singapore[c]	95	Informal	Uncertain
38. South Korea	529	Bilateral	Uncertain
39. Taiwan[c]	302	Informal	Uncertain
40. Thailand	130	Bilateral	No
Mideast			
41. Israel[c]	108	Informal	Yes/Uncertain
Others[d]			

Source for GDP data: International Monetary Funds 2003 estimates.

[a] 'Yes' means that constitutional orders are mature, at least twenty years old. 'Uncertain' means that a country has a constitutional order less than twenty years

old, or it appears to have achieved an initial constitutional breakthrough, but uncertainties about it persist.

[b] The United States has suspended military relations with New Zealand until it reverses its policy on US nuclear power ship visits.

[c] Taiwan, Singapore, and Israel have strong informal military ties to the United States.

[d] Micronesia, the Marshall Islands, and Palau are formally US military defence responsibilities, but they have been omitted. They and many other small countries – e.g., Caribbean island states – have been left out because even in the aggregate they add very little to the power of the American empire although many of them technically could be included and some, but not all, would choose to be included.

Source: Dujarric, *America's Inadvertent Empire.* p. 40

The countries within the American empire account for 70 per cent of the gross world product. Pakistan is another state which is always willing to be a part of the American *imperium*. If the Odom and Dujjaric study had been published in 2004, when Washington declared Pakistan a non-NATO ally, they would have added Pakistan to the category of 'willing vassals'. Afghanistan remained outside of the US for a long time, but was eventually brought into the fold by force of arms.

IV

In contemplating the Greco-Roman period, and going through European and Islamic empires, including the Umayyad, Abbasid, and Ottoman one learns a few useful lessons: 1) Empires do not last forever; sooner or later they collapse 2) The trick is to prolong their tenure as much as humanly possible. This enormous responsibility imposes upon the empire-builders a heavy burden of statesmanship, calling for far-sightedness, a degree of patience and tolerance for the interests of 'friends' and 'foes'. The ability to bludgeon the foes into submission creates the hubris of invincibility, which encourages the start of endless military interventions.

Another major danger to the empire comes from several sources: 1) the imperial urge to expand in order to impose imperial (disguised as God-ordained) values; 2) the irresistible urge to intervene far and wide for 'humanitarian reasons'—the US Army alone operates in 120 countries, creating the potential to be sucked into many non-strategic bushfire wars; 3) counter-attacks by the subordinated populations, often called the barbarians. (These barbaraians were very substantially responsible for the fall of the Roman empire); 4) implosion under the weight of internal contradictions – the Soviet Union was the best example of this self-made harm; and 5) finally the exhaustion spawned by these debilitating internal and external catalysts.

What are the less-powerful states to do in the face of this colossus? Developed states in Europe, in the process of achieving unity in the European Union, have the capability to defy American power. Moreover China, Russia, and India to some degree have the capacity to follow an independent foreign policy. In some distant future China might appear as a countervailing force to American power. Some scholars speculate the European Union to be a third pole of power in international power structure.

Other less developed countries like Pakistan and Afghanistan have to learn the diplomatic skills to be on the right side of the American *imperium*. If the US is in a position to dictate terms on larger geo-political issues, they too can exploit their 'weak position' to extract as many economic, industrial, and educational benefits as possible. As long as these two countries remain politically unstable and fail to evolve stable political systems which best suit their national character, they will remain tempting playgrounds for other more powerful states.

Modern diplomatic history presents several examples where less powerful states fully 'exploited' more powerful states to improve their economies and industrial capacity. These opportunities developed when the powerful states for the attainment of their own strategic objectives decided to help regional states with substantial investments in their economies: I) At the end of the nineteenth century Britain invested in Japan and transferred technology in order to strengthen Japan's potential to contain the expansion of Czarist Russia in the Far East. II) In the wake of World War I and the Soviet Revolution of 1917 Germany and the Soviet Union signed the Treaty of Rapallo of 16 April 1922 under which each renounced all territorial and financial claims against each other. A secret annex signed on 29 July allowed Germany to train its military in the Soviet Union and violate other provisions of the Treaty of Versailles, which forbade 'the armed forces of Germany not to include any military or naval air forces', in addition to renouncing the right to manufacture aircraft and tanks. Working secretly German technicians helped to restructure the Soviet defence industries. The celebrated designer of the MIG aircrafts Artem Mikoyan acquired the technical skill for aircraft designing from the German engineers.

III) In the 1950s the Soviet Union built a large number of industries in China. The countries relations deteriorated in 1962 when during the India-China War the Soviet Union supported India at the expense of China, a fellow 'communist state.'

IV) In 1971 the US under President Richard Nixon abandoned its well-known policy of isolating China, which had been in place since the communist victory ended the civil war in 1950.

Since the 1970s US private industrial investment has been absolutely phenomenal. China entered into a new economic partnership with the US, and has accelerated in industrial development with US and other foreign capital.

V) In order to raise India as a countervailing force to the rising power of China, the US will help India's economic and industrial development for at least the next ten years. Pakistan may not benefit from the US as India would; yet Pakistan's gains can be substantial if it develops the skills to 'exploit' American 'generosity'.

To do this successfully Pakistan needs to put its political house in order; and Afghanistan needs to reconstruct itself into a viable state.

NOTES

1. Edward Gibbon, *The Decline and Fall of the Roman Empire*, Vol. I (New York: Modern Library, n.d.), p. 25.
2. Henry Kissinger, *Does America Need a Foreign Policy* (New York: Simon and Shuster, 2001), p. 17.
3. Ibid., pp. 25-26.
4. Trudy J. Kuehner, *The New Perspectives on the Genesis of the US* (Philadelphia: Foreign Policy Research Institute, September 2004), p. 1.
5. Hans J. Morgenthau, *Politics Among Nations* (New York: Alfred A. Knopf, 1963), p. 11.
6. United States Central Intelligence Agency, *The World Fact Book*, 2005, <https://www.cia.gov/cia/publications/factbook/rankorder/2067rank.html> (18 September 2006).
7. United States Central Intelligence Agency, 'The United States', *The World Fact Book*, 2005, <https://www.cia.gov/cia/publications/factbook/rankorder/2067rank.html> (18 September 2006).
8. Ibid.
9. Robert M. Hathaway, 'Unfinished Passage: India, Indian Americans and the US Congress', *The Wilson Quarterly* (Spring 2001), p. 21.
10. For the most reliable information on the Jewish community's political role, see L. Sandy Maisel and Ira N. Forman, eds., *Jews in American Politics* (NY: Rowman and Littlefield, 2001), p. 273.
11. Ibid., page
12. For a very brilliant exposition of the American civil religion see, McDougall, *Freedom Just Around the Corner*.
13. Michael Hudson, *Super Imperialism* (London: Pluto Press, 2003), p. 38.
14. Hunter, op. cit., p. 197.
15. 'Lag in Disbursements: World Bank Criticized on LCD's Operations', *Journal of Commerce* (20 February 1973).
16. *US Aid History*, (Washington DC: The Department of State, June, 2003), p. 4.
17. Ibid.
18. Ibid.
19. WTO, *Understanding the World Trade Organization* (Geneva: Media Relations Division, 2003), pp. 9-10.
20. Ibid.
21. Hudson, op. cit., p. 201.
22. David Sanger, 'Playing the Trade Card', *The New York Times*, 17 February 1997.
23. Ibid.
24. Ibid.
25. Robert J. Art, *A Grand Strategy for America* (Ithaca: Cornell University Press, 2003), p. 15.

26. See Robert Kagan, *Of Paradise and Power: America and the New World Order* (New York: Knopf, 2003); Jean Bethke Elshtair, *Just War Against Terror: The Burden of American Power in a Violent World* (New York: Basic Books, 2003); Niall Ferguson, *The Rise and the Demise of the British World Order and the Lessons for Global Power* (New York: Basic Books, 2003).

27. Michael Hardt and Antonio Negri, *Empire* (Cambridge: Harvard University Press, 2000), pp. 182, 198-9.

28. Andrew J. Bacevich, *American Empire* (Cambridge: Harvard University Press, 2002), p. 3.

29. Ibid., pp. 215-220.

30. Charles Krauthammer, *Democratic Realism: An American Foreign Policy for a Unipolar World* (Washington DC: The American Enterprise Institute, 2004), pp. 2-3.

31. Zbigniew Brzezinski, *The Grand Chessboard: American Primacy and its Geostrategic Imperatives* (New York: Basic Books, 1997), p. 40.

32. Richard Haass, 'Imperial America', paper delivered at the Atlanta Conference, 11 November 2000.
    < http://www.brookings.edu/views/Articles/Haass/2000imperial.htm>.

33. Tom Clancy with General Zinni (Retd.), *Battle Ready* (New York: G.P. Putnam's Sons, 2003), p. 322.

34. William E. Odom and Robert Dujarric, *America's Inadvertent Empire* (New Haven: Yale University Press, 2004), pp. 39-40.

3

The US Withdrawal from Afghanistan and Pakistan

Nine years and forty-nine days after the Soviet troops marched into Afghanistan, they completed their withdrawal on 15 February 1989. Almost simultaneously the US lost interest in Afghanistan and Pakistan. The US locked its embassy in Kabul because of the absence of law and order there, and the war that started between the seven militias (the so-called Mujahideen), who failed to share power with each other. The Mujahideen's conflict in reality was an ethnic struggle between the Pashtuns and five major minority ethnic groups.

US relations with Pakistan soured over the nuclear issue. A series of sanctions were imposed which made life for Pakistan quite difficult. With American withdrawal from Afghanistan, Pakistan found the latter very receptive to its influence and very helpful in sustaining the struggle for Kashmir. Pakistan began to play its role independently of US concerns, and perceived Afghanistan as its 'strategic depth'. Here these issues are discussed: 1) the geostrategic environment at the global level, which led the US to withdraw its interest from Afghanistan, 2) the rise of the Taliban and the emergence of a failed state, 3) strained relations between the US and Pakistan.

I

GEO-STRATEGIC ENVIRONMENT

The period 1989-90 proved to be truly filled with a 'revolution': it witnessed the demolition of the Berlin Wall and the roll-back of Marxism-Leninism and the Soviet regime in Eastern Europe and the three Baltic States. In October 1989, President Mikhail S. Gorbachev declared that the Soviet Union had no moral or political right to interfere in the affairs of its East European neighbours. Consequently, he gave up the traditional superpower prerogative of intervention by military means. On 4 February 1990 Gorbachev called on the Soviet Union's Communist Party to foreswear its constitutional monopoly on power, and to accept the prospect of rival political parties. This shift of power led to the rise of Boris N. Yeltsin to the Presidency of Russia, and the collapse of the Soviet Union in December 1991. This development became the catalyst for the disintegration of the Communist Party, which held together the heterogeneous population of the Soviet Union. The crash of the old world order in Eastern Europe occurred along with the demise of the USSR.

In the post-Soviet period two revolutions were underway: one was primarily nationalistic, the other was essentially democratic, which emphasized the free market economy of capitalism. Russia sank into the position of a secondary state as it inherited from the Soviet Union a reduced number of assets: 90 per cent of the oil, nearly 80 per cent of the natural gas, 62 per cent of the electricity, 70 per cent of the gold and 70 per cent of the trained technical workers.[1] Russia also inherited 80 per cent of the industries, including metallurgy, aeronautics, space and nuclear industries. In addition to those reduced resources Russia inherited 60 per cent of the Soviet territory and a wide variety of problems with its neighbours.

The US viewed the collapse of the Soviet challenge with equanimity since it occurred without any direct military involvement of its armed forces. With this dramatic Soviet collapse China's army and nuclear arsenal became less threatening to the US. There was a vast discrepancy in economic power between the US and China in 1993. The US GNP was $5.7 trillion, and China's $700 billion. Since the 1970s China had put economic development before military modernization, its defence budget was reduced from 15.4 per cent of the budget in 1981 to 8.2 per cent in 1989. Its 1992 defence budget rose to 9.45 per cent of the total, but the $6.72 billion outlay was only 2.27 per cent of America's defence budget. China faced no foreign military threat nor did it pose a threat to the interests of the US. Since President Jimmy Carter established diplomatic relations with China (and withdrew diplomatic recognition from Taiwan) relations between the US and China had improved progressively. 'Between 1983 and 1993, China's exports to the US rose from $2.5 billion to $40 billion, and its trade surplus from $3 billion to $15 billion.'[2] While the Soviet Union's collapse eliminated Moscow's military threat, China's geopolitical importance correspondingly diminished. Washington no longer needed to use the China card to contain Moscow. By 1996 China had also joined institutions that form the foundation of an international capitalist economy, the World Bank, the IMF, the Asian Development Bank, and the Pacific Economic Cooperation Conference. China's economic interests are at present consistent with those of the US, creating economic interdependence.

The end of the Soviet Union called into question India's basic policy of non-alignment, which had been the cornerstone of its security and foreign policy. The Soviet Union was its supplier of technology and weapons. According to one estimate 'the Indian Army was nearly 80 per cent reliant on the Soviet Union.'[3] The Soviet Union conducted barter trade, which tremendously benefited India. After 1991 Russia wanted payments in hard currency, and was unable to supply spare parts for the weapons that it had earlier supplied. India was forced to review its foreign policy, especially under the leadership of Prime Minister Atal Bihari Vajpayee, who declared in 1998 that

India and the US were 'natural allies'. Vajpayee was critical of the US preference for Pakistan's military rulers, its alliance with communist China, its indifference to 'terrorism in Kashmir', and its refusal to accept 'India's compulsion to acquire weapons'. If the US paid attention to India's legitimate concerns, India would be 'the newest ally of the United States in the twenty-first century'.[4] Despite this expressed desire for friendship US, India had remained sympathetic to the Soviet military intervention in Afghanistan. This pro-Soviet orientation was a sour point in her relations with the US but India was not perceived to be a threat to America's core interests and values.

Against this background it made sense for the US to withdraw its interests from Afghanistan and Pakistan and leave them to settle their affairs on their own. In reality this policy of disengagement spawned a vacuum of power which Pakistan was unable to fill. The US did not foresee the unintended consequences of its policy, spawning an 'Islamic' fundamentalist terror movement led by Osama bin Laden in close collaboration with the Taliban. In any case the US paid a heavy price in the tragedy of 11 September 2001.

II

THE RISE OF THE TALIBAN MOVEMENT

The appearance of the Taliban, an unknown Islamic Student Movement, flashed across the Afghan horizon in late 1994. Two years later, in September 1996, the Taliban took Kabul and hanged Najibullah, the Soviet-sponsored former president, in a public square. Subsequently, they banned female access to education and employment, and imposed draconian Islamic laws including stoning proven adulterers to death and amputating thieves' hands and feet. Their rapid conquests, imposition of harsh punishments, and uncompromising commitment to their interpretation of Islam brought to the surface in the West all the frightful stereotypes about Islam. One observer called the

Taliban's movement 'Islamic Maoism', blending Chairman Mao's 'serve the people' doctrine with Sunni Muslim beliefs. A more benign description suggested that the Taliban 'in the tradition of the Pashtun reactionary movements recurrent in Afghan history.'[5] Another assessment was that the Taliban victory 'did more to change the world' than the 'Israeli-Palestinian', because the Taliban had one single-minded aim: the redemption of the 'entire Islamic world of one billion people.'[6] Had they succeeded in Afghanistan, their impact would be expected to be felt not only in Pakistan, Uzbekistan, and Kirghistan, but also in Russia, Iran, and India.

In these regions the Taliban's impact, religious or political, could not be ignored. In response, the governments of these countries re-oriented their foreign policies in relation to each other and to Afghanistan. The Taliban's zeal was generally described as that of Islamic fundamentalism, a kind of transitional street force with the potential to topple established governments through agitation or to spread indiscriminate terror even against the big powers. Increasingly, fear of Islamic fundamentalism replaced the old dread of Communism. However, it may be kept in mind that the exploitation of some religious ideas to promote political interests can also be observed in other religious communities.

THE TALIBAN'S PARADIGM OF ISLAMIC FUNDAMENTALISM

The Taliban circulated a substantial amount of information about their view of Islam, and explained their political and social policies in its light. Their religious, political, and social policies can thus be profiled.

To begin with the term, Taliban is derived from the Persian and Pashto plural of the Arabic word *talib*, 'seeker of knowledge'. The Prophet Muhammad (PBUH) is known to have urged the believers to seek knowledge, even if it meant going to China. Historically, it was practical for Afghan students to travel to

India until 1947, when India was partitioned, and then to Pakistan. In India, their favorite *madrasa*, an institute of higher learning, was the *Dar al-`ulum* of Deoband in Uttar Pradesh, which had been established in 1862. The Deoband Dar al-`ulum was known for its anti-British orientation and stood for the independence of a united India, but also retained a strong anti-Aligarh Muslim University policy. The latter was a modernist private university, which was established by Sir Sayyid Ahmad Khan (1817-1898) with the cooperation of the British.[7] While Aligarh Muslim University offered a Western education to middle-class students, the Deoband Dar al-`ulum trained young working and lower-middle-class Muslims, who received a traditional religious education, and joined the ranks of 'big' and small 'mullas in *masajid* (mosques)'.

Intellectually the Taliban were heir to the traditional affinity between the Deoband *Dar al-`ulum* and the Afghan *ulema*. However, after 1947 the leading Deobandi *ulema* in Pakistan, as well as other sectarian religious leaders, established *Dar al-`ulum* in all the provinces of Pakistan, including Azad Kashmir and the northern areas. The regional and sectarian distribution is given in Table 1. The number of graduates of different levels of education from these institutions, especially from 1982 to 1987, is impressive (see Table 2).

TABLE 1: REGIONAL AND SECTARIAN DISTRIBUTION OF *DAR AL-`ULUM* (UP TO 1988)

	Deobandi	Barelvi	Ahle Hadith	Shi`a	Others
Punjab	590	548	118	21	43
NWFP	631	32	5	2	8
Sindh	208	61	6	10	6
Balochistan	278	34	3	1	31
Azad Kashmir	51	20	2	-	3
Islamabad	51	20	-	2	3
Northern Areas	60	2	27	11	3

Source: *Dini Madaris Pakistan ki Jam e Report 1988*, Islamic Education Research Cell, Ministry of Education, Government of Pakistan, Islamabad, 1989.

TABLE 2: DEGREES AWARDED FROM *DAR AL-`ULUM*

	Nazerah	Hifz	Tajweed o Qirat	Daura-e-Hadith
Punjab	169,688	39,704	21,399	12,252
NWFP	68,529	7,129	9,510	27,906
Sindh	73,623	7,755	18,280	2,552
Balochistan	32,830	4,545	5,789	2,616
Azad Kashmir	12,460	1,066	1,212	337
Islamabad	3,877	154	367	-
Northern Areas	10,898	243	275	28

Source: *Dini Madaris Pakistan ki Jam e Report 1988*, Islamic Education Research Cell, Ministry of Education, Government of Pakistan, Islamabad, 1989.

During the years 1982-7, the *Dar al-`ulum* of North-West Frontier Province (NWFP), an area contiguous to Afghanistan, awarded an abnormally large number of the highest degrees. This development coincided 'with the influx of Afghan refugees and the Mujahideen at the height of Afghan jihad'[8] against the Soviet Union.

The Taliban leaders were the product of these theological seminaries. The governor of Jalalabad, bordering Pakistan, was a graduate of Dar al`ulum Haqqani of Akora Khattak. The judge of Jalalabad High Court and its *qadis* were the former scholars of another *madrassa*. The Taliban's ambassador to the UN, Maulana Abdul Hakim Mujahid, though not officially acknowledged by the United Nations, was an alumnus of the *Dar al-`ulum* of Binnori Town, Karachi. The Taliban government's ambassador to Pakistan was Mufti Ma'sum, who was a graduate of the same *Dar al-`ulum*. Some of the top echelon of the Taliban leaders were accomplished traditional Islamic scholars, while other had not completed their education.

Their education, however, was frozen in time, an apt description given by a Pakistani scholar. Unlike the Shi`a *Dar al-`ulum*, all Sunni theological institutions curricula are based upon Dars-i Nizamya. The eighteenth-century scholar, Mullah

Nizam ud-Din, who established this curriculum, flourished during the post-Aurangzeb period: the Mughal emperor died in 1707.[9] This system of education teaches young students: (1) Arabic grammar (2) syntax (3) rhetoric (4) philosophy of logic (5) dialectical theology (*Ilm al-Kalam*) (6) Tafsir (Qur'anic exegesis) (7) Fiqh (Islamic laws) (8) Usul al-Fiqu (Islamic jurisprudence) (9) Hadith (the Prophet's statements (PBUH)), and (10) mathematics. Strangely enough, none of these disciplines includes nineteenth-century texts, let alone contemporary works produced by modern scholars in the East or West. One cannot expect a modern outlook on religious and political matters from graduates of these studies. The Taliban's *Weltanschauung* was determined by this education, which is petrified in a pre-modern mould.

The Taliban's political structure reflected, according to them, the early Caliphate of Khulfa-i Rashidin (632-662), the four 'rightly-guided' caliphs who succeeded the Prophet Muhammad (PBUH).[10] The Taliban were 'committed to establishing an exemplary Islamic rule' for the world and especially for the Muslim states, and they were impervious to the possibility that their 'exemplary' Islamic paradigm may produce negative stereotypes of Islam.

Emulating the early Caliphate, the Taliban created a supreme council (*majlis-i shura*) consisting of twenty individuals and, in a fairly representative congregation of 1,500 Sunni ulema (religious scholars), who represented various ethnic tribes, elected 35-year-old Mulla Muhammad Umar the Amir al-Muminin, the Commander of the Faithful. The majority of the council members were Pashtuns; fourteen of them had lost parts of their body fighting against the Soviet Union. Mulla Umar had lost one of his eyes.

Despite their commitment to the pristine purity of Islam, the Pashtun ethnic composition of the Taliban turned their jihad into a struggle for power against the Tajiks in the Panjsher Valley and the Uzbeks in the north. The first group was led by former President Burhan-ud-Din Rabbani and the well-known military commander Ahmad Shah Massoud. The latter was led by the Uzbek General, Rashid Dostem, who had previously collaborated with the Soviet expeditionary forces and then shifted his allegiance in January 1992 to the Mujahiddin, a seven- party coalition which had been supported by the US and Pakistan in their war against the Soviet Union. The Taliban emphatically denied the ethnic bias of their movement, saying that their true jihad was the war between right (which they espouse), and wrong (which is represented by their opposition). It was a titanic struggle between virtue and vice, with 'no place in it for racial predjudice'.

In consonance with their concept of Islamic virtue, they established a department of moral control—Amar bil Ma'ruf Nahi Anil Munkar—which 'enforced good and forbade evil'. This department enforced Hudood punishments ordained by the Qur'an or the Sunna, including whipping of 100 strokes or death by stoning for having sexual intercourse without being married to the partner. Homosexuality as a capital offence was make punishable by the wall-toppling method, when a fifteen-foot brick wall was toppled over the guilty person to kill him.[11] Thieves must have their hands and feet amputated. Television stations, 'being against the shari'a', were closed, and photography, singing, and music were eliminated. Those who did not pray five times a day or did not fast for thirty days during the month of Ramadan were imprisoned; shaving off the beard or trimming it to less than a fistful was prohibited, as too was having a Western-style haircut. Gambling, betting, pigeon-keeping and flying, and dog racing were forbidden.[12]

The Taliban's repressive policy towards women evoked the strongest possible indignation from some Muslim countries, and from the West. The Taliban dogmatically asserted that Allah defined and determined women's rights—not the US, or the United Nations or the European states. They rejected 'the Western-bestowed rights of women', and described their critics' attitude as 'entirely absurd and stupid'. Islam, according to them, has placed full responsibility for a woman's maintenance upon the man. If a man could not pay her dowry (*Mahr*), or bear her expenses, then his marriage was not valid. If the husband died, the woman had the right to remarry, or she could live with her parents, who were responsible for her maintenance. Islam made woman an heir of her parents' wealth, as well as to her husband's estate. Also, she was an heir to her children's property. Contrary to these provisions, the Taliban asserted that 'the West has made a woman an object of man's lust and desires'. They are also 'dragged' into the offices and factories, restaurants and stores. Consequently Western women had lost their 'personality and identity'. Addressing Europeans, the Taliban stated that they had no right to force upon others their own failed values. 'Your parliament passes a bill which makes it legal for a man to marry another man, for a son-in-law to marry his wife's mother, i.e. his mother-in-law. Why do you compel us to do the same?'

In addition to these cultural polemics, the Taliban explained their policy towards women's employment and education. Indeed, female education and employment were adversely affected in cities, especially in Kabul. Women were forced to observe purdah (seclusion and concealment), and to stay at home, thus losing their jobs. The Taliban asserted that Kabuli women were divided into two categories: those who were linked to the Communist movement and those who had been sent to Moscow. In Moscow, they learned 'all the vices', and then returned 'bent upon destroying the Islamic environment of Afghanistan' and were appointed to different jobs in the government offices. These women 'belonged to the Communists, heretics and atheists', and enjoyed the United Nations' patronage. Their husbands were sent to the war fronts to go into the certain mouth of death. Then these women became the object of 'leaders' lust'.

All of these Kabuli women were removed from their jobs, the Taliban asserted, with full salaries; they were not denied the right to their livelihood. The denial of education was not permanent. Women would receive education in Islamic madrasas 'from which [they] emerge as an epitome of honour and decency, grace and dignity'. When would these female madrasas be established? The answer was to 'wait till the end of the civil war'! Consequently, the present generation of young girls was denied the benefits of education at all levels.

For nearly two years after the capture of Kabul, the Taliban demonstrated no anti-Western reflexes, and the US generally maintained an attitude of benign neglect. After spending approximately $10 billion supporting the Mujahideen against the Soviet Union, the US also cancelled the last of its civilian aid programmes for Afghanistan, apart from an $800,000 grant to a private agency which distributed emergency winter (1995) supplies in Kabul. Meanwhile, Pakistan switched its backing to the Taliban from the hard-line Mujahideen leader, Gulbuddin Hikmatyar, who had become the prime minister by virtue of the Islamabad agreement of 7 March 1993. This agreement was ceremoniously signed on 12 March 1993 in Mecca, one of Islam's holiest places, where King Fahd of Saudi Arabia and Prime Minister Nawaz Sharif of Pakistan personally guaranteed the power-sharing agreement among the political parties of the Mujahideen.[13] However, the warlords, including Ahmad Shah Masoud and General Rashid Dostem, had not signed the agreement. Predictably, this sanctified agreement fell apart.

In pursuit of personal and ethnic domination, even before the last Soviet troops were withdrawn in 1989, the Mujahideen resistance leaders were at war with each other, and had carved Afghanistan up into a jigsaw puzzle of lawless fiefs.[14] It is in this treacherous Hobbesian political environment that the Taliban rode to victory in Kabul, winning in the process Pakistan's support and US acquiescence. With a large Pashtun population in its own NWFP, Pakistan was indeed eager to have a Pashtun-dominated government in Kabul.

Other regional powers also started to support different ethnic groups. Iran backed the Shi`a ethnic Hazara, who were now led by the Iran-sponsored party Hizb-i Wahdat. They maintained small but effective military forces in western Kabul and across central Afghanistan. General Dostem, who led Uzbeks in northern Afghanistan, benefited from close ties with Uzbekistan and to some extent with Russia. Saudi Arabia initially supported Abdul Rabb Rasul Sayyaf, a Kharruti Pashtun whose forces controlled some strategic territory north-west of Kabul. However, when the Taliban had established control over 90 per cent of Afghan territory, Saudi Arabia extended them diplomatic recognition.

In addition to its pro-Pashtun policy, Pakistan's relations with the Tajiks were soured by President Rabbani of Afghanistan's policy towards India. From 1947-1979 when the Soviet Union and India maintained an entente cordiale with monarchical Afghanistan, the latter pressed territorial claims on Pakistan. Consequently, Pakistan felt squeezed by the two neighbours. Rabbani's overtures to India recreated the same old fears in Pakistan's establishment. Rabbani sent Hedayat Amin Arsala, his minister of foreign affairs, to India in July 1993 to ask it to reopen its embassy in Kabul and to provide 'humanitarian aid,' including training facilities for Afghan students in India. Also, he denied that Afghans were involved in the Muslim campaign for self-determination in Kashmir. Arsala then added, 'Let bygones be bygones' in reference to India's support for the Soviet sponsored leader, Najibullah, and India's benign tolerance of the Soviet invasion of Afghanistan.[15]

By 1998, the lines of confrontation were clearly drawn. Pakistan and Saudi Arabia supported the Taliban against the Mujahideen, the Afghan coalition which had fought against the Soviet Union from 1979 to 1989 with the help of the US Pakistan, and Saudi Arabia. The Mujahideen were now part of the Northern Alliance, including the Tajik President Rabbani and the Uzbek warlord, Rashid Dostem, and were supported by Iran, Tajikistan, Uzbekistan, and Russia.

Ten thousand miles away, the victor of the cold war, the US stood aloof, impervious to the outcome of the conflict between the northern alliance and the Taliban. From a position of moral superiority and splendid detachment, it castigated the Taliban and the northern alliance headed by President Rabbani for their violation of human rights in Afghanistan.[16]

RUSSIA'S REASSERTION OF POWER IN EURASIA AND REGIONAL REALIGNMENTS

Despite the Taliban's control of 90 per cent of Afghanistan's territory, President Rabbani's government, which controlled 10 per cent of the territory in the north, controlled most of the country's embassies abroad, and retained Afghanistan's United Nations seat after the UN General Assembly deferred a decision on Afghanistan's credentials in September 1997. Indeed in the Taliban's non-recognition by the world community, the US played the decisive role. As of January 1999, only Saudi Arabia, Pakistan, and the United Arab Emirates diplomatically recognized the Taliban's government and maintained their embassies in Kabul.

Indifferent to their diplomatic isolation, the Taliban dogmatically divided the global state system into four zones: (1) *dar al kuffar*, the lands of the infidels, including India, Russia, and other non-Muslim states; (2) *dar al munafiqin*, the states of the hypocrites, including Iran; (3) irreligious countries, including Turkey; and (4) *dar al-Islam*, 'good Muslim' states including Pakistan, Saudi Arabia, and the United Arab Emirates, as well as others which had not yet taken their decisions for the Taliban's recognition. Most of the states in the world did not recognize the Taliban's government because 'they are the true followers of Islam and are extremely sincere in implementing the Islamic system'. This was the Taliban's explanation for their diplomatic isolation. The fact that most of the countries were appalled by their violation of human rights and religious extremism was irrelevant to them. They, on the other hand called Rabbani a 'traitor', and Ahmad Shah Massoud 'a Communist, who belonged to the *Shola-i Javid* faction of Afghanistan's communist movement'. Their lukewarm Islamicness made them, they believed, acceptable to the US and other countries.

Much of the Taliban's invective was reserved for their archenemy, the Tajik Ahmad Shah Massoud, who organized the Northern Alliance and at first invited his 'Pashtun father', Hikmatyar, to join the war against them, then asked his Uzbek 'grandfather', General Dostem, to join him, and then 'begged his great-grandfathers, India, Iran Tajikistan' for help. No one could save him. He was driven out of Kabul. Indeed, the Taliban's self-confidence was buttressed by their victories against the Northern Alliance, and by blind faith that 'God and Islam are with them'.

The dogmatic aspect of the Taliban's religio-political thinking alarmed Afghanistan's neighbours in Eurasia. Galvanized by the urge to reassert itself in Central Asia, Russia became actively involved in Tajikistan and Afghanistan, as well as reviving its strategic partnership with India. These developments led Pakistan to actively support the Taliban in order to checkmate the Russian influence, and to keep India out of Afghanistan's affairs. Between February 1996 and July 1998, Russia was back in Afghanistan, supporting its former enemies, the Mujahideen of the Northern Alliance under the leadership of President Rabbani and Ahmad Shah Massoud. By 1996, Russia had built a new bridge over the Amu Darya River on the Tajikistan border. This allowed Russian arms convoys to travel to Kabul (which was still under Rabbani-Massoud control) through areas controlled by Massoud, bypassing the city of Mazar-i-Sharif, which was then held by Massoud's Uzbek rival, General Dostem. Russia also built an airport at Taloqan as a strategic rear base for Massoud in the eventuality of his ouster from Kabul by the Taliban.[17] Russian and Indian technicians were engaged to upgrade facilities at Kabul's Bagram airport, where Massoud was then based.

By 1996, Russia had also stationed 20,000 troops in Tajikistan to protect the Tajik government against its domestic rebels and to 'seal' its borders with Afghanistan. Three geo-strategic considerations brought about a broad relationship between Russia and Iran: (1) both states wanted to curb US influence and that of American oil companies in the Caspian oil basin; (2) Iran and Russia wanted to ensure that many of the planned Caspian oil pipelines would traverse Iranian and Russian territories; (3) both states' support to the Northern Alliance would create a buffer between the Taliban and the Afghan border with the former Soviet republics, while the continuation of war in Afghanistan would prevent Western oil companies from building pipelines across Afghani and Pakistani territories.[18]

Finally, the Taliban's Islamic fundamentalism and their virulent anti-Shi`aism led Iran and Russia to conclude that Sunni fundamentalism would spill over into Central Asia and even into Russia, where at least eleven of the twenty-two autonomous republics in the Caucasus and Volga Ural basin are Muslim. Consequently, Russia started to supply heavy weapons, training, and logistical support to the northern alliance, while Iran supplied arms, fuel, and other resources. Moreover, Russia and Uzbekistan started to support General Rashid Dostem, who then controlled Mazar-i Sharif and the surrounding Uzbek territories. The Tajik leaders of the Northern Alliance, Rabbani and Massoud, who controlled the Panjsher Valley, started to strengthen their relations with Tajikistan.

At present, Tajikistan is not a viable country and is almost completely dependent on Russia and Uzbekistan. With a non-functioning economy, its government is weak and faces periodic rebellions. Territorially the smallest of the Central Asian states, Tajikistan's population is about 5.2 million. Tajiks comprise 59 per cent of the population and Uzbeks 23 per cent; the rest consists of nineteen different ethnic groups.[19] Uzbekistan also contains at least 2 million Tajiks in its territory.[20] Consequently, Tajikistan has become a zone of conflict and a sphere of influence for Russia and Uzbekistan. Islam Karimov, the President of Uzbekistan, was conducting an 'independent' national policy trying to dislodge Russia from his country's southern flanks, as if to tell Russia: 'This is our border, this is our zone of responsibility, these are our interests, and you have no business here.'[21] Karimov conveyed the same message to Tajikistan, Uzbek General Dostem, and Rabbani and Massoud, the Tajik members of the Northern Alliance.

Karimov vociferously attacked Islamic fundamentalism within Uzbekistan[22] and Afghanistan, and constantly lambasted the Russian intelligence services for unrest in certain Central Asian states whenever it was convenient for the promotion of Uzbekistan's interests. In November 1998, when rebellion erupted in the northern part of Tajikistan, Emomali Rakhmonov, Tajikistan's president, blamed the Uzbeks for provoking the rebellion. Karimov retorted with much larger accusations: the Tajik government was involved in large-scale drug trafficking; it was dividing power between Rahkmanov's cohorts and the United Tajik opposition; and keeping out from power-sharing 'certain people from Kulyab, who with the help of Russian intelligence services organized the latest attack by Makhmud Khudoiberdiyev's detachment'.[23]

Clearly, the Taliban's divided opposition was aided by very divided supporters, who, as a matter of convenience and due to a limited convergence of interests, supported the Northern Alliance. Against this political landscape, it is no wonder that the Taliban overran Mazar-i Sharif, General Dostem's stronghold, on 8 August 1998 and then pushed forward to capture Bamiyan city and province in central Afghanistan. In this conquest, the Taliban killed eleven Iranian diplomats, and the existence and location of several dozen Iranians could not be determined. Iran charged that the Taliban were holding the living Iranians as 'hostages.' This episode strained Irani-Pakistan relations, because Pakistan had assured Iran on the day of the attack that the Taliban had given an assurance about the safety of Iranian diplomats in Mazar-i Sharif. During 1998-9, Shi`a-Sunni relations deteriorated in Pakistan when Sunni Muslims attacked Shi`a mosques and killed a large number of Shi`a Muslims—all in the name of Islam. Very justifiably, Iranian President Muhammad Khatami condemned on 4 January 1999 'all terrorist acts whether in Iran or Pakistan', and denounced the Taliban's 'outlaw attitude', as they had taken no concrete action to bring Iranian diplomats' murderers to justice.[24]

Outraged by the Taliban's conduct, Iran concentrated nearly 200,000 troops on Afghanistan's borders and put pressure on Pakistan to moderate the Taliban's behaviour. The Iranian diplomats' bodies were returned to Iran and the crisis subsided.

Despite friendly relations over a period of fifty years, Irani and Pakistani policies over Afghanistan have substantially diverged. As a Shi`a Muslim state, Iran apprehends an encirclement of Sunni Muslim states, and resented the Taliban's discriminatory policy towards its Shi`a minority and its claim to be a true 'Muslim state'. Also, Iran saw Pakistan as an accomplice in the Taliban's enterprise.

It is an irony of international politics, which demonstrates the validity of a well-known diplomatic cliché – there are no permanent friends and no permanent enemies—that over developments in Afghanistan the US and Iran came to a limited agreement including: non-diplomatic recognition of the Taliban's government; denial of UN membership to the Taliban; and a demand for a genuine power-sharing agreement between the Northern Alliance and the Taliban. The Taliban, on the other hand rejected any such power-sharing negotiations. Instead, they offered the opposition leaders participation in the government, rejecting also the possibility of establishing a federal constitution in Afghanistan.

However, the US added two more grievances of its own against the Taliban: they were supporting their regime partially from their profits in the opium trade and directly taxing growers as well as traders trafficking in narcotics; and they were sheltereing the Saudi-born terrorist, Osama bin Laden, who was linked to the bombing in August 1998 of two US embassies in Africa where more than 300 people had been killed and another 500 wounded. Consequently, the United States wanted Osama bin Laden to be extradited to the US. In retaliation, US cruise missiles attacked in August training sites in Afghanistan to punish Osama bin Laden.[25]

The Taliban countered the US's accusation by asserting that the former President Rabbani had invited Osama bin Laden to Afghanistan. They inherited this problem, and would cooperate with the US government if the evidence of bin Laden's culpability could be conclusively demonstrated. On this issue, the dialogue between the US government and the Taliban remained inconclusive.[26]

Russia, frustrated by its own inability to decisively shape geopolitical realities in Central Asia and Afghanistan, and chafing under the US's hegemonic role at the global level, was interested in developing a counterweight to the US in alliance with China and India. In December 1998, Prime Minister Yevgeny Primakov visited India. Describing India as a great power, which was exhilarating music to his hosts' ears, he proposed a 'strategic triangle' that would involve Russia, India, and China to build 'peace and security'. Immediately, China rejected the proposed tripartite strategic relationship,[27] while the US downplayed almost contemptuously the importance of any Indo-Russian strategic agreement.[28]

Regarding the rise and fall of the Taliban power a question may be asked: why did Pakistan become the patron saint of the Taliban? Several explanations may be offered. First, during the war in Afghanistan against the Soviet Union, Pakistan's favorite was Gulbuddin Hikmatyar, a Pashtun, who had moved to Pakistan in 1974. Before and after the Soviet withdrawal, Hikmatyar proved to be an unscrupulous soldier of fortune, quickly forfeiting the support of the Pashtun population in Afghanistan and the government of Pakistan. Being primarily a Pashtun movement, the Taliban appeared most appropriate for Pakistan's support. The Taliban were quite popular with the Pashtun refugees in Pakistan, and had a vast reservoir of following among the young Pashtun students at madrasas in Pakistan, especially at Dar al-ulum Haqqania of Maulana Sami-ud-Haq, who was also a senator. Moreover the Taliban enjoyed extensive support in southern Afghanistan, areas contiguous to Pakistan, where their military bases could support the insurgents in Kashmir.

The Taliban had established their control in 90 per cent of Afghanistan's territory and maintained law and order and general peace. Ideologically, they were very close to Saudi Arabia's official creed of Wahabism, which was most welcome to the

Saudi monarchy, and acceptable to the government of the United Arab Emirates. Consequently, the three like-minded governments on this issue recognized the Taliban. However, Pakistan remained the major supplier of funds and advisement to the Taliban. As an example, in 1999 Pakistan paid the salary of the Taliban government's employees for a period of two to three months.[29]

Another important factor which led Pakistan to bet on the Taliban was her plan to expand trade and economic relations with the Central Asian republics, especially the gas-rich republic of Turkmenistan. Clearly this could not be done without the active cooperation of a friendly government in Afghanistan. A plan to lay a pipeline from Turkmenistan through Afghanistan and Pakistan, and eventually leading to India, has been on the planning board for some years. Such a pipeline would unite the economies of the three countries, and hopefully spawn cooperative relations between India and Pakistan.

Finally, the Pakistan Army's strategic thinkers have always looked upon Afghanistan as 'Pakistan's strategic depth', and doggedly pursued policies that might make this dream a reality. In the early 1960s the same idea under the name of 'confederation' was pursued diplomatically with the ill-fated Sardar Daud, who is reported to have remarked: 'a confederation was the correct step to realize our common destiny...We shall be a republic, if Pakistan so desired. Both sides would maintain internal autonomy, but they would form a central government for defence, foreign policy, foreign trade and communications. The prime ministers would rotate.'[30] These developments did not come to pass, but who knows what might happen in the future. The geo-political relations always persist in history; human will can certainly mould them.

US PAKISTAN TENSIONS

Pakistan's civil and military elites have always sought to establish stable and long-lasting relations with the US. This aspiration found the earliest expression in the foreign policy calculation of the founder of Pakistan, Muhammad Ali Jinnah, who sent a secret mission to Washington DC in October 1947 to ask the US government for economic aid (a loan) to purchase military equipment in the US. History has demonstrated that Pakistan's geo-strategic location in Central and South Asia has brought the two countries together into alliances as the US interests have repeatedly converged with those of Pakistan's. However, tensions also developed as Pakistan perceived its interests to be at variance with those of its senior partner US. The period 1989-2001 was filled with acute clashes of interest over four very significant issues: 1) Pakistan's pursuit of nuclear weapons, 2) the sanctions that the US imposed in retaliation, 3) Pakistan's unsatisfied territorial claims on Kashmir, which had been spawned by the partition of India in August 1947, and finally 4) Pakistan's support of the Taliban and the recognition of their government in Afghanistan.

I

THE NUCLEAR ISSUE AND SANCTIONS

Pakistan has claimed that its nuclear programme was spurred on by India's rapidly growing capability in the 1960s. In 1948 India established its Atomic Energy Commission under the internationally known scientist Dr Bhabha, who directly reported to the Indian Prime Minister. In 1960 India was able to get a MW plutonium production reactor called the Canada-India Reactor (CIR) without safeguards. In 1964 India completed a processing plant with the assistance of the British and American suppliers. India could extract 13 kg of weapons grade plutonium, the equivalent of two or three bombs per year, by the mid-1960s.[31] Pakistan had established its Atomic Energy Institute in 1955, and had significantly benefited from President Eisenhower's 'atom for peace' programme; specifically the US government gave Pakistan about 70,000 items of information about atomic energy.

This was a boost to the atomic energy constituency in Pakistan.[32] In the 1950s the training of nuclear physicists and engineers was accomplished. During 1960-71 the atomic energy programme moved to a higher stage of development, when the emphasis shifted to starting a nuclear reactor programme in Pakistan. Compared to the Indian nuclear programme, Pakistan's development was indeed very modest. Prime Minister Zulfiqar Ali Bhutto (1971-1977), as an Indian scholar, Ashok Kapur, stated, 'mobilized nuclear nationalism in Pakistan'.[33] Consequently, nuclear weapons, as a deterrent against India's overwhelming power, entered the social psyche of Pakistan's political leadership, strategic planners, and the general public. With the unexpected appearance of Dr A.Q. Khan on the scene in 1974, Bhutto was made to realize the potential of an enrichment technology, the so-called uranium route to weapons.

After the 1974 detonations of nuclear devices by India, no amount of external pressure could have prevailed upon Bhutto's determination to arm Pakistan with nuclear weapons. Also Pakistan refused to adhere to the Nuclear Nonproliferation Treaty. In reacting to these developments in April 1979 the US cut off all aid to Pakistan under Section 699 (Symington Amendment) of the Foreign Assistance Act of 1961. However, the Soviet invasion of Afghanistan in December 1979 once again spawned convergence of interest to confront the Soviet Union in Afghanistan. Although Bhutto had been overthrown by General Ziaul Haq, the Army Chief of Staff, US subordinated its ideological commitment to democracy and human rights, and found a way to bypass the nuclear issue with Pakistan. General Zia gave assurances to the United States that Pakistan would not explode a nuclear device or embarrass it. He interpreted this policy to mean that Pakistan could quietly continue to develop its nuclear technology and capability without exploding a nuclear device.

The US Congress had a different view. In 1985 the US Senate passed the Pressler Amendment requiring the president to certify annually that Pakistan did not possess a nuclear device as a precondition for allocation of economic aid. When the Soviet troops finally withdrew from Afghanistan in February 1989, the US strategic objective had been achieved. US pressure on Pakistan increased, demanding the roll-back of its nuclear capability. Pakistan refused the demand. In consequence, the US President refused to certify to Congress that it did not possess the nuclear device. Subsequently Pakistan offered assurances to the United States that it 1) did not have nuclear weapons, 2) would not conduct a nuclear explosion, and 3) would not make weapon-grade highly enriched uranium, or 4) transfer nuclear technology to a third party. These assurances failed to convince the US Congress. Actually the President did not have the authority to exercise a waiver with respect to the Pressler Amendment.

Consequently US-Pakistan relations deteriorated, especially at a time when the Mujahideen were fighting among themselves and against the Taliban. There was at the same time instability in Central Asia, and in India-Pakistan relations over Kashmir. The Clinton Administration attempted to limit the damage of the Pressler Amendment with the passage of the Brown Amendment. This change made it possible for the US to resume limited cooperation with Pakistan in some areas, and to find a solution for compensating her for the non-delivery of F-16 aircrafts, some of which had been fully paid for.

While Pakistan's diplomacy repeatedly made attempts to get around the sanctions trap, India exploded three nuclear devices on 11 May 1998 under the Thar Desert in Rajasthan, approximately 70 miles from the borders of Pakistan. Surprisingly, the CIA failed to notice the Indian preparations, and to inform President Clinton in advance of the event. Two week later Pakistan responded in kind and tested nuclear weapons for the first time in Balochistan. President Clinton made forceful attempts to persuade Prime Minister Nawaz Sharif not to follow in India's footsteps. But he failed. In addition to sending Strobe Talbott to Pakistan to prevent the nuclear tests,

President Clinton called Prime Minister Nawaz Sharif four times. In his last call on 28 May 1998 President Clinton 'all but begged him not to detonate a nuclear weapon', and offered him a 'changed relationship' with Pakistan, which would include the delivery of twenty-eight F-16 fighter jets that Pakistan had paid for, but never received. Also Clinton would try to 'cut through the knot' of laws blocking military and economic aid to Pakistan, and would keep trying unilaterally to 'get closer in security terms'.

Then the conversation took on a personal note. President Clinton said, 'If you do this, we can do great things together. We can work on your economy; we can give you tools you need to help defend your country.' After hearing Clinton out, Sharif responded,

> you have said all the right things, but the rest of the world is filing its fingernails. The failure of most of the world to punish India for its tests made it impossible for me not to follow suit...I wish I did not have these [domestic] forces acting on me, but people are demonstrating in the streets, the editorialists and the opposition are demanding I test. You have to understand my position...my hands are tied.

Clinton responded: 'The test would force me to impose sanctions that could cost Pakistan billions and cripple its economy. If you do this [testing], Nawaz, I have to do this, and it'll hurt you a lot more than it'll hurt India. If your hands are tied, so are mine.'[34]

In May 1998 President Clinton resorted to punitive sanctions, which were imposed on India and Pakistan. Initially he maintained symmetry of sanctions when the 1998 Indian-Pakistan Relief Act (Brownback I Amendment) was passed. However, when the Brownback II Amendment (waiver of some sanctions) was passed in 1999, President Clinton decided to waive almost all economic sanctions which had been imposed on India, but lifted only two sanctions on Pakistan, i.e. agricultural credits and lending by US commercial banks. The

Brownback II Amendment invested an indefinite authority in the President to waive the Pressler Amendment. Despite appeals from the Pakistan government, and pressure from the Pakistani-American community, President Clinton refused to exercise this waiver authority in Pakistan's favour. Pakistanis demonstrated very strongly to urge the repeal of the Pressler Amendment to ensure non-discriminatory treatment of Pakistan.

From June 1998 to September 2000 the US conducted an extensive dialogue with India. Deputy Secretary of State Strobe Talbott and India's Minister of External Affairs Jaswant Singh 'met 14 times in seven countries on three continents'. They discussed items on the security and nonproliferation agenda, as well as their visions for US-Indian relations and the potential for economic and strategic cooperation between the two countries. Talbott has published his version, *Engaging India: Diplomacy, Democracy, and the Bomb* (Washington DC: Brookings Institution, 2004).

Even before the publications of this very informative book, Talbott explained on 16 January 1999 in a lecture to the Stanford-Harvard Prevention Defence Project at Palo Alto what the US wanted India to do in addition to dealing with the issue of Kashmir. India could take four steps in the security field:

- First, by adhering to the Comprehensive Test Ban Treaty
- Second, by making possible a moratorium on the further production of fissile material
- Third, by demonstrating prudence and restraint in the development, flight testing and storage of ballistic missiles and nuclear-capable aircraft
- Fourth, by strengthening export controls.[35]

Jaswant Singh spun circles around Strobe Talbott in their diplomatic parlays. India refused to sign the CTBT, and informed the US of its decision when the second Clinton term was about to end. Pakistan simply followed a wait and see policy and was satisfied that its nuclear dilemma was solved by India's 'successful' negotiations with the US.

However, the US pressure on Pakistan about its nuclear programme did not decrease. The newly installed Bush administration sent Assistant Secretary of State Christine Rocca to Pakistan in the first weeks of August 2001. Secretary Rocca stated forthrightly in Islamabad that nuclear- and democracy-related sanctions prevented the US from pursuing cooperation with Pakistan. Especially the democracy-related sanctions 'could only be lifted when democracy was fully restored.'[36] Rocca added that the US supported a high-level dialogue between India and Pakistan. Like President Clinton, his successor President George W. Bush had recognized the need for sustained dialogue between the two South Asian powers.

On 11 September 2001 the political dynamics changed radically. Due to the developments in Afghanistan, Pakistan moved back to a closely allied position with the United States, as consequence of the 9/11 tragedy. President Bush cleared the way for US arms and military assistance to Pakistan on 22 September and 27 October 2001 when he waived separate sets of sanctions prohibiting such exports. One set of sanctions was for developing and testing nuclear weapons, and the second related to the October 1999 military coup by which President General Pervez Musharraf took power. Critics of US foreign policy contend that the so-called commitment to democracy and the promotion of democratic institutions in foreign lands is not a high value, but is merely a tool of US foreign policy. Whenever the instrument stands in the way of national interest it is blithely jettisoned. Nevertheless in dealing with non-friendly and non-democratic states it comes in handy to bludgeon the local rulers.

NOTES

1. Vladislav Zubok, 'Tyranny of the Weak', *World Policy Journal* Vol. IX, No. 2, (Spring 1992), p. 195.

2. Wilson R. Nester, 'The Far East Ménage à Trois', in the *Roles of the United States, Russia and China in the New World Order*, ed. Hafeez Malik (London: Macmillan Co., 1997), p. 83.

3. Shirin R. Tahir-Kheli, *India, Pakistan and the United States* (New York Council on Foreign Relations, 1997), p. 8.

4. C. Raja Mohan, *Crossing the Rubicon; The Shaping of India's New Foreign Policy* (New York: Palgrave Macmillan, 2003), pp. 49-50.

5. Oliver Tirard-Collect, 'The Taliban in Afghanistan: A French Approach', *Middle East Studies Bulletin* (1997), p. 148.

6. Franz Schuzman, 'Afghanistan's Taliban Rebels Blend Islam and Maoism', *Jinn Magazine* (San Francisco), 30 September 1996.

7. Hafeez Malik, *Sir Sayyid Ahmad Khan and Muslim Modernization in India and Pakistan* (New York: Columbia University Press, 1980), See, Chapter 5.

8. See an excellent study of these institutions, A.H. Nayyar, 'Madrasah Education Frozen in Time', in *Fifty Years of Pakistan: Education and the States*, ed. Pervez Hoodbhoy (Karachi: Oxford University Press, 1998), pp. 215-50.

9. For Mullah Nizam-ud-Din's life and work and other issues see a series of articles contributed by Mufti Muhammad Rida Ansari, Baniy Dars-i Nizami: 'Mullah Nizam-ud-Din Muhammad', *Ma'arif* (Azamgarh: October 1970).

10. Shah Waliy Allah, *Izalat al Khafa' 'Un Khilafat al-Khalfa'*, Trans. Into Urdu by Abdul Shakur and Insha Allah (Karachi: Matba'-i Sa'idiy, n.d.), vol. 1, 39; see also an excellent study by Wilfred Madelung, *The Succession to Muhammad: A Study of the Early Caliphate* (Cambridge: Cambridge University Press, 1997) p. 326.

11. For cases of this punishment being administered, see 'Execution by Taliban: Crushed Under Wall', *The New York Times*, 16 January 1999.

12. See 'The Movement of the Taliban', an authoritative statement filed by the Taliban with the internet, <http://www.Taliban.com>.

13. *The Nation*, 13 March 1993.

14. For details on these lawless fiefs see a detailed study by Barnett R. Rubin, *The Fragmentatiion of Afghanistan* (New Haven: Yale University Press, 1995), pp. 274-84.

15. *Frontier Post*, 21 July 1993.

16. US Department of State, *Afghanistan Country Report on Human Rights Practices for 1992* (Washington DC: 30 January 1998).

17. Ahmad Rashid, 'A new Proxy War: Foreign Powers again Feeding Irons to Factions', *Far Eastern Economic Review* (1 February 1996).

18. James Risen, 'Russian are Back in Afghanistan, Aiding Rebels', *The New York Times*, 27 July 1998.
19. For details see, Hafeez Malik, ed., *Central Asia: Its Strategic Importance and Future Prospects* (New York: St. Martin's Press, 1994), p. 125.
20. Mohammad Reza Djalili et al; eds., *Tajikistan: The Trails of Independence* (New York: St. Martin's Press, 1997), p. 102.
21. Aleksei Novikov, 'Uzbek to Aid in Afghanistan', *Novaya Yezhednevnaya Gazata* (Moscow), 15 January 1994, p. 3.
22. Karimov believes that Islamic fundamentalists aim 'to discredit democracy, the secular state, and a multi-national and multi-confessional society'. Islam Karimov, *Uzbekistan: On the Threshold of the Twentieth Century* (New York: St. Martin's Press, 1998), pp. 24-8.
23. Yevgeny Krutkov, 'Islam Karimov accuses Russian Intelligence Services', *Sevodnya* (Moscow), 2 December 1998, p. 2.
24. *Dawn* (Karachi), 4 and 5 January 1999.
25. For details on these developments see, *The New York Times*, 6 and 21 September 1998.
26. US Institute of Peace, Special Report, *The Taliban and Afghanistan, Implications for Regional Security and Options for International Action* (Washington DC: November, 1998).
27. *The New York Times*, 22 and 23 December 1998.
28. *Dawn*, 29 December 1998.
29. Interview with Pakistani diplomats in Kabul during my visit to Afghanistan in March 2000.
30. For further details on the Confederation Project see twice Ambassador to Afghanistan's memoirs: Muhammad Aslam Khattak, *A Pathan Odyssey*, (Karachi: Oxford University Press, 2004), pp. 100-102.
31. Munir Ahmad Khan, 'Development and Significance of Pakistan's Nuclear Capability', in *Founders' Aspirations and Today's Realities*, ed. Hafeez Malik (Karachi: Oxford University Press, 2001), p. 150.
32. Ashok Kapur, *Pakistan's Nuclear Development* (London: Croom Helm, 1989), p. 36.
33. Ibid., p. 57.
34. Tim Weiner, 'Nuclear Anxiety: In Washington, After an Anguished Phone Call, Clinton Analyzes Pakistan', *The New York Times*, 29 May 1998.
35. Strobe Talbott, *Dialogue, Democracy and Nuclear Weapons in South Asia* (Washington DC: Department of State, 1999), p. 2.
36. Syed Talat Hussain, 'Lifting of Sanctions Linked to Democracy', *Dawn*, 3 August 2001.

4

Pakistani Territorial Claims on Kashmir and Relations with India

Kashmir has remained a flashpoint of conflict between India and Pakistan. Despite India's repeated endeavours to make it an ordinary bilateral dispute between the two states, Kashmir has continued to be a matter of concern for the great powers. A fresh look at the origins of this dispute might shed some light on the intensity of emotions which exist about it in Pakistan and India.

I

At the dawn of independence in 1947 there were almost 600 princely states within British India. The last British viceroy, Lord Mountbatten, advised the hereditary rulers of these states to join India or Pakistan, keeping in view the geographical location of the state, and the demographic composition (i.e. Hindu or Muslim) of the population. Only three large states — Kashmir, Hyderabad (Deccan) and Junagadh — defied this advice. Another related issue was: did the people of the state or their unelected and hereditary rulers have the right to make the decision of accession to India or Pakistan. While the All-India National Congress emphasized the right of the citizens to choose between the two new states, the Muslim League leadership accepted the ruler's right to decide. Quaid-i-Azam Muhammad Ali Jinnah issued his judgment reaffirming this on 19 June 1947.

This was a fatal mistake for the national interest of Pakistan. Defying the imperatives of the geography and demography of his state of Junagadh, lying in the Kathiawar district of Gujarat and with a Hindu majority, its Muslim ruler decided to join Pakistan on 14 August 1947 and Pakistan accepted his instrument of accession on 20 September. The Hindu ruler of Kashmir, disregarding the Muslim population of the state, decided to join India. India accepted the accession offer on 27 October 1947.[1]

Within Kashmir political dynamics convulsed very rapidly during 1947. In the spring a Muslim uprising took place in Poonch, an autonomous principality within Kashmir. The uprising was spawned by the militant Hindu organizations, especially the Rashtriya Swayamsevak Sangh (RSS), which had infiltrated the state. They were tacitly supported by Maharaja Hari Singh, the ruler of Kashmir. They had started riots by attacking Muslim neighbourhoods in different districts of Poonch. Poonch was a source of recruits for the British-Indian imperial army. A total of 71,667 men from Kashmir had served in the army during World War II; 60,402 were Muslims from Poonch.[2] Encouraged by the success of this revolt, which had achieved control of the entire Poonch principality, the leaders in the western Jammu districts, including Muzaffarabad, Poonch, and Mirpur established a provisional government of Azad (Free) Jammu and Kashmir on 3 October 1947. This was a direct challenge to Shaikh Muhammad Abdullah's All-Jammu and Kashmir National Conference, which had a considerable following in the Kashmir Valley. While these events rocked the state the Hindu ruler concluded a standstill agreement with the government of Pakistan. The agreement established Pakistan's management of Kashmir's post and telegraph system, with an obligation to provide the foodstuffs and other essential commodities.

To add fuel to the fire of instability in Poonch, several thousand Pashtun tribesmen from the North-West Frontier Province of Pakistan invaded Kashmir on 21 October 1947. Clearly their objective was to force the ruler's decision of accession in Pakistan's favour. On 24 October the ruler telegraphed his request to the Indian government for military aid to repulse the Pashtun raiders. On 27 October Lord Mountbatten replied 'accepting accession, but noted that once law and order had been restored and the 'invader' expelled, the accession should be ratified by a reference to the people [of Kashmir].' Speaking for the representative government of newly independent India, Jawaharlal Nehru declared on 2 November 1947 his government's 'pledge,' given 'not only to the people of Kashmir but to the world' to 'hold a referendum under international auspices such as the United Nations'; and if the people of Kashmir and Jammu decided to 'part company with us, they can go their way and we shall go our way.'[3]

Prime Minister of India Jawaharlal Nehru declared on 2 November 1947 India's pledge, 'not only to the people of Kashmir, but to the world' to 'hold a referendum under international auspices such as the United Nations,' to determine if the people of Kashmir wanted to remain with India or join Pakistan

As the war between India and Pakistan's armies raged in Kashmir, India brought the Kashmir issue to the UN Security Council in January 1948. The UNSC passed an extensive resolution, providing for the establishment of a UN Commission for India and Pakistan to play a mediating role. It urged the government of Pakistan to 'use its best endeavours' to withdraw tribesmen and other nationals from Kashmir. Once the withdrawal had occurred India was to withdraw its own forces from Kashmir, and to reduce them to the minimum strength required for the support of the civil power in the maintenance of law and order. Once the requirements were satisfied a Plebiscite Administrator was to be appointed to ascertain the wishes of the people of Kashmir on the question of the accession of the state to India or Pakistan.[4]

The ceasefire line was established in January 1948, and remained in place until 1971. It was renamed the Line of Control (LoC) in 1972. In the war of 1971 Pakistan lost 341 square miles of territory, including the Haji Pir Pass in the tribal sector. Pakistan gained 59 square miles in the Chhamb Jorian Sector.

Unsuccessful negotiations were conducted between 1949 and 1956 by India and Pakistan to devise mechanisms for the implementation of the UN SC resolutions of 1949. In September 1954 Pakistan joined the US-sponsored military alliance, to which the Soviet Union strenuously objected. The Soviet leaders Nikita Khrushchev and Nikolai Bulganin came to India and visited Kashmir in November 1955. Khrushchev called Kashmir 'one of the states of India', and Bulganin called Kashmir's population 'part of the Indian people'.[5] Reneging on its commitment, India then declared that a state-wide unsupervised plebiscite was no longer relevant.[6] India also used Pakistan's alliance with the US as an additional reason for upsetting the India-Pakistan equilibrium, and renounced its commitment to holding a plebiscite in Kashmir. Since then a bitter stalemate has persisted.

Let us now examine the manner and style of the Muslim League leadership, especially the way it dealt with Kashmir, and the issue of the state's accession to India or Pakistan.

II

With the collapse of the Cabinet Mission Plan in 1946, conceptually the two independent states – India and Pakistan, had come into existence. It was announced on 20 February 1947. Yet, there is no evidence available to suggest that the Muslim League leadership had developed any cohesive strategy to deal with the issue of the princely states' accession, and especially that of Kashmir to Pakistan. In July 1947 the Indian Independence Act created two *de jure* states, which was an occasion to rethink the negotiating strategy. That the transfer of power to India was to be accomplished no later than June 1948. Jinnah was no longer negotiating with a political party, but with the sovereign and independent state of India. While the issue of states' accession was rooted in the governance of British India, that the accession of states to India would be achieved through Machiavellian techniques remained beyond the Muslim League's intellectual horizon.

Like an accomplished lawyer, Jinnah attempted to tackle the accession issue in a legal framework. Yet the strategy in the transformed political milieu called for the technique of *realpolitik*. This implied that the Muslim League leadership should have bargained with the Indian leadership: giving to India what at that time India wanted most – smooth and non-disruptive transfer of the states of Junagadh and Hyderabad where Pakistan exercised decisive influence, and in a quid pro quo receiving Kashmir, if not all, then those parts of this heterogeneous state which were predominantly Muslim. Jinnah had already accepted the principal of partition within partition, that is, the division of the Punjab and Bengal, along the line of the Hindu-Muslim divide. This led him to call the new Muslim state 'a moth eaten Pakistan'. Mortally afraid of India's 'balkanization', the Congress leadership would have been in all probability receptive to this bargain. This is not merely a conjecture; a great deal of circumstantial evidence lends credence to this thesis.

Granted that the state of Jammu and Kashmir had a population of 4,021,160 (in 1949) of which 75-80 per cent was Muslim. But this Muslim population was concentrated in certain parts: Gilgit, Hunza, Baltistan, Poonch, and the Kashmir valley. Jammu province was predominantly Hindu, with the exception of two or three Muslim districts. Ladakh, where the population is ethnically related to the Tibetans was (and still is) Buddhist. Following the principle of self-determination, the Ladakhis should belong to neither India nor Pakistan. The Kashmir Valley is no more than 10 per cent of the total area of the historical Kashmir state. Currently, Pakistan retains control over Gilgit, Hunza, and Baltistan, the re-designated northern areas, and Azad Kashmir, which includes parts of Poonch. Pakistan's real loss has been the Kashmir valley, which was incorporated into the

Indian Union by force. This loss could have been avoided in quid pro quo negotiations with India before August 1947.

Instead of territorial bargaining, Jinnah accepted in a statement on 19 June 1947:

> ...the Indian [princely] states will be independent sovereign states on the termination of [British] paramountcy...it is open to them to join the Hindustan Constituent Assembly or the Pakistan Constituent Assembly, or to decide to remain independent...we do not wish to interfere with the internal affairs of any state, for that is a matter primarily to be resolved between the rulers and the peoples of the states.[7]

In legal terms this meant that a ruler could sign an instrument of accession to join either India or Pakistan. On 14 August 1947 Junagadh state announced its decision to accede to Pakistan, while the Hindu ruler of Kashmir joined India on 26 October 1947.

In Junagadh the population was overwhelmingly Hindu, the ruler was indeed Muslim, and the reverse was true in Kashmir. However, Junagadh was sacred to Hindu sentiment because it was believed to be the death-place of Lord Krishna, and is the site of the famous Temple of Somnath, which was sacked by Sultan Mahmud Ghazanvi in 1024. (Incidentally, when India took over Junagadh the temple was restored 'at great expense'.)[8] India, as well as Pakistan, rejected the accessions of Junagadh and Kashmir.

In a court of law, Jinnah would have successfully argued his case by striking a plea bargain: Pakistan withdraws its claims to Junagadh, and India should do the same in regard to Kashmir. Jinnah's tactical and legal shrewdness would have paid off. But this case was not in a British court of law. Here two sovereigns were playing a zero-sum game for high geo-strategic advantages. On the other hand, a political strategy of demanding plebiscites in disputed areas, especially in Kashmir, Junagadh (and in Hyderabad) might have secured the Kashmir valley for Pakistan in light of the principle of partition within partition. This approach could not be considered outlandish since the Indian leadership had successfully insisted on a plebiscite before 15 August 1947 in Pakistan's NWFP.

For this strategy to have a chance of success, Jinnah needed to have the goodwill of Lord Mountbatten. Their relations were problematic: two titanic egos had a head-on collision, both determined to protect their place in the sun. One represented the waning imperial power, operating in collusion with Indian the leadership, and presiding over an established state which had inherited the material and intellectual resources of the British Raj; the other, who considered himself the equal of Mountbatten, if not superior, was confident of his political skills and unchallenged leadership over Muslims, who were completely mesmerized by his charisma. Mountbatten had offended Jinnah by using the principle of partition within partition in the case of the Punjab and Bengal. Jinnah wounded Mountbatten's ego by denying him the opportunity to be even the part-time Governor-General of Pakistan. How bitter their relationship was can be gathered from a dialogue, which was recorded by Mountbatten on 2 July 1947:

> Mountbatten: I pointed out to him that if he became the constitutional Governor-General of Pakistan his powers would be constitutionally restricted, and that he would act only on advice, but that as Prime Minister he could run Pakistan.
>
> Jinnah: In my position it is I who will give the advice, and others will act on it.
>
> Mountbatten: Do you realize what this will cost you?
>
> Jinnah: It may cost me several crores of rupees in assets.
>
> Mountbatten: I replied somewhat acidly: It may well cost you the whole of your assets, and the future of Pakistan. I then gave up and left the room.

What was the major cost to Pakistan? Kashmir! India, with Mountbatten's collaboration, managed to obtain Kashmir's accession and cheated Pakistan out of its legitimate inheritance. Kashmir's disposition in this unjust manner sowed the seeds of enmity and distrust between the two states, and Mountbatten must be held responsible in large measure for this unfortunate consequence. On a personal level, Mountbatten turned the table on Jinnah and hoisted him with his own petard in a face to face conversation of three and a half hours over Kashmir on 1 November 1947 at Lahore:

> Jinnah: Expressed surprise at the remarkable speed at which we [Government of India] had been able to organize sending troops into the Srinagar plain...
>
> Continuing: The accession was not a bona fide one since it rested on 'fraud and violence' and would never be accepted by Pakistan.
>
> Mountbatten: I asked him to explain why he used the term 'fraud', since the Maharajah was fully entitled in accordance with Pakistan's own official statement about Junagadh—to make such accession. It was, therefore, perfectly legal and valid.'
>
> Jinnah: This accession was the end to a long intrigue and that it had been brought about by violence.
>
> Mountbatten: I entirely agree that the accession had been brought about by violence; I knew the Maharajah was most anxious to remain independent, and nothing but the terror of violence could have made him accede to either dominion...the violence had come from tribes for whom Pakistan was responsible.

Mountbatten not only exercised his imperial prestige with the rulers of the princely states, he also tampered with the boundary award which had been given by a British jurist Sir Cyril Radcliffe. In February of 1992 Radcliffe's former secretary, Christopher Beaumont, 'provided the *Daily Telegraph* (London) with a memorandum he had prepared many years earlier on the commission's [boundary] deliberations' that confirmed the fact that 'frontiers had been secretly redrawn to Pakistan's disadvantage.'[9] Beaumont stated that Radcliffe 'yielded to overwhelming political expediency, by agreeing after he had decided the line, to the transfer of Ferozepur and Zira sub-division in Punjab from Pakistan to India...under pressure from Mountbatten who was in turn under pressure from Nehru and almost certainly from the Maharaja of Bikaner whose state would have been adversely affected if the Canal Headworks in Ferozepur had gone to Pakistan.'[10]

The Indian Independence Act spelled out the partition of the Punjab and Bengal provinces and clearly enumerated by name the districts that were awarded to India and Pakistan. In the new scheme of state formation the district of Gurdaspur occupied a strategic place, and was awarded to India. Radcliffe by his catastrophic generosity severed the sub-districts (*tehsils*) of Pathankot and Gurdaspur and attached them to Indian territory, and thus made Kashmir contiguous to India and accessible through an all-weather road. Radcliffe denied any external pressure on him for his bisection of the district of Gurdaspur, but offered no plausible explanation for this favour to India.

To inflict further damage on Pakistan, Mountbatten also interfered with the work of the Boundary Commission. As he himself admitted, Kashmir's accession to India would be 'a practical proposition' only if the three eastern *tehsils* (sub-districts) of Gurdaspur district were allotted to India, which would make Kashmir a contiguous territory with India. The first schedule of the Indian Independence Act of 18 July 1947 had given the entire district to Pakistan. In the final Boundary Commission award of 12 August which was not published until 15 August 1947, through Mountbatten's intervention, the three *tehsils* of Gurdaspur were awarded to India. This cartographic dishonesty created a safe and all year round route from India to Kashmir!

Mountbatten lived up to his words: 'Mr Jinnah, it may well cost you the whole of your assets, and the future of Pakistan.'[11] It did!

In addition to Kashmir, Junagadh and Hyderabad (Deccan), the Muslim League leadership considered some contiguous and some non-contiguous Hindu states possible for inclusion in Pakistan. The Hindu rulers of these states were entitled to declare their independence, and to join Pakistan after August 1947. Technically, the ruler's decisions would be legal. Prominent among these states were Indore in Maharashtra, Travancore, (now part of Kerala) and Jodhpur in Rajasthtan. The Ruler of Travancore made preliminary terms with Jinnah, including a trade agreement. The Hindu Ruler of Jodhpur, whose state's population was predominantly Hindu, had several meetings with Jinnah, who had handed him 'a blank sheet of paper on which to write all concessions'[12] he wanted from the government of Pakistan. Specifically Jinnah offered him the use of Karachi as a free port, free import of arms, jurisdiction over the Jodhpur-Hyderabad (Sindh) railway, and a large supply of grain for famine relief. All this on one condition, that Jodhpur would declare its independence on 15 August 1947, and then join Pakistan. The Ruler of Jodhpur came very close to acceding to Pakistan.

In dealing with the princely states, Indian leaders had secured Mountbatten's personal assistance. Knowing the servile mentality of these princes, they believed that the rulers would be overawed by Mountbatten's personality, prestige, and royal connections. Mountbatten was more than willing to help. Very skilfully he checkmated Jinnah's shrewdness, and persuaded these rulers not to fall into his 'trap'. Mountbatten played the same game in Kashmir, and Pakistan lost.

The partitioning of India was not a velvet divorce between two consenting partners, like the one that took place between the Czech Republic and Slovakia. An undetermined number of Hindus and Muslims lost their lives in 1947 as they moved across the boundary lines between the two states. A weaker and disorganized Pakistan licked some of its self-inflicted wounds, and nursed some plausible and some far-fetched grievances against India. The two states being inherently unequal was unacceptable to the psyche of the Pakistani elites who wanted the past glory of the Muslim rule over India to miraculously repeat itself. The myth of the martial races of India, comprised mostly of Muslims, was nurtured to right the wrongs of 1947. India for the first time was able to establish its military superiority over the Muslims, and resented the fact that so many of them escaped to Pakistan. India's policy after 1947 was determined to cut Pakistan to a smaller size by encouraging East Bengal's cessation from Pakistan. Drunk with power, the unwise generals of Pakistan provided a remarkably good opportunity to India to satisfy its strategic objective in 1971. Today hardly anyone in Pakistan bemoans the loss of East Pakistan, but the defeat of 1971-72 rankles in the hearts of Pakistanis. Indian leaders, on the contrary, believe that Pakistan's grand strategy is to place as many obstacles as possible in India's quest for a great power status.

A territorially dissatisfied state, and threatened by India's rising power, Pakistan followed the strategy of periodic conflicts with India to challenge the status quo in Kashmir, combined with peaceful negotiations through the benign intervention of major powers, especially the US when its global interests converged with that of Pakistan.

There has never been a shortage of bilateral negotiations between India and Pakistan. Each unsuccessful round degenerated into military confrontation. In the late 1940s and 1950s the United Nations' mediations ran their course, then US President Truman and the British Prime Minister Clement Atlee's representatives attempted to find mutually acceptable solutions. None of their bilateral negotiations were successful. The Soviet Union took its turn at peace-making in 1965, when it organized a peace conference in Tashkent. The conference merely re-established the status quo ante bellum of 1964. The spirit of Tashkent died very quickly and Kashmir once again became the centrepiece of their conflict.

At the end of these negotiations came frustrations, which spawned internal convulsions in Kashmir in 1989. The Kashmiri uprising which caused the death of 7,000-8,000 Kashmiri youths was supported by Pakistan. The Afghan *jihad* supported by the US, Saudi Arabia, China, and Pakistan gave birth to the *jihadi* movements, that directed their guns toward the Indian forces after the Soviet withdrawal from Afghanistan.

During the 1990s attempts were made to re-start India-Pakistan dialogues. This time the initiative was taken by

Pakistan's Prime Minister, Nawaz Sharif. He committed himself to creating friendly relations with India in his election campaign. In an interview given to an Indian journalist of international reputation, Sharif expressed the desire for a meeting with the Indian Prime Minister Atal Bihari Vajpayee. Vajpayee was quick in accepting the proposal, and offered to take a bus ride, on a route which was to be inaugurated between India and Pakistan. Sharif was an attractive Pakistani leader to Vajpayee for three reasons: Sharif's public commitment of establishing friendly relations with India; his personal contacts with Indian leaders, including the former prime ministers Chandra Shekhar and Nara Simha Rao, and I. K. Gujral; and Sharif's desire to critically examine with India the implications of the nuclear programme.[13] Also Vajpayee's image in Pakistan was attractively positive.

The opportune moment to open the dialogue came in February 1997, when Sharif's Muslim League had won a two-thirds majority (140/200) in the National Assembly. India's Prime Minister, H.D. Deve Gowda, instead of receiving a formal acknowledgment of his congratulatory letter to Sharif, found a proposal to start 'negotiations at the foreign secretaries level, if possible before the end of 1997'. Deve Gowda wrote back to say: 'we are ready.' Consequently, the foreign secretaries met on 28-31 March and then on 19-23 June for the second time, and identified eight subjects including Kashmir for the eight working groups. Within India strong objections were raised by the political elite to 'India agreeing to a separate working group on Kashmir'. The issues at (A) and (B) within the eight subjects were to be dealt with by the foreign secretaries, who were to coordinate and monitor the projects of all the working groups. (A) included issues of peace and security and confidence-building measures (B) included Jammu and Kashmir. The rest covered Siachen, the Wuller Barrage project, Sir Creek, terrorism, and drug trafficking.

In May 1998 the nuclear explosions took place. Now the major powers became involved in the India-Pakistan dialogue. They began to realize that without serious negotiations on

Kashmir, the nuclear issues posing a challenge to international security would remain unresolved. At the Non-Aligned Movement's summit in August 1998 in Durban the foreign secretaries of India and Pakistan agreed to revive the 23 June 1997 formula. They agreed to do preparatory work for their prime ministers' meeting in New York in September 1998 on the sidelines of the UN General Assembly's Session. It was at the UN meetings that the bus service between India and Pakistan was agreed upon.

Speaking in Hindi at a regal dinner in his honor at the resplendent Mughal Fort in the heart of Lahore, Vajpayee declared: *dushmani bahut ho chuki. Ab dosti karni chahiye. Dosti kay liye mushkil faislay karnay hain. Dosti kay liye Kashmir per baat karni hai.* (Enough of enmity. Now we must cultivate friendship. Difficult decisions will have to be taken to achieve that. We will have to talk on Kashmir in order to forge the friendship.) In addition to the expression of effusive desires for friendly relations some fairly significant decisions were made: (1) to take immediate steps for reducing the risk of accidental or unauthorized use of nuclear weapons; (2) to discuss concepts and doctrines in order to adopt measures for confidence-building in the nuclear and conventional arms fields to prevent the outbreak of conflict; (3) Vajpayee did not repeat the traditional Indian view that Kashmir was an integral part of India; (4) the establishment of a back-channel to explore a viable solution(s) for the Kashmir dispute. Pakistan nominated a veteran diplomat, Niaz A. Naik, and India designated R. Mishra. Both diplomats met each other in November-December 1998. Since this was back-channel diplomacy no official record of their meetings is available, although it is hard to believe that they did not produce anything in the form of personal memoranda of understanding for their leaders' benefit. A fairly reliable source of information is an interview which Sartaj Aziz, former Foreign Minister to Nawaz Sharif, gave to a very reputable Indian journalist, A.G. Noorani, in 2002. Actually this interview confirmed and elaborated what Amit Baruah had reported in *The Hindu* on

3 April 1999. Noorani's analytical insights are indeed most informative.

EMERGENCE OF THE CHENAB FORMULA

Niaz A. Naik was assisted in formulating Pakistan's exploratory proposals by the Kashmir Study Group, which included two former military officials—Admiral K. K. Nayar and General K. M. Arif. Some features of the formula were highlighted:

- The framework of these proposals was to 'have a designated district-wise referendum' in Kashmir.
- Expectations were that the Hindu-majority areas in Jammu, and Buddhist-majority Ladakh would go to India.
- India did not accept a communal-based or religious-based referendum.
- Alternatively the exploratory proposal used neutral geographic terminology, advancing the view that the Chenab River would become the dividing line. In reality the geographic line also underlined the communal divide. All the Hindu-majority areas were west of the Chenab River, and all the Muslim-majority areas were east of the Chenab.
- Consequently, the area east of the Chenab River and Ladakh would go to India.
- Azad Kashmir, already under Pakistan's control, and the Northern Areas (i.e. Gilgit and Hunza) would remain with Pakistan. (They had been part of Pakistan since 1947.)
- India would give the Kashmir Valley maximum autonomy. However, the scope of the autonomy remained nebulous. Three interpretations were offered:
  1. In the initial study it was proposed that the maximum autonomy would exclude defence and foreign affairs, 'which would be jointly managed' by India and Pakistan 'as a condominium'.

2. In the next proposal it was stated that 'since areas join the independent entity from both sides, each side could administer that area under its sovereignty'.

3. The Valley of Kashmir would not be partitioned. On the contrary, it would become larger as a political unit.

4. Some districts located outside its current jurisdiction would have the option to join the Valley. (Presumably these districts would include the three Muslim-majority districts—Doda, Rajourni and Poonch—of Indian Jammu.)

5. The LoC would remain, but some alterations would take place 'as areas on both sides would be part of a new entity.'[14]

How many of these exploratory proposals for the development of negotiating positions were accepted by Mishra remains unknown. On the positive side both states appeared to be altering their well-known traditional legalistic and politically worn-out positions, enabling them to finally resolve this problem. J. N. Dixit, who became the National Security Advisor of the Manmohan Singh government, lead by the Congress Party in 2004, elaborated his own version of the Chenab formula. His proposed solution is based upon the ground realities in Kashmir; the LoC remains intact 'with some adjustments (as far as Pakistan is concerned), and qualitatively responsive to political arrangements for the governance of Jammu and Kashmir, and responsive to the aspiration of the people of that state.'[15] Much the same offer had been made to Pakistan by Nehru in 1948-9.

THE KARGIL INCURSION: AN EXERCISE IN FUTILITY; TENSIONS WITH THE US AND INDIA

Three and a half months after the Lahore Summit the 'peace bus', as Vajpayee described it, 'collided with the peaks of Kargil and was shattered to pieces'. India also called it the 'betrayal' of the Lahore process, and 'a stab in the back'. In the aftermath the US became involved in the affairs of both states fairly heavily, but the Indian reaction was entirely different. India was receptive to the US involvement.

First, why the Kargil episode; what was to be gained by Pakistan? Who planned it, and what were the expectations? Probably Pakistan looked upon the peaks of Kargil as another Siachin glacier, parts of which India had occupied in 1984.

The Kargil conflict took place between 8 May 1999 when Pakistani forces and Kashmiri militants numbering about 5,000 were detected atop the Kargil ridges, and 14 July when both sides ceased military operations. By June 1999, Indian troop strength in the region had reached 730,000. The build-up included the deployment of around sixty frontline aircraft. For these operations, the US sources further believed that the generals had obtained only 'in principle concurrence without any specifics', from Prime Minister Nawaz Sharif.

The Pakistan Army probably calculated that even if the intrusions were discovered in early May, the Indian Army's reaction would be slow and limited. If effective, the operations would enable Pakistani troops to secure a number of dominating heights from where the Srinigar-Leh National Highway 1A could be interdicted at a number of places. If successful the operations would give Pakistan control over tracts of strategic land across the LoC, enabling Pakistan to negotiate from a position of strength. The intrusion would irrevocably alter the status of the LoC.

As retaliation from the Indian Army, Air Force and Navy (indicating the broadening of the conflict) gathered momentum, and Pakistani forces atop the Kargil were about to be completely ejected, the outbreak of an India-Pakistan war across the international boundary became a distinct possibility. At this point in time, Sharif realized that Pakistan was left with six days of fuel to sustain itself if a full fledged war broke out.

Since the Kargil conflict took place after the nuclear explosions, Pakistan's calculation was that it would involve the world community, and especially the US, which might benefit Pakistan. (Incidentally in the same manner Pakistan had miscalculated in 1967 in the second Kashmir war.) Much to Pakistan's chagrin the US held Pakistan responsible for violating the LoC and occupying 'the evacuated position of the Indians' in the Kargil peaks.[16] The US also stated that the expeditionary forces included 'Pakistani-backed militants and regular army'. Initially Pakistan admitted to supporting only the Kashmiri 'freedom-fighters'. As the conflict was underway along a 150-kilometre front, the claim was not taken seriously.

Clearly, the Pakistan Army must have planned the attack months before Vajpayee's arrival in Lahore. Sharif and his supporters have refused to own up to his approval or consent for the Kashmir incursion, and demanded the establishment of an independent commission of inquiry into the totality of the Kargil expedition. Pakistan's army has contradicted the Sharif contention, and has let it be known that he was repeatedly briefed by the generals, including: 1) 29 January 1999 briefing in Skardu; 2) 5 February in Kel (relating to the interdiction taking place from the Indian side of the LoC); 3) the ISI briefed him on 12 March 1999; 4) the Military Operations Directorate at GHQ briefed him on 17 May 2 June and 22 June 5) and the Chiefs of the Army, Navy and Air Force briefed Sharif's Defence Committee of the Cabinet on 2 July 1999.[17] These facts demonstrate that Sharif was indeed the leading figure in the decision-making mechanism of war and peace, especially about the Kargil expedition.

Why didn't he stop the Kargil planning, if he had firmly resolved to achieve rapprochement with India? Clearly the policy of war and peace could not be pursued simultaneously. Raised as a politician by the Pakistan Army under General Zia-ul-Haq's rule, Sharif gained substantial political experience first as the Chief Minister of the Punjab, and then as the Prime Minister of Pakistan. Unfortunately through experience he acquired no wisdom. In his second term (17 February 1997 to 12 October 1999) as the Prime Minister Sharif's Muslim League had won a two-thirds majority which like an intoxicant went straight to his head, leading him to believe that power and wisdom are the same thing. First, he attempted to control the Supreme Court where the spunky but restless Chief Justice came close to convicting him for the offence of contempt of court. To demonstrate his judicial activism, Chief Justice Sajjad Ali Shah had entertained an appeal for which hearings were conducted with a view to striking down the Thirteenth Amendment to the Constitution, which incidentally had been adopted unanimously in the National Assembly. If the amendment were to have been set aside it would have enabled the president to dismiss the prime minister. To intimidate the Chief Justice and other Supreme Court judges, Sharif's party organized an attack on the Supreme Court building on 27-28 November 1997.[18] Hurriedly the judges vacated their chamber and sought protection in fleeing. The Chief Justice requested the Army Chief to protect the court.

To cap all these misadventures Sharif also sought, through a constitutional amendment in August 1998, what he called in his Parliamentary speech the implementation of Islamic laws 'where the Qur'an and *sunna* are supreme'. Critics charged that in the name of Islam he was attempting to 'establish a fascist rule', and to 'buttress his power'.[19] Some critics charged that Sharif was determined to become, like Mulla Umar the Taliban leader, *Amir-al-Muminin* (the commander of the faithful). There was a general impression at the time in Pakistan that Prime Minister Sharif was tremendously impressed by the Taliban successfully establishing an Islamic Emirate of Afghanistan where the Qur'an and *sunna* had become the foundation of the Emirate's political system. It was in reality an attempt to outshine the Taliban in Pakistan. This accumulated hubris produced the Kargil adventure.

By late May and early June 1999 a serious mini-war was raging in the mountains above Kargil. The US was convinced that the conflict might escalate into an all-out war, where Pakistan might seek support from China and the Arab states, and India from Russia and Israel. The horror of nuclear cataclysm added to this anxiety.

DIPLOMACY OF CRISIS

Some Pakistani scholars who have presented essentially the Pakistan Army's perspective highlighted an interesting development. The military leadership came to believe that India was willing to negotiate the Kargil crisis with Pakistan in the middle of June 1999. The back-channel parleys between Niaz Naik and P.K. Mishra had made some undefined headway to diffuse the conflict. On 27 June 1999 indications appeared that an understanding had been reached 'on the final settlement of the Kargil conflict'. The settlement was to be signed in New Delhi by the Prime Minister of India and Pakistan. To mobilize international support, Sharif visited China on 27 June. India suggested that Sharif might make an impromptu stop in New Delhi on his way back from Beijing. That is why, it is speculated, Sharif cut short his visit to China. 'Once he did this, the Indian offer was suddenly cancelled, which left Sharif cooling his heels off in Hong Kong.'[20] Evidently India demanded nothing less than the complete withdrawal of Pakistani forces from the mountains of Kargil. She was encouraged in this by the fact that the United States accepted the Indian viewpoint, and so did China.

When Sharif visited China on 28 June 1999, China stated in general principle support for Pakistan 'in its efforts to de-escalate the situation along the Line of Control'. Also China advised India and Pakistan to find a peaceful solution for their dispute over Kashmir. A week earlier on 18-20 June 1999 the G8 Cologne Summit had described military action to change the status quo along the LoC as irresponsible. On 24-25 June the Clinton Administration sent General Anthony Zinni, the Commander-in-Chief of the Central Command to urge Sharif to withdraw Pakistani forces from Kargil. Addressing Sharif, General Zinni stated as recorded in his memoirs: 'If you don't pull back, you are going to bring war and nuclear annihilation down on your country.'[21] This blunt statement by the no-nonsense American general unnerved Sharif, but he delayed the process of withdrawing control after his meeting with President Clinton.

Actually relations with the US had already considerably soured over Afghanistan and Osama bin Laden.

PROBLEMS WITH AFGHANISTAN AND FEAR OF TERRORISM

Indeed the Taliban were under the protective wing of Pakistan. The US had issued in September 1998 a stern warning to the Taliban that they would be held directly responsible for any attacks on Americans wherever they occurred, even if they were carried out by Osama bin Laden's network, 'as long as they continued to give sanctuary to it'.[22] Also, the US government believed that 'Pakistan was the nation that held the key to his [bin Laden's] ability to use Afghanistan as a base for war against the United States.'[23] It was widely believed in US intelligence circles, especially the National Security Counterterrorism Office, that Pakistan's ISI was training Kashmiri *jihadists* in one of the camps which had been hit by US missiles. At this point in time the State Department's Counterterrorism Coordinator advised the Secretary of State Madeleine Albright 'to designate Pakistan as a state sponsor of terrorism'.[24] Secretary Albright rejected this recommendation because it would damage already tense relations in the wake of the May 1998 nuclear tests.

The US government encouraged the Saudi government to press Sharif with regard to the Taliban and Osama bin Laden. In October 1998 Crown Prince Abdullah put a

> tremendous amount of heat on Sharif. President Clinton invited Sharif to Washington, and confronted him on December 2, 1999. When Sharif returned to Pakistan Clinton called him on December 18. Sharif only promised to talk to the Taliban. Clinton called Sharif again in June 1999 to urge Sharif to persuade the Taliban to expel bin Laden from Afghanistan.[25]

Against this tense background, one can imagine how isolated Sharif was diplomatically when General Zinni confronted him in Islamabad. In the last days of June 1999 Sharif began to ask to see President Clinton in order to present his case on the Kargil conflict. Clinton consulted Prime Minister Vajpayee, who demanded the withdrawal of Pakistani forces to the LoC and no negotiations under the threat of 'aggression.' Clinton assured Vajpayee that: 1) he would not countenance Pakistani aggression; 2) he would not reward Pakistan for violating the LoC; 3) he would stand for US commitment to the Lahore process; 4) direct talks between India and Pakistan were the only solution to the Kashmir issue, and 5) there would be no third party intervention.[26] This was a shining moment of success for Indian diplomacy. For the first time the US government had completely jettisoned support for Pakistan over its conflict with India.

On 22 July Sharif called President Clinton, and appealed for US intervention to stop India's counter-attacks. Clinton advised Sharif to withdraw completely from the Kargil hills. Sharif became desperate, and called Clinton again on 3 July and asked for a meeting. Clinton was blunt: 'come only if you are ready to withdraw.' Yet he advised Sharif to consider carefully the wisdom of his trip to Washington under these constraints. Sharif literally invited himself to Washington and came to see Clinton on 4 July and brought his wife and children with him. The US estimated that Sharif was afraid that the Pakistani Army might be telling him to leave, if the summit failed.

Sharif's flight landed at Dulles Airport, a substantial distance from Washington. No one from the US government came to welcome him, only the Saudi Ambassador Bandar bin Sultan was there to greet him and his family. In fact, Clinton had asked the Saudi Ambassador to receive Sharif to weigh in forcefully with him on the ride to Blair House, a US government guest house across the street from the White House. Bandar had secured Prince Abdullah's support for the US position. The US had also obtained British Prime Minister Tony Blair's and China's support for force-point US policy for the Kargil conflict. Distraught and completely isolated, Sharif perceived a threat from his military chiefs, who were pressing for a bold and tough stand on Kargil.

In the meeting Clinton treated Sharif like an errant school-boy, when with the wave of his hand he brushed aside his request for a one on one private meeting. Bruce Riedel, a staff officer on US National Security, remained in their meeting, and recorded the minutes of their dialogue. Sharif wanted to withdraw Pakistani forces with some cover. Clinton denied him that too. Fuming with anger Clinton then dropped a bombshell on Sharif: 'Do you know that your military was preparing their nuclear tipped missiles' against the Indian forces? Sharif was taken aback and denied that he had ordered the preparation of their missile force. Clinton sensed that Sharif was worried for his life. At that point he bluntly chastised him for ignoring his requests to bring Osama bin Laden to justice from Afghanistan.

Finally, Sharif capitulated and an agreement was reached, including the key sentence: 'The Prime Minister has agreed to take concrete and immediate steps for the restoration of the Line of Control.' The statement also called for a ceasefire once the withdrawal was completed, and restoration of the Lahore process. Clinton added a sentence to reaffirm his long-standing plans to visit South Asia. After consulting his Foreign Secretary, Shamshad Ahmad, Sharif asked Clinton to add one more sentence to the statement: 'the President would take personal interest to encourage an expeditious resumption and intensifica-tions of bilateral efforts [i.e. the Lahore process] once the sanctity of the Line of Control had been fully restored.'

Clinton called Vajpayee to preview the agreement, which he approved, and the matter was clinched. The Kargil expedition, an exercise in futility, was over. Full of anxiety and trepidation Sharif returned home and declared publicly a pyrrhic victory: from now on the President of the United States will take an interest in the Kashmir problem. In reality it was a big victory for India both militarily and politically. Relations between Sharif and the Pakistani military were poisoned, and both started to plan against the other.

What was the strategic result of the Blair-White House Summit? It had a profound impact on Indo-US relations. Riedel stated:

'Doors opened in New Delhi to Americans that had been shut for years. The Indian elite—including the military—and the Indian public began to shed long held negative perceptions of the US. The stage was set for the unprecedented back to back summits between President Clinton and Prime Minister Vajpayee in 2000'.[27]

Exactly three months and eight days after Sharif's arrival back home, Army Chief Pervez Musharraf, an intrepid and swash-buckling general who was excessively rich in self-esteem, toppled Sharif's government in a bloodless coup. Sharif contributed generously to his own political demise by his well-known political clumsiness. While General Musharraf was flying from Sri Lanka, back to Pakistan on 12 October 1999, Nawaz Sharif fired him from his job, and appointed an ISI General to be Chief of the Army. Evidently, Musharraf and his supporters in the army had prepared a counter coup, which succeeded. And Pakistan was back under army rule.

US SHUNNING MUSHARRAF AND TILTING TOWARD INDIA

From the coup of 12 October 1999 to the tragedy of 11 September 2001, the period of one year and nine months was filled with a great deal of tensions between the US and Pakistan, and some degree of relaxation of tensions between Pakistan and India. After 11 September 2001 the political dimensions changed rapidly.

First with India: Why did Vajpayee extend an invitation to Musharraf for a summit meeting with him in Agra on 24 May 2001 after his repeated declarations that India would not deal with the military government in Pakistan that had come to power by unconstitutional means in October 1999? Several factors explained this change in policy. 1) Despite the withdrawal of forces from Kargil across the LoC the *jihadis* and Kashmiri freedom-fighters had continued the conflict in the Indian section of Kashmir. 2) India's attempts to parley with Kashmir's political parties, including the Hurriyet parties (dedicated to achieving national self-determination), were not successful. 3) India was under 'friendly pressure' the US and other major powers to resume dialogue with Pakistan on issues related to Kashmir and nuclear reduction. 4) The US had assured India that it had changed its attitude toward the Kashmir dispute.[28] Also there is a strong Indian business lobby. It was interested in a gas pipeline originating in Iran or Turkmenistan and coming to India through Pakistan and knew that the route through Pakistan was the shortest. It was also interested in the Pakistani market.

J.N. Dixit offered an additional economic explanation of Musharraf's acceptance of Vajpayee's invitation with great alacrity on 27 May. India presumed that 'economically [Pakistan] was on the verge of bankruptcy, and serious political instability.'[29] The economic problems India reasoned, might have persuaded the General to seek a 'practical compromise' on Kashmir, and normalize relations with India.

On the eve of his departure, Musharraf elevated himself to the position of President of Pakistan, by pushing aside the Sharif-era, pliable and gentle President, Rafiq Tarer. This second coup against an elected president, which elicited no protest, convinced India that Musharraf had the support or at least general acquiescence of Pakistan's public.

The Agra Summit was held on 15 and 16 July 2001. Very vigorously Musharraf presented Pakistan's viewpoint on Kashmir, but showed scant interest in other issues, what India likes to describe as the 'composite dialogue.' India believes that if all the outstanding disputes are resolved, the political climate in south Asia would become so congenial that Pakistan would cease 'this obsession' with Kashmir. This may be wishful thinking, but India has never stopped trying to lure Pakistan into this protracted dialogue. On the contrary Pakistan's repeatedly stated position is that the only real problem between India and Pakistan is the Kashmir dispute. Resolve this dispute and all the issues will fall into place.

These two orientations clashed in Agra. At the summit, Musharraf realized that for India the Kashmir Valley is non-negotiable, but other changes could be discussed. Moreover, India separated all other issues from Kashmir, including notably the war in Siachen and the Wular Barrage being constructed on the River Chenab in Jammu, which Pakistan maintained was in violation of the 1960 Indus Waters Treaty negotiated with the help of the World Bank. The Indian agenda proposed other issues—the Sir Creek demarcation in the Rann of Kutch, terrorism, economic cooperation, and promotion of friendly exchanges.

In Delhi, Musharraf invited Kashmiri Hurriyat leaders to a reception in the Pakistan Embassy. Disapprovingly, India sent only a low-ranking official of the Foreign Service. Musharraf also gave a press conference to the editors of the Indian newspapers. Focusing on Kashmir, he proposed that India and Pakistan should consider making some areas of Kashmir independent, placing them under joint Indian-Pakistani control or putting them under the administration of the UN. These suggestions presupposed demilitarization of the Kashmiri regions. With this proposal he gave up Pakistan's traditional stance demanding the implementation of the UN Resolutions. India refused to sign the final communiqué that included specifically the urgency to resolve the Kashmir dispute. However, it did agree that further meetings among high-level ministers should take place in the near future, and Vajpayee agreed to visit Pakistan later in the year. Dissatisfied with this inconclusive summit, Musharraf returned home.

NOTES

1. For an excellent analysis of the Kashmir dispute, see Sumantra Bose, *Roots of Conflict: Paths to Peace* (Cambridge: Harvard University Press, 2003), p. 38.
2. *The Statesman* (Calcutta), 4 February 1948; Bose, p. 32.
3. Bose, p. 36; Bhushan Dasgupta, *Jammu and Kashmir* (The Hague: Martinus Nijhoff, 1968), p. 226; Alastair Lamb, *Crisis in Kashmir, 1947-1966* (London: Routledge and Kagan Paul, 1966), p. 109.

4. Lamb, p. 408.
5. For details on the Soviet leaders' visit to Kashmir and India, see Hafeez Malik, *Soviet-Pakistan Relations and Post-Soviet Dynamics* (New York: St. Martin's Press; London: Macmillan, 1996).
6. Aziz Ahmad (Minister of State), *Line of Control*, Statement of December 11, 1972 in the National Assembly (an unpublished personal copy).
7. *The Indian Annual Register*, (Delhi: 1947), p. 112.
8. H.V. Hodson, *The Great Divide* (New York: Oxford University Press, 1997), p. 428.
9. Karl E. Meyer, 'The Invention of Pakistan: How the British Raj Surrendered', *World Policy Journal* (Spring 2003), p. 82.
10. Ayaz Daudzai, 'Kashmir: Historic Facts Can't Be Altered', *The Mirror of the World* (Moscow), 14 May 2005,
< http://iraqwar.mirror-world.ru/article/49979>; see also, Meyer, op. cit.
11. Stanley Wolpert, *Jinnah of Pakistan* (New York: Oxford University Press, 1984), p. 370.
12. Hodson, *The Creat Divide* p. 380.
13. J.N. Dixit, *India-Pakistan in War and Peace* (New York: Routledge, 2002), p. 366.
14. For details see A. G. Noorani, 'The Truth about the Lahore Summit', *Frontline* (Vol. 19, Issue 4) 16 February -1 March 2002, pp. 1-10.
15. J.N. Dixit, *India-Pakistan* p. 382.
16. Bruce Riedel, *American Diplomacy and the 1999 Kargil Summit at Blair House* (Philadelphia: Policy Paper Series, 2002), pp. 2-3.
17. Shireen M. Mazari, *The Kargil Conflict, 1999* (Islamabad: The Institute of Strategic Studies, 2003), pp. 57-8.
18. Sajjad Ali Shah, Chief Justice, *An Autobiography: Law Courts in Glass House* (Karachi: Oxford University Press, 2001), p. 509.
19. 'Pakistan Premier Proposes an Islamic Society Based on Koran', *The New York Times*, 29 August 1998.
20. Mazari, pp 58-59; Nasim Zehra, 'Was There a Deal that Delhi Went Back on?' *The News*, 27 June 1999; see also Zehra's article, 'Nawaz Sharif and Kargil', *The News*, 29 July 2004.
21. General Anthony Zinni and Tom Clancy, *Battle Ready* (New York: G.P. Putnam and Sons, 2004), p. 347.
22. DOS Cable, Islamabad 06863, 'Afghanistan Demarche to Taliban on bin Laden Threat', 12 September 1998; *The 9/11 Commission Report* (Washington DC, 2003).
23. Ibid., p. 63.
24. Ibid., p. 122.
25. Ibid., p. 126.
26. Bruce Riedel, *American Diplomacy and the 1999 Kargil Summit at Blair House* (Philadelphia: Policy Paper Series, 2002).
27. Riedel, American Diplomacy p. 9.

28. C. Raja Mohan, *Crossing the Rubicon: The shaping of India's New Foreign Policy* (London: Palgrave Macmillan, 2003), p. 190.
29. Dixit, India-Pakistan p. 403.

5

The US Tilt Towards India

Signalling a major foreign policy orientation, President Clinton visited India for five days and Pakistan for five hours during his week-long visit of 19 -24 March 2000. His visit to India was designed to lay the foundations for 'a positive long-term relationship'. For his reluctant visit to Pakistan, Clinton had four specific objectives: 'to encourage an early return to civilian rule; a lessening of tensions over Kashmir; to urge General Musharraf not to execute the deposed Prime Minister, Nawaz Sharif, who was on trial for his life and to press Musharraf to cooperate with the US on bin Laden and Al Qaeda.'[1] Musharraf gave an assurance that Sharif would not be executed, but remained 'non-committal on other issues'.[2]

Clinton's visit to India was most significant. He offered no geostrategic explanation for his decision to visit, other than to say that the US had wasted too much time since December 1991. This explanation is indeed inadequate. Clinton did not have an epiphany one fine morning on his brief walk from the residential part of the White House to the Oval Office and recognize that it was high time to enlist India as a strategic partner. In the cold war period India had sided with the Soviet Union primarily as a counterweight to China and the US. Since the collapse of the Soviet Union in 1991 US policy toward South Asia was in gestation. The catalytic factors were: 1) the rise of China; 2) Russian endeavours to create another pole of power, which might not be a perfect counterbalance to the US but would at least provide a semblance of equilibrium; 3) destabilizing developments in Afghanistan under the Taliban, and Pakistan's intricate relationship with them; 4) the never-ending conflict over Kashmir between India and Pakistan and 5) last but not least, the Indian-American community's role in creating a strategic partnership with India. These five factors shaped the US's new foreign policy orientation, and they deserve to be explored.

THE RISE OF CHINA

By the dawn of the twenty-first century China had become by far the strongest power in Eurasia. China's rise in political prestige began in the late 1970s when the US withdrew diplomatic recognition from its loyal protégé Taiwan and agreed to the one China policy that was re-confirmed by subsequent communiqués issued by both the US and China. Yet as a hedge, the US Congress passed the Taiwan Act in 1979, which obligated the US government to protect Taiwan; it also made it exceptionally difficult for China to achieve unification with Taiwan as Section 2a (5) of the Act states that it is the responsibility of the US 'to provide Taiwan arms of defensive character'.

Postponing its efforts for unification, China under Deng Xiaoping's leadership in the 1980s initiated a policy of economic reforms establishing a 'socialist market economy'. By 2000 China's economic performance had surpassed India's in terms of the standard of living of the population. It also succeeded in integrating its economy with the world economy.[3] Now China's economy is doubling in size every ten years, and personal incomes have been rising steadily. Its trade with the US played a major role in China's growth. Investors around the world poured money into Chinese industries that manufactured goods sold in the American markets. As a mark of high confidence foreign direct investment in China during 1979-1993 came to $221 billion ($111 billion in 1993 alone).[4] China benefited enormously from American consumers' demand for less expensive Chinese goods, and has become dependent on them. It needs a prosperous America with economic policies that avoid protectionism. Also, China needs secure sea lanes, and like other

Asian states implicitly relies upon the US navy to protect its oil import.[5] In the light of China's economic growth, it is not surprising that now it 'is set to complete a transition from aid recipient to international donor in 2005'.[6]

Even in 2001 the Chinese Prime Minister Zhu Rongji, on his 14-20 May visit to Pakistan, signed six agreements and a Memorandum of Understanding providing for financial assistance on a variety of projects, including an assistance package of $100 million to develop the country's railroad system.[7] However, China's economic activity in South-east Asia was much more impressive. Some viewed it 'as the beginning of an inescapable process of China replacing the United States as the dominant power in Asia.'[8] In 2002, it was estimated that China's trade was growing at a faster rate than Japan's growth during its boom years in the late 1960s and 1970s, and China's surplus in its trade with the US was $103.1 billion and $129.4 billion in 2003 (see following Table).

TABLE

US Merchandise Trade with China: 1988-2002 and Estimate for 2003   ($billions)

Year	US Exports	US Imports	US Trade Balance
1988	5.0	8.5	-3.5
1989	5.8	12.0	-6.2
1990	4.8	15.2	-10.4
1991	6.3	19.0	-12.7
1992	7.5	25.7	-18.2
1993	8.8	31.5	-22.8
1994	9.3	38.8	-29.5
1995	11.7	45.6	-33.8
1996	12.0	51.5	-39.5
1997	12.8	62.6	-49.7
1998	14.3	71.2	-56.9
1999	13.1	81.8	-68.7
2000	16.3	100.1	-83.8
2001	19.2	102.3	-83.1
2002	22.1	125.2	-103.1
2003 projection*	27.4	156.5	-129.4

Source: US Department of Commerce.
*Projections for 2003 based on actual data for January-July 2003.

Indonesia buried age old hostility as it wooed the Chinese government for the award of a $9 billion liquid natural gas contract to power the industries of southern China.

In January 2001, the Chinese state-owned offshore oil company, CNOOC, bought the lucrative Indonesian oil and gas fields owned by the Spanish company, Repsol-YPF, for $585 million. In May 2002, the Petro China Company outbid four rivals to buy the Indonesian assets of Devon Energy Corporation for $262 million. The little Asian tiger, Singapore, had lost by 2002 more than 42,000 jobs over the last five years in trade with China.

China also turned its attention to Central Asia and the Middle East. In 2003 it signed the China Kazakhstan Pipeline Agreement, worth $3.5 billion, and around the same time also signed a mega-gas deal with Iran worth $100 billion. The deal entails the annual export of some 10 million tons of Iranian liquefied natural gas for a period of twenty-five years. In 1993 for a 2,760 km pipeline, with more than 700 km traversing Pakistani territory the Iran-China agreement could create a real 'peace pipeline'.

Last but not least China expanded its public diplomacy in Asia. In 2003, 2,563 Indonesian students received visas to go to China for education. By comparison only 133 Indonesian students received visas for study in American universities. While the US was mired in fear of terrorism, and was launching a 'crusade for democracy' in Iraq, China was quietly expanding its cultural and intellectual enterprises.

President Clinton's policy was what he called constructive engagement, implying integrating China into the global economy through its admission into the World Trade Organization. This policy also envisaged increased cooperation with China to: stop the spread of weapons of mass destruction, work together on the peaceful use of nuclear energy, and 3) fight organized crime and drug trafficking.[9] This cooperative policy, however, does not mean that Clinton had ignored geopolitical imperatives of power. The Taiwan Act was honoured, and the policy of paying lip service to the concept of one China was also maintained. In 1996

China conducted military exercises in waters close to Taiwan in an apparent effort at intimidation. Clinton dispatched two aircraft carrier battle groups to the region to discourage the Chinese aggressive posture. Subsequently, tension in the Taiwan Strait diminished. To balance the expanding power of China, Clinton initiated the new Indian policy; it was not an epiphany.

The pendulum swung the other way under George W. Bush, who succeeded Clinton. In July 2002 the US Department of Defence issued a study that stated that China was rapidly modernizing its military with the objective of countering American power in the Pacific, and pressing Taiwan to accept unification on China's terms. The study asserted that China's military modernization would pose a threat to Japan and the Philippines, as well as to Taiwan. It estimated that China's military budget was $65 billion a year – much more than the $20 billion per year that China publicly reported. Then the report catalogued various types of missiles and submarines that were being replaced by more modern varieties.[10] The Republican stalwarts began to say that the report's conclusions about China's ballistic missile programme should trigger alarm bells. The report's harsh tone was also in keeping with the Republican Party's conservative wing, which excoriated President Clinton and Congressional Democrats for being soft on China.

ATTEMPTS TO CREATE A COUNTERVAILING POLE OF POWER

Russia, diminished in size and economic resources, and China, the more resourceful economic power, China, made serious efforts during the 1990s to create an alliance that would be respected by the US. In 1996 at their first summit meeting in Shanghai, China and Russia invited the leaders of Tajikistan, Kazakhstan, and Kyrgyzstan to establish what was euphemistically named the Shanghai Forum. They signed an agreement on military confidence-building measures in the region of their common borders. Subsequently, they expanded their cooperation to include efforts to combat ethnic separatism, international terrorism, and crime and regional extremism. Also, they announced that the Forum was open to other countries with similar concerns, and let it be known that they wanted to become a serious 'club' whose influence would extend far beyond their region.

On 6 July 2000 the members of Shanghai Forum, met in Dushanbe, Tajikistan at the fifth summit of the Shanghai Forum. The Uzbek President Islam Karimov participated in the Dushanbe talks as a guest. He declared that as long as armed confrontation continued in Afghanistan, producing a new generation of terrorists and militants, they would have no assurance against aggressive tendencies and regional extremism. The Russian President Vladimir Putin examined his Russian border troops of the 201st Russian Division in Tajikistan in July, and bluntly stated: 'the most important thing right now is to establish a Russian military base, and reinforce Russia's military presence in Tajikistan'. Two years earlier Tashkent had not liked the Russian military presence in Tajikistan, but in 2000 its attitude had changed.

Three days before the summit meeting in Dushanbe, Chinese President Jiang Zemin made an official visit on 3 July 2000 to Tajikistan, and signed a border treaty, a legal cooperation treaty, and a declaration on the regional situation. In their joint declaration they expressed concern over the condition in Afghanistan, and underlined their common interest in combating separatism and Islamic fundamentalism. For Tajikistan, cooperation with China amounted to a recognition of that country's importance in Central Asia. For China, collaborating with Tajikistan was an additional trump card in its hands to fight against separatists in the Xinjiang Uygur Autonomous Region, which is contiguous to Tajikistan and Pakistan and is a traditional homeland of Muslim Uygurs. It was then wellknown that about 1,000 Uygur separatists were in the training camps of Osama bin Laden in Afghanistan. To receive Chinese military and economic help Tajikistan completed building a highway from Dushanbe to Kulyab (Kelob) via Kurgan-Tyube.

The Dushanbe declaration signed by the five heads of state in 2000 pointedly reminded the US and NATO that it was inadmissible to interfere in the internal affairs of other states 'on the pretext of humanitarian intervention, and protecting human rights'.[11] In this subtle way, Russia's actions in Chechnya were supported, and the Chinese position on Taiwan. China opposed any plans which would include Taiwan in a theatre missile defence system.

However, as the Shanghai Forum countries, now known as the Shanghai Cooperation Organization, met in Beijing in January 2002 they asserted that the fall of the Taliban did not end the terrorist threat, and that their governments would continue to work together against terrorism, separatism, and extremism to promote regional stability. On a broader level this meeting represented an effort by China and Russia to form a counterweight to growing US influence in Eurasia. Even before the tragedy of 9/11 President Clinton was aware of these developments, and wooing India was, therefore, timely and appropriate.

DESTABILIZING DEVELOPMENTS IN AFGHANISTAN: OSAMA BIN LADEN'S ROLE

The Clinton administration had two serious problems with Afghanistan: that the Taliban government itself was composed of religious zealots, and that it was sheltering Osama bin Laden. Well before the 11 September 2001 attacks the Taliban's partnership with bin Laden's Al Qaeda organization had become the Clinton administration's overriding concern in US policy toward Afghanistan. In August 1998 Al Qaeda activists bombed the US embassies in Kenya and Tanzania. President Clinton increasingly exercised more pressure on both the Taliban and Pakistan's Prime Minister Nawaz Sharif to extradite bin Laden. The US was convinced that Sharif was deliberately not helping in its difficult relations with Afghanistan.

To deal with the Taliban the US adopted a strategy of applying sanctions, the threat of some military action, and the continuation of diplomatic efforts.

The US Ambassador to the United Nations Bill Richardson was sent to Afghanistan in April 1998. He asked the Taliban to hand over bin Laden to the US; the Taliban flatly refused.

In retaliation for the bombing of the US embassies in Kenya and Tanzania, on 20 August 1999 Clinton authorized the firing of seventy-five Tomahawk cruise missiles into Zawhar Kili's rock gorges. On the night of 20 August in Islamabad, General Joseph Ralston, Vice Chairman of the US Joint Chiefs of Staff, sat down to dinner with General Jahangir Karamat, Pakistan's Army Chief. Ralston's main responsibility was to assure General Karamat that the incoming 'friendly' missiles were American, and not an Indian nuclear missile attack. This dinner further muddied the troubled waters. One account suggested that Ralston told Karamat forthrightly that cruise missiles were in the air. Another maintained that Ralston was not so forthcoming and told Karamat in general terms that a 'retaliatory action' was being planned by the US. Actually Ralston left Pakistani airspace before the missiles arrived, 'infuriating Karamat, who felt the Americans had failed to take him adequately into their confidence.'

A very detailed investigative study reported that 'Sharif meanwhile was angry that the United States talked directly to the Army about the attack rather than to Pakistan's supposedly supreme civilian authority, and he was also angry at Karamat, believing that the General deceived him or let him down.'[12] President Clinton, however, described this episode matter-of-factly: 'Ralston would tell him [General Karamat] what was happening a few minutes before our missiles invaded Pakistani airspace, too late to alert the Taliban or Al Qaeda, but in time to avoid having them shot down or sparking a counterattack on India.'[13] When Pakistan discovered that some of the missiles had fallen inside its territory and caused Pakistani casualties, it denounced the attack in public and private.

In order to create additional economic pressure Clinton imposed a ban on US trade with Afghanistan on 4 July 1999, and blocked the Taliban's assets (which were not many) in US financial institutions.

On 15 October 1999 the US succeeded in convincing the UN Security Council to pass its first resolution sanctioning the Taliban regime. The resolution banned flights outside Afghanistan by Ariana Airlines (most planes were not technically fit to fly), and directed UN member states to freeze Taliban assets.

On 19 December 2000 under US initiative the UN Security Council adopted another resolution that was directed specifically at Pakistan as well as the Taliban. This called for a worldwide prohibition against the provision of arms or military advice to the Taliban, a reduction of Taliban diplomatic representation abroad, and a ban on foreign travel by senior Taliban officials.

On 30 July 2001 the UN Security Council adopted a third resolution that was once again aimed directly at Pakistan. It provided for the posting of monitors there to ensure that no weapons or military advice was being given to the Taliban.

After 1997 the US also started to push for covert operations against bin Laden and the Taliban. Contacts were renewed with Ahmad Shah Massoud, the legendary Tajik military commander of the Northern Alliance, with a hope that he might help in delivering bin Laden to the US. Massoud urged the US to recognize the danger spawned by the alliance of the Taliban with the Pakistani ISI and the Osama terror infrastructure. He did not want the US to have an exaggerated view of his military capability. Sharif, who came to power in 1997, had a tacit agreement with the establishment that he would leave the army and the ISI alone, and not interfere with the course of policy being pursued by them.

Yet at the first opportunity that came his way Sharif eased the Army Chief, General Jahangir Karamat, out of office. A gentle and thoughtful general, Karamat had made a speech at a naval school in Lahore where he proposed the creation of a National Security Council with armed forces representatives as a policy-making forum for defence and national security. Clearly this was a power-sharing proposal between the civilian-led democracy and the Pakistani military. Reflecting his flawed judgment of character, Sharif appointed Pervez Musharraf to head the army, and General Zia-ud-Din as the Director General of the ISI. It was generally believed in Lahore that General Zia-ud-Din, who belonged to the Engineering Corps, had wormed his way into Abaji's (Sharif's dear father) heart. With his appointment to run the ISI, people thought that Sharif had singled out his own man to protect him. General Pervez Musharraf and Corps Commanders could not have ignored General Karamat's 'ouster,' and General Zia-ud-Din's prominent promotion, as signs of Sharif's determination to subordinate the army to his rule.

By the fall of 1998 the Clinton Administration was convinced that Pakistan's regional objectives included bleeding Indian forces in Kashmir and supporting the Taliban in its war against Massoud's ragtag army. The Taliban believed that it would take one more year of war to defeat Massoud.[14] The US perception was that an unholy alliance, principally supported by Pakistan, was supporting terrorism directed at the United States and threatening to provoke a nuclear war over Kashmir.[15]

Sharif visited Clinton in December 1998 in Washington and the ISI Director General Zia-ud-Din was a member of his entourage. In the White House Cabinet Room Clinton had a one on one brief chat with General Zia-ud-Din, and then announced to the others that Zia-ud-Din had just offered to set up a squad to go after bin Laden. The White House approved the plan. 'Through the Islamabad station, the CIA paid salaries and supplied communication and other gear, as directed by Zia-ud-Din.' Subsequently, the US charged that 'on paper the CIA-funded a secret commando team was being trained for action against bin Laden in Afghanistan,' but in reality the elite strike force was loyal to Pakistan's Prime Minister and the ISI agency was prepared to protect them against any future army coup against them.[16] Clearly this was a double-cross deal that did not endear Sharif or his protégé General Zia-ud-Din to President Clinton and his White House staff.

CONFLICT OVER KASHMIR

In the 1990s the Kashmiri population in effect took control of its destiny, and rebelled against the Indian government. A thoughtful Indian scholar, Sumantra Bose, has stated that by 1990 the government authority in the Kashmir Valley had collapsed 'and insurrection took hold'.[17] Bose divided the insurgency into three distinct phases:

> the *intifada* or uprising phase, which lasted from 1990 until 1995; a period of demoralization and atrophy (1996-1998); and the *fidayeen* phase (1999-2002), marked by the renewal of insurgency with a radical Islamist ideological color and ascendancy of Pakistan-based militant groups using *fidayeen* (suicide-squad) tactics against Indian forces.[18]

During the first two phases the US considered the insurgency a political expression of the Kashmiri people's urge for self-determination, which was threatened by India. However, in the third phase its perceptions began to change. By 1998 the US clearly saw a linkage between Afghanistan, Pakistan, and the insurgency in Kashmir. The counter-terrorism centres in the White House and the CIA believed that 'Pakistan spawned the Taliban, [and] nurtured it...'[19] The Taliban, they assessed, served a dual purpose for Pakistan. 1987, they created a strategic depth for it 'in its confrontation with India'. Paul A. Pillar, who served for several years as the Deputy Chief of Counterterrorist Center at the CIA during the Clinton Administration, explained the second: 'this is how the problem in Afghanistan relates to the one in Kashmir – the Taliban and groups based in the territory it controls (including ones associated with bin Laden) provide major support to the Kashmiri insurgency, in the form of both training facilities and manpower.'[20] President Clinton adopted the same view as he stated in his memoirs: 'The Pakistan intelligence service used some of the same camps that bin Laden and Al Qaeda did to train the Taliban and insurgents who fought in Kashmir.'[21]

In the latter part of the third phase, especially after the 9/11 attacks on American targets in New York and Washington DC, the US government started to view all forms of political violence in any part of the world as acts of terrorism.

THE INDIAN AMERICAN COMMUNITY'S ROLE

President Clinton paid handsome compliments to the Indian–American community for its remarkable success in the US. When Indian Prime Minister Atal Bihari Vajpayee visited the US in September 2000, President Clinton gave a state dinner in his honour to which 700 Indian-Americans were invited. (Hardly more than 7 Pakistani-Americans have ever been invited to White House dinners on a similar occasion.) These invitees were there because the US wanted 'to focus attention on the enormous contributions being made by the Indian-American community.' Clinton invited a large number of Indian-Americans to fly with him when he visited India; there they participated in festivities held in his honour in New Delhi and Bombay. In recognition of their importance to India, the Vajpayee government had created the position of an Additional Secretary in the Ministry of External Affairs to promote closer relations with them.

Also, on 18 August 2000 the government of India appointed a High Level Commission (HLC) to examine India's relations with the Indian diaspora. L.M. Singhvi, a former Ambassador to Britain, was made the Chairman with the rank of a Cabinet Minister. After several months of international travel Singhvi and his four colleagues submitted an exhaustive review of overseas Indians' adaptation to the cultures of foreign lands. Focusing on the US, they divided the Indians' migration into three categories: 1) those from agricultural backgrounds, that is Punjabi Sikhs and some Hindus, who moved from British Columbia to California; 2) entrepreneurs, store-owners, self-employed businessmen, who came to the US mainly in the 1960s; 3) professionals—doctors, engineers (the 1960s), software engineers, management consultants, financial experts and media persons who came in the 1980s and continue to migrate to the US.[22]

Even during the Cold War period, when relations remained frigid, India conducted robust programmes of public diplomacy with the US. In the 1950s-60s, Indian students enrolled in American universities in large numbers, where they were most conspicuous in the departments of hard sciences. An undetermined number of these highly-trained Indians settled in the US.

By 1980 there were 387,000 Indian-Americans in the US, but by 1990 this figure had risen to 815,447, and the 2000 Census recorded the phenomenal growth of 105.87 per cent at 1,678,967. In 2005, their number was estimated to be 2 million. (The Pakistani-American community, by comparison, is only a small fraction of the Indian number, estimated in 2005 at no more than 400,000.) After the tragedy of 9/11, thousands of Pakistanis in the US who were not legal residents were deported. So the size of the Pakistani-American community has substantially dwindled. The educational achievement and economic status of the Indian-American community is equally striking in 2005.

- A median income of $60,093, double that of all American families
- 200,000 Indian-American millionaires
- 58 per cent of Indian-Americans were over the age of 25 and had a college degree
- 43.6 per cent of Indian-Americans in the workforce employed as managers or professionals
- 35,000 Indian-American physicians.
- 300,000 Indian-Americans working in high-tech industries
- 15 per cent of Silicon Valley start-up firms owned by Indian-Americans
- More than 5,000 Indian-Americans on the faculties at American universities.

• 74,603 Indians studying in the US—making Indians the largest group of foreign students in the country[23]

'Reflecting their concentration in the medical, scientific and computer fields, the per capita income of Indian-Americans exceeds that of every other group in the country (including whites) except Japanese Americans.'[24] The per capita income of the Indian-American community in 2001 was estimated at $60, 093 compared to the per capita income of US citizens of $38,885.[25]

This wealth and success has now been converted into political clout. Indian-Americans raised $4 million on behalf of political candidates during the 1992 election; in 1998 this figure almost doubled to more than $7 million. In the 2000 elections the number was much higher. Senator Sam Brownback (Republican-Kansas) observed: 'By their engagement and aggressiveness they are able to influence things beyond their numbers.'[26] While Indian-Americans are located in practically all the states, they are largely concentrated in ten: New York, New Jersey, Pennsylvania, California, Michigan, Ohio, Illinois, Texas, Florida, and Massachusetts. One example of their political clout is sufficient. When in 1999 the House International Relations Committee discussed the resolution dealing with the Pakistan-backed incursion into the Kargil sector of Kashmir, Indian-American computer specialists in a 24-hour period generated 400 email letters of condemnation against Pakistan. The Committee was bound to notice this avalanche of support for India.

The American Association of Physicians of Indian Origin, the Indian American Friendship Council, the Asian-American Hotel Owners Association, and other professional groups host legislative conferences in Washington each year, which prominent US lawmakers are invited to address. The 1999 Indian American Friendship Council Conference was attended by almost forty US such lawmakers. The theme of these meetings is generally—'India, the largest democracy, and the US, the oldest democracy are natural allies.' This drumbeat of democracy resonates in the White House, on Capitol Hill, and with the general public. Pakistan comes out as a citadel of military rule, and a state filled with religious intolerance and zealotry—all anti-democratic attributes.

The Indian-American Community played a significant role in creating a Congressional Caucus for India, especially after 1992 when a well-known advocate for India, Representative Stephen J. Solarz (Democrat-NY), was defeated in his bid for re-election. This was due to the redrawing of congressional districts in New York City, his loss of voter confidence after the House Ethics Committee named him as one of the worst abusers of the House of Representatives Bank—writing 743 overdrawn checks in a thirty-nine month period, and finally the determined efforts of the Pakistani-American Community. With a large Indian-American population in his congressional district in New Jersey, Congressman Frank Pollone then roped in some other Democrats and Republicans to organize the India Caucus. In 1999, the Caucus had a membership of 115 members; more than a quarter of the entire House. Since then membership has exceeded 200 and the leadership has shifted to other Congressmen. The India Caucus promotes Indo-US relations and other issues of concern to the Indian-Americans. Its is also an institutional base of support for India on Capitol Hill. Despite the fact that most members are Democrats and only a few are Republican, the Caucus is a formidable force to be reckoned with. At present it is well-nigh impossible to have an anti-India measure passed by the House of Representatives. In fact, a very high level of support exists in the Congress for India's inclusion as a permanent member of the UN Security Council.

In addition to the Indian Caucus, an intimately cordial collaborative relationship has been cultivated between the Indian Embassy, the Indian-American Community, and the Indian Congressional Caucus. The Indian Embassy remains exceptionally receptive to the activities of the community's activists. Indian Ambassadors are known to receive the calls of Indian-Americans directly, rather than have them routed through their secretaries.

This triangular interaction is the envy of many other nationalities.

India has, however, added another dimension of support structure to its diplomacy in Washington. In May 2003, the then-Indian National Security Advisor, Brajesh Mishra, addressed the American-Jewish Committee regarding the need for joint action by the US, India and Israel. In September 2002 President Bush stated in a gathering:

> I am pleased to see so many distinguished members of the United States Congress here today. They are friends of Israel. They are also friends of India. The Caucus on India and Indian-Americans in the House of Representatives has nearly 160 members...The increasing contact between the American-Jewish Committee and Indian-American Community organizations is another positive reflection of the shared values of our people.[27]

Commenting on three aspects of this new dimension of relationship an Indian analyst offered his assessment:

> This commonality of interests, therefore, has both national and international implications. 1) Domestically, it allows the Indian-American Community to harness the skills of a larger and more skillful lobbying group to help attain mutual goals. 2) Internationally, it may allow India to procure weapons that have been denied by the United States to China – one of India's regional competitors. 3) From the Israeli perspective, it strengthens both military-strategic and diplomatic ties with India. This not only provides Israel with an important regional ally in the fight against radical Islamic groups but also weans away Indian diplomatic support to the Arab states.[28]

Clearly this emerging relationship between Israel and India has President Bush's support. But it also has an anti-Pakistan dimension. During the Kargil War Israel supplied within 24 hours UAVs for high-altitude surveillance, laser-guided systems, and many other items to India. Israel has emerged as India's number two weapon supplier after Russia. Some of India's recent defence purchases from Israel are as follows:[29]

- artillery Guns 130mm upgradation to 155mm-180 (to be done in Israel)
- artillery Guns 130mm upgradation to 155mm-250 (to be done in India)
- battlefield surveillance radars (Artillery) - 250
- battlefield surveillance radars hand held (Infantry) – unspecified
- fast attack naval craft Super Davora – 2 plus four to be built in India
- electronic warfare system for INS VIRAT (aircraft carrier)
- 160mm mortar ammunition – 30,000 rounds
- 125mm shells (for tanks) – 100,000 rounds
- 5.56mm ammunition for rifles—unspecified
- Unmanned Aerial Vehicles (UAVs)—8 in 1999 for surveillance purposes (Army) – 20 in 2000
- Indian Navy UAV requirements (shipborne)—50
- Russian MI 35 helicopter prototype upgradation—25 with Israeli avionic and night vision devices

Prime Minister Ariel Sharon of Israel visited India in September 2003; Vajpayee referred to Israel the same way he had earlier described the United States as 'a natural ally in the war against terrorism.' Israel sold three Phalcon early warning radar systems mounted on Russian Illyushin aircrafts to India for $1 billion. This purchase would enable India to detect aircraft and missile launches deep inside Pakistani airspace. Even though the US retained the right to exercise a veto on the deal because US technology was incorporated into Phalcon, the US gave its approval.[30]

Alarmed by these transactions, Pakistan's Foreign Minister Khursheed Mahmud Kasuri stated that 'Sharon's visit to India symbolized a threat to the security balance in the region.'[31] President Musharraf termed as 'extremely threatening to his country's interest the visit of Ariel Sharon to India.'[32] He then added that if Sharon, Vajpayee, and Bush were trying to unite in an anti-Muslim military alliance, then it was the 'saddest day in the history of the world'. Then he hastened to add a self-consoling pacifier that 'I do not think that Israel and the United States are doing that at all.'[33]

Shrunk in size and disorganized, the Pakistani-American Community has now to confront a goliath of an alliance between the Indian Congressional Caucus, the Indian-American Community's several well-organized lobbies, and the Jewish Community's very effective lobbies. In the US various ethnic and business lobbies constantly enter into alliances and joint activities to exercise influence on US legislators and policy makers, and they are protected by law in their efforts to win friends and influence people in the echelons of US government. More resourceful and organized lobbies win and benefit their clients as they mould US domestic and foreign policies. In this struggle for influence, the Pakistani Embassy's role in Washington has been less than successful ever since the advent of Pakistan in 1947. Several explanations for this poor performance can be offered.

Whenever political relations between the US and Pakistan were cordial and Pakistan was a US ally, especially during the Cold War, the Embassy felt no need to bother with the Pakistani-American community. Trained and educated as diplomats at the Fletcher School of Law and Diplomacy of Tufts University, Pakistan's diplomats cultivated the mannerism of high political functionaries of the defunct Empires. One example among many would suffice to illustrate this point. In the late 1950s, a young Third Secretary brought a cook from Pakistan and had him trained as a driver. The cook turned driver performed two roles. He cooked meals for the young man's family, and drove the stiff-necked Third Secretary to his office in the morning, and picked him up again after office hours. He was severely chastised if he did not rush to open the car door for the diplomat at the

Chancery's entrance. The diplomat boasted that he spoke the Queen's English and wrote it as well.

During this early period, the Pakistan Embassy always arranged two receptions on Pakistan Day as well as on other significant occasions. One reception was attended by the Ambassador and other Pakistani diplomats, and the invitees were always white Americans. No African-American was ever invited and non-official Pakistanis were not invited either. The explanation was: 'Those Pakistanis do not have polished manners, and they do not know how to behave.' One additional caveat was offered: 'The Pakistan Embassy's function is to cultivate and entertain Americans, not Pakistanis.' The second reception was arranged for the local Pakistani-Americans.

This grotesque attitude continued until Zulfiqar Ali Bhutto was elected President in 1971. His populist style not only changed relations between the government and the people, but forcefully changed the nineteenth century stiffness of the Pakistani ambassadors, and the subordinate diplomats. Moreover, his government liberally issued passports to young Pakistani professionals and workers, which made it possible for them to migrate to the US. With Bhutto's support, the Pakistani-American community began to grow. The years 1971-2 were exceptionally difficult for Pakistan over the Bangladesh debacle. Desperately, the Pakistan Embassy sought the help of Pakistani-Americans to influence public opinion; however, it was unable to put together even a group of a dozen individuals who could effectively lobby in support of the Pakistani position on the issue. They did not have the political experience or the contacts on Capitol Hill. Ambassadors, however, wanted the Pakistani-American community to convey to their Prime Minister that 'Pakistan's Ambassador is a world class diplomat'.

The early 1970s marked a period of isolation for Pakistan in the US. But after Bhutto was overthrown in 1977 and General Zia-ul-Haq became the Martial Law President, the Pakistan Embassy needed no public diplomacy in Washington. The Soviet Union, in a sense, became the best lobby for Pakistan, especially when it invaded Afghanistan in 1979. Zia engaged a retired US Senator from Pennsylvania to communicate with the US Congress. He did not need the Pakistani-American Community. Once he commented to this author (H. Malik): 'When the US needs Pakistan, it creates a benign image of us in America.' How right he was!

When President Clinton visited India and Pakistan in 2000 another military coup had taken place in Pakistan. At this time no amount of intensive public diplomacy could have created a favourable image of Pakistan in the US. All the sanctions were in place; additional sanctions related to the nuclear explosion of 1998 had been added. Pakistan was, as the expression goes, in the doghouse.

CLINTON IN INDIA AND PAKISTAN

President Clinton's visit to India in March 2000 had been in active preparation since his election as President 1997. He had asked a national security team to do a comprehensive review of policy toward South Asia. By mid-1997, the policy review was concluded and had recommended that Relations with India should not be viewed exclusively through the prism of the US non-proliferation policy. 'A multi-basket' approach should be adopted to deal with India across a wide range of issues, including economies and trade, energy, regional security, the environment, and climate change. Each issue should be dealt with independently 'without holding any one hostage to progress on the others.' Clinton explained this new approach to India's Prime Minister I. K. Gujral at a meeting at the UN General Assembly.

India conducted nuclear tests in 1998. Instead of visiting India, Clinton imposed Congressionally-mandated sanctions known as the Glen Amendments on India, and also on Pakistan for its own nuclear explosions. So US relations with India slid back to the single issue of proliferation and arms control. Meanwhile Vajpayee had embarked upon a new policy of relaxation of tensions with Pakistan. Shortly thereafter the conflict over the Kargil Hills erupted, which was resolved by Clinton after his meeting with Sharif in July 1999 at Blair House. Kargil led India to believe that the US had changed its traditional policy of support to Pakistan. India began to perceive the US as a potential partner.

After the collapse of the Soviet Union, India's basic orientation of its foreign and domestic policy changed during the 1990s. India de-emphasized progressively its *de facto* alliance with Russia, its policy of state socialism, and its leading role in the Non-Aligned Movement. For international security Indian leaders, supported by US neo-conservatives, began to project a new architectural design of relations for the US, namely that India is squeezed between the regions of the Middle East, a hotbed of instability, and China, a rising power in the Far East to challenge the US power and presence in that region. These threatening regions in the Middle and far East can be contained by a countervailing power of democratic stability that would include Turkey, Israel, and India. Clinton's advisors began to present India as a global player, whose influence would be felt everywhere in the twenty-first century. That is why Clinton decided to visit India in the last year of his presidency.

Clinton and his foreign policy advisors believed that they created a new architecture for sustaining a broad engagement with India. This was laid out in the jointly agreed vision statement. Specifically the US committed to 1) annual foreign ministers. meetings; 2) creating a new science and technology forum to promote cooperation between Indian and American scientists; 3) creating an Asian Center for democratic governance, a non-governmental committee to be housed in New Delhi to promote democracy throughout Asia; 4) a US-India financial and economic forum agreement that sets up annual meetings of the top leadership of economic teams on both sides.

Speaking before the Indian Parliament, where he was received most cordially and enthusiastically, Clinton emphasized that India's May 1998 nuclear tests were a mistake. Incidentally it is the same message that he delivered in Islamabad on state television, since the National Assembly did not exist. On Kashmir he spoke repeatedly before his Indian hosts, and emphasized respect for the LoC (which was music to the Indians' ears), restraint by both countries, rejection of violence, and renewal of dialogue.

After his triumphal visit to India, Clinton hopped over to Pakistan amid exceptional security precautions. Pakistanis had cleared an area one mile wide around the runway to make certain that his plane could not be hit by a shoulder-fired missile. In his televised address Clinton asked Pakistan to turn away from terror in Kashmir and nuclear weapons, and opt for a dialogue with India over Kashmir to sign the test ban treaty, and to invest in education, health, and development rather than arms.[34] In his one meeting with Musharraf, Clinton lectured him: 'I thought terrorism would eventually destroy Pakistan from within if he didn't move against it.'[35] Also he made it clear to him that the US would not attempt to mediate the bitter dispute over Kashmir. After uttering these wise counsels to Musharraf he flew to Geneva to meet with President Assad of Syria. No agreement or protocols on military or economic matters were signed as they had been in India. In slightly less than five hours Clinton's 'state' visit was over.

To strengthen his courtship of India, Clinton invited Vajpayee to make a state visit to the US before his term expired. Vajpayee came to Washington in March 2000 to a cordial reception 'fit for a king.' A year before his arrival, Congress had passed a bill, which Clinton signed in 1999, authorizing the Government of India to create a memorial garden (at 21st Street NW) in which to install Mahatma Gandhi's statue. On 16 September 2000 a larger-than-life sculpture was officially dedicated by President Bill Clinton and Prime Minister Vajpayee. Other statues of Mahatma Gandhi have been erected in other cities, including New York, San Francisco, Salt Lake City, Houston, and St. Louis. Clinton chimed in that no other country 'has been more influenced by India than the United States.'[36]

In a welcome ceremony to the White House, Clinton praised Vajpayee's commitment to forgo nuclear testing, and then added: 'It is not only India's democracy, but India's manner of achieving democracy that will forever inspire America.' He called India a 'rising economic leader, making breathtaking strides in information technology,' and hailed this as a time of 'new hope and new opportunities in Indo-American ties'. Physically exhausted, and suffering from an ailment, Vajpayee gallantly addressed a joint session of the US Congress while sitting in a chair, as his painful knee did not let him stand up. Six years before him a Prime Minister of India had addressed the US Congress and, like an academic teaching a Literature 101 course, had talked about Henry David Thoreau, Walt Whitman, and his own Mahatma Gandhi, and then finally the end of the Cold War. Pragmatic Congressman attuned to local politics, were noticed to be snoozing during the learned discourse.

This time, Vajpayee's speech urged closer economic and political ties, which would erase the 'shadow of hesitation' that still persisted between India and the US. Yet he did not accede to American pressure to curb India's nuclear weapons programme. Without mentioning China he stated that 'security issues have cast a shadow on our relationship. I believe this unnecessary.' He continued to emphasize the economic component of US-India relations, boasting of India's recent efforts to open its banking, insurance, and telecommunications sectors to outside investment. Finally he delivered the punch line: 'We have much in common and no clash of interests. Let us remove the shadow of hesitation that lies between us and our joint vision.'[37]

Vajpayee's warm reception in Washington contrasted sharply with the treatment accorded General Pervez Musharraf during his trip to New York for the UN Millennium Summit a week earlier. Once upon a time the most allied ally of the US, Pakistan had run afoul of the United States for its links to radical Islam, including Afghanistan's ruling Taliban government and Osama bin Laden's movement. Musharraf, who had overthrown an inept elected Prime Minister, was rebuffed in his efforts to see

President Clinton in New York. The State Department had let it be known that Musharraf's meeting with the US President would give the appearance that the US government endorsed the military regime.

To make matters worse, Musharraf and Vajpayee slung belligerent barbs at each other at the UN General Assembly. In a paternal style, Vajpayee reminded Musharraf that 'terrorism and dialogue do not go together.' Vajpayee called Pakistan the major 'source of terrorism' in South Asia, while Musharraf charged that Indian democracy was undermined by 'human rights abuses and the country's caste system', and ridiculed the concepts of democracy and secularism while on a visit to the US, where both are considered sacred. Musharraf also drew an unexpected and humiliating snub from Bangladesh's Prime Minister Sheikh Hasina Wajad. She condemned military dictatorships and demanded trials of Pakistanis for abuses during the 1971 war over Bangladesh. In retaliation, Musharraf cancelled planned talks with her.[38]

PRESIDENT GEORGE W. BUSH'S STRATEGIC ARCHITECTURE: FROM JANUARY 2001 TO 11 SEPTEMBER 2001

The conservative Bush administration, which came to the White House in January 2001, was determined to substantially alter the US strategic plan for four distinctly separate regions:

1) relations with the European Union
2) new security architecture and its scope
3) new approach for China: from constructive engagement to strategic competition
4) strengthening relations with India and downgrading the traditional relations with Pakistan

1. RELATIONS WITH THE EUROPEAN UNION (EU)

Soon after his inauguration as President, Bush was preoccupied with the European countries march toward union: would this drive be compatible with US interests. Since the Soviet Union had collapsed, the incentive for US policy to encourage European states to unify had considerably diminished if not entirely evaporated. After all, the 27-nation EU with a 460 million population weighs in with $12.82 trillion in economic output, roughly on par with the US. It is conceivable that one day the euro may replace the dollar as the dominant means of exchange. Since 9/11 Europeans have confabulated in their security conferences about the possibility of downgrading the trans-Atlantic partnership of NATO and replacing it with an EU military structure. President Bush's conservative advisers advised him that the EU would build itself up as a counterweight to American power. It would be easier for the US to deal with European states one by one rather than confront an equal power.

A united Europe would very likely be guided (if not dominated) by Germany and France. Following the tradition of its diplomacy during the 1815-1939 period, Britain would attempt to be a balancer between the EU and the US. These developments are almost natural. In history large coalitions like NATO always came into existence when there was a widely shared perception of threat; when the threat disappeared, so did the coalitions. Reflecting this new bent of mind Chancellor Gerhard Schröeder of Germany (without consulting his European colleagues) stated in February 2005 before President Bush's visit to Brussels: '[NATO] is no longer the primary venue where trans-Atlantic partners discuss and coordinate strategies.' He then charged that the dialogue between the US and the EU did not take into account the bloc's 'growing importance.' However, President Jacques Chirac of France has irritated President Bush and his Administration most often. Early in February 2005, when several American senators visited him in the Elysée Palace, President Chirac told them that the 'arms embargo was an insult to China'.[39] Then he openly criticized the US for 'over arming Taiwan',[40] implying that this policy was making the negotiations for unity between China and Taiwan an exercise in futility. Needless to say Bush's decision to invade Iraq was strongly opposed by France and Germany.

2. POTENTIAL CONFLICT WITH CHINA

Barely five months into its first term, the Bush administration announced a new approach toward China, which left no doubt that the US considered her a threat to its global reach. The new administration projected 'China as a partner on some issues and a competitor on others.' This concept replaced President Clinton's policy of constructive engagement with a deliberately crafted nebulous policy. When questioned by a member of the Senate Subcommittee on East Asian and Pacific Affairs on 1 May 2001, the Assistant Secretary of State refined the concept of US relations with China to almost total nothingness. He said: 'China is a kind of a friend. I would certainly agree that it is not a kind of an enemy. I would also state that it's certainly not our ally.'

The Bush administration added five issues in its relations with China where serious differences existed: 1) Taiwan; 2) Tibet; 3) Hong Kong; 4) National Missile Defence System (NMD); 5) trade issues, human rights, and religious freedom. Clearly the first three very sensitive issues related to the territorial integrity of China. The NMD system impacted on the security of the mainland and Taiwan. The last category of economic issues impacted on the well-being and economic development of China. Moreover, the Bush Administration's tone was harsh and considerably aggressive.

Within the first three months of Bush's inauguration as President, the relationship between the US and China took a nose dive. At a hastily gathered news conference on 2 April 2001 Bush made a statement concerning the mid-air collision of a US EP-3 reconnaissance plane with a Chinese fighter jet. The US plane was forced to land on Hainan Island in China. Bush insisted that the naval maritime plane was on a 'routine surveillance mission in international airspace over the South China Sea.' He demanded that all twenty-four crew members and the aircraft be returned promptly, along with the plane's state of the art spying equipment without 'further damaging or tampering.' One of the Chinese fighter jets that were shadowing the US plane was damaged. The Chinese plane had crashed with the loss of its pilot. Bush offered search-and-rescue assistance to locate the plane and the pilot.

The Chinese claimed that the American plane was on a spy mission in their airspace, listening in on the Chinese military. They mined the plane's military secrets, although the crew had been able to destroy or disable some of the equipment. The US had spent billions of dollars and decades perfecting the technology on the Aries spy plane. No other country could copy the reconnaissance capabilities of this aircraft.

Only nine days before this incident a Chinese warship had chased a US naval ship out of international waters in the Yellow Sea. The Chinese claimed that it was within their territorial waters. Regarding the spy plane China insisted that it had constantly opposed US spy flights off its coast, which had been occurring for several years. They warned that on the resumption of such flights China would lodge 'serious representations'.

China demanded an apology for the plane collision and asked the US to take responsibility for the incident. Until this happened, the Chinese stated that the twenty-four crew members of the surveillance plane would not be returned. Republican Congressmen took an increasingly tough line arguing that a link should be made between China's actions and two key bilateral issues—the question of new US weapons sales to Taiwan, and the status of China's trade relations with the US.

Finally China announced on 11 April 2001 the release of the twenty-four US crew members after it received a letter of regret from President Bush, acknowledging 'We are sorry the entering of China's airspace and the landing did not have clearance, but very pleased that the crew landed safely. We appreciate China's efforts to see to the well-being of our crew.'[41] However, after the Chinese inspection of the aircraft was completed it was in such bad shape that it had to be dismantled and returned in crates.

This standoff once again thrust Taiwan into the limelight of US politics. Bush made it clear in his discussion of arms sales that the US would continue to provide defensive weapons to Taiwan to defend itself against China. Following the policy of status quo in the Far East, the US was determined to protect the territorial integrity and interests of Japan, South Korea, Australia and Taiwan. China was made to understand that the US would preserve the existing distribution of power.

The Congressional testimonies also highlighted at this time that China's military preparations had Taiwan and the US as their focus. China had 300 missiles near the Taiwan Strait. A Pentagon report of 2001 claimed that 'China will probably have the ability to conquer Taiwan by 2005.' Bush reacted on a television programme that the US would do 'whatever it took' to help Taiwan defend itself, 'up to and including military force'.[42] More recently, Bush opposed the sale of weapons to China when he was on a visit to Europe in February 2005. This time he offered a geostrategic explanation that lifting the EU's arms embargo on China would change the 'balance of relations' between China and Taiwan. This embargo had been imposed in 1989 after China's crackdown on pro-democracy protestors in Tiananmen Square in Beijing.

In addition to lucrative sales for European weapons, the lifting of the embargo would be an important way to forge close ties with China. The EU sees China as another pole of power, with which it has to deal with in a cooperative manner. It is generally assumed that in the coming years China will be a 'big' spender for weapons. In 2005 the Pentagon estimated China's spending at $50 billion to $70 billion. By contrast the US, with the largest military budget in the world, was expected to spend $500 billion on the military and its operations in Iraq and Afghanistan.[43]

A few days after his return from Europe, Bush invited on 1 March 2005 the Chairman of the Senate Foreign Relations

Committee, Senator Richerd G. Lugar, and Senate Minority Leader Senator Joseph R. Biden Jr., to the White House and sought their help in warning Europe that if it lifted its ban on arms sales to China, the US might retaliate with severe restrictions on technology sales to European companies. Bush's insistence was based on a new American intelligence assessment that China was rapidly becoming better equipped to carry out a sophisticated invasion of Taiwan. Also China would be able to counter any effort by the US or to react to such an attack. In supporting President Bush, Senator Lugar stated that Congress could react with 'a prohibition on a great number of technical skills and materials, or products, being available to Europeans.' Biden called the lifting of the ban 'a non-starter with the Congress.' During the last five years, while Bush had been in office, new intelligence reports indicated that China had raced ahead with one of the most ambitious military build-ups in the world, including twenty-three new amphibious assault ships that could ferry tanks, armoured vehicles, and troops across the 100 miles to Taiwan, and thirteen new attack submarines. 'Their amphibious assault shipbuilding alone equals the entire US Navy shipbuilding since 2002',[44] the intelligence indicated. Almost simultaneously Taiwan's President Chen Shui-bian warned the EU against lifting the arms embargo on China, saying it could tilt the military balance and threaten regional security'.[45]

Clearly European leaders do not look upon China as a challenge or a threat. In the future she might be a counterweight to the pre-eminent power of the US. For the sales of weapons to China the European states also offered a logical argument to rebut the US position. They argued that the sanctions were to punish China because of its killing of pro-democracy demonstrators in Tiananmen Square sixteen years previously, not because China was a rising military power. Now that a new generation of leaders had taken over power in Beijing, the specific cause of the sanctions was removed.

In the name of Taiwan, the missile defence system, human rights and religious freedoms, trade surplus and democracy a titanic struggle for power is underway between China and the US. China perceives the US as an arrogant and expansionist *imperium*, which is hostile to China's strategic interests and its adversary all across the board. China is driven by strong nationalism. With a slight twist by the government this could easily turn into anti-imperialism and anti-Americanism, both wrapped up into one explosive mix.

Inspired by its own messianic zeal, the US has planned a security architecture to 'contain' China, which consists of several elements. It wants China 1) to accept the American-led security architecture in Asia; 2) not to endeavour to undermine or disrupt it; 3) to undertake military modernization in a gradual and non-threatening way; and finally 4) not to attempt to build its relations with Russia, Europe, or India into an anti-American alliance, which might alter the balance of power in a fundamental manner.

In the defence of human rights and religious freedom the US took up the cause of Tibet and Hong Kong. In Tibet the Bush Administration pressed China for an end to religious restrictions against Tibetan Buddhists, and to let them preserve their unique cultural, religious, and linguistic heritage. In Hong Kong, where more than 50,000 Americans live and do business, the US was interested in maintaining its special status.[46]

In matters of security President Bush placed the proposed national missile defence system near the top of his priorities as he settled into his first week in the White House. He authorized ground breaking for new missile silos in Alaska. In Russia this initiative was viewed as another humiliating sign that Russia, with its 6,000 nuclear weapons, was no longer the strategic equal of the US. President Bush heightened Russians anxiety by a policy declaration that the US would withdraw from the outdated 1972 Anti-ballistic Missile Treaty 'at a time convenient to America'.[47] In the development of missiles the Russians and Chinese challenge to the US was seen in January 2001 in the following terms: Russia (plus Ukraine, Kazakhstan and Belarus) 1,207; China 20 North Korea 1-5. In addition to Russia the

Chinese and the European states (with the exception of Britain) described the NMD system 'as yet another manifestation of America's threatening hegemonistic tendencies.'[48] China's main concern was that such a system could also be used to protect Taiwan, Japan, and US troops in South Korea. However, President Bush maintained that the NMD system would be targeted at 'rogue states', such as North Korea, Iran, and Iraq. It may be pointed out that the 1999 National Missile Defence Act provided for the deployment of the NMD system as soon as it was technologically available.

The policies of the US, Taiwan and China are leading to a confrontation. To discourage Taiwan from declaring formal independence China took steps to craft an anti-secession law, which defined Taiwan as 'an inalienable part of China'. The detailed text of the draft was approved by the Central Standing Committee of China's National Congress in 2004. Beijing enacted the anti-secession law on 8 March 2005. The Act may also compel Chinese leaders to use force against Taiwan if they suspect the Taiwanese leaders of any (rather vaguely defined) 'separatist activities'.[49] The Act defined the Taiwan issue as 'one that is left over from China's civil war of the late 1940s'; and posited the unification of Taiwan with China through negotiations. The anti-secession law is in reality a stern warning to Taiwan, and its patron saint, the US: for the US to discourage Taiwan from claiming independence and sovereignty, and for Taiwan not to cross over the red line of separation. Defiance of the Chinese warning would lead to armed conflict, and the US would have the unpalatable option of standing by or joining the war with unpredictable consequences.

In addition to these geostrategic considerations, US trade with China under Bush became a significant issue of concern. China joined the WTO in December 2001. Trade between the two countries increased from $4.8 billion in 1980 to $94.9 billion in 1999. However, in 2003 China had a trade surplus with the US of $124 billion.

In the steady erosion of US-China relations, as the US strategic architecture is fleshed out, US policy is bound to tilt in the direction of India and Taiwan. Relations with Pakistan will be downgraded, as happened under Clinton and Bush before the tragedy of 9/11. This tragedy's impact was so overwhelming that strategic planning had to be redirected in favour of Pakistan—but not for very long.

Also a convergence of interests has developed between the US, India, and Japan. Japan is supportive of India's case for its permanent position in the UN Security Council. To Japan freedom of navigation and security in the Indian Ocean are of great importance, since Japan depends upon the Gulf area for 90 per cent of its crude imports. The Japanese asserted in 2004 that 'once the Japanese vessels cross the Malacca Strait and navigate westbound, they find that India is literally the only country that has a reliable navy.' Consequently defence cooperation, in particular navy to navy cooperation, had been strengthened during the previous five years.[50]

3. NEW SECURITY ARCHITECTURE

Very vigorously Bush explained early in his first term the national missile defence system (NMD), and the strategic thinking that underscored it. The plan was to transform the parameters within which the Cold War strategic architecture was built. It implied that the doctrine of mutually assured destruction would be abandoned. On the positive side the new concept suggested that a new cooperative global security regime would be created, and targets would be the so-called rogue states, and terrorists. These new threats, replacing the Soviet threat, are the disruptive elements openly challenging the concept of global power distributions, which might be established through negotiations or the threat of force generally accepted when couched in diplomatic terminology. Naturally this new distribution of power would reflect each state's rank determined by its economic resources, industrial and technological development, territory, population, and commitment to human rights and democracy.

The Indian reaction to Bush's concept of the new world order was enthusiastically supportive; Europe's was cool, and the Chinese opposition was loud and clear. China saw that the implications of this strategic design were directed to inhibiting its growth as a military superpower. Why was India so enthusiastic? Several explanations can be offered: 1) India wanted the US to lift the sanctions imposed over nuclear explosions; 2) India wanted US support to gain a permanent seat on the UN Security Council; 3) India was keen to replace Pakistan as Washington's strategic partner in South Asia; 4) India desired to capitalize on growing economic ties between the two countries, driven by the increasing contributions of Indian-American' engineers and entrepreneurs in the high-technology sector.[51]

4. STRENGTHENING RELATIONS WITH INDIA AND DOWNGRADING THE TRADITIONAL RELATIONS WITH PAKISTAN

By June 2001 the Bush Administration had taken significant steps to improve the relationship with India. In the military to military dimension the US initiated one joint military exercise or engagement each month. These exercises covered a wide range of military skills and attempted to improve the capacity for combined military operations across the board – by Special Forces against terrorists, maritime interdiction, search and rescue, airlift support, logistics transport, and airborne assault. In June and July 2002, the Indian Navy ships *Sukanya* and *Sharda* conducted escort patrols for American ships through the Malacca Straits, in support of Operation Enduring Freedom Afghanistan. American warships began to refuel in Chennai and Mumbai. The largest ever US-India naval exercise was conducted in September 2002. In 2003 more than 180 high-ranking leaders from the Indian security community attended conferences sponsored by the US Department of Defence.

Delivering a luncheon address before the Confederation of Indian Industry in New Delhi in 2003, the US Ambassador Robert D. Blackwill paid the most flattering compliment to the Indian military: 'Indian and American soldiers are warriors. Their central mission is to fight and win wars. How many armies can one say that about today?' While during 2001-2 many Pakistanis were deported from the US, during the same period the US consular offices in four Indian cities issued more than half a million business and tourist visas to Indian citizens. The visa issuance rate for India was the same as it had been before 9/11.[52]

In May 2001 Deputy Secretary of State Richard Armitage, to add insult to injury to Pakistan, just barely stopped short of directly naming Pakistan as a rogue state in a press conference in India. Asked to name rogue states, he referred to Libya, Iraq, North Korea, and other countries 'in your neighborhood'. When pressed to elaborate, he said: 'We have questions about Pakistan which are wellknown, and of which you are equally aware.'[53] Armitage was in New Delhi to seek support from the Indian government for Bush's ideas on the new strategic framework for global security. He declared the start of a new relationship between India and the US. He called on Prime Minister Vajpayee and handed over a letter from Bush accepting the invitation to visit India in the near future. Also Bush assured Vajpayee that he intended to work closely with him to 'promote common interests in Asia and beyond.'[54]

'FALSE RELATIONSHIP' WITH PAKISTAN

It was left to Armitage to articulate the new relations with Pakistan. He did so with his customary bluntness. In an interview to an Indian correspondent he stated:

For years we had an unbalanced policy in South Asia...People would look at it superficially and say we had a great relationship with Pakistan, but it was in a way a false relationship because in the first instance it was built against the India-Soviet Union axis, and then latterly it was against the Soviet occupation in Afghanistan...So we didn't have a policy for Pakistan, we had a policy with Pakistan directed at something else...what we are desirous of is for our Pakistani friends to try to develop a relationship about Pakistan.'[55]

If false relationships were to be replaced by the positive content of bilateral relations, what were they supposed to be? Some of these dots were connected by the Assistant Secretary of State, Christine Rocca, who appeared before the annual session of the Pakistan-American Congress at the Sam Rayburn Building on 27 June 2001. The Assistant Secretary, highlighted some positive and some negative aspects of US relations with Pakistan. On the positive side she did not fail to underline the geostrategic significance of Pakistan as 'a central place at the crossroads of Asia.' Actually, it is this strategic importance which draws the US (and China) to close relations with Pakistan, despite its chronic political instability and lack of democracy. Rocca added two more attributes of Pakistan's geography. It bridges China to the north-east, and the Persian Gulf to the south-west.

Moreover Pakistan is a bridge to Afghanistan, which connects the Asian land mass to South Asia and the Persian Gulf. These attributes are the permanent factors contributing to Pakistan's significance in world politics. In reality all states acquire strategic significance, especially for the grand strategies of major powers, by virtue of their geography, and natural resources. As a functionary of diplomatic practice, Armitage had probably never carefully studied the craft of statesmanship, which would have made him sensitive to the intrinsic value of geography. Indeed the bitter lesson of 9/11 brought home to him the strategic importance of Pakistan.

On the negative side Rocca added several developments. The US government was 'concerned', when General Musharraf named himself President of Pakistan through a special order rather than allowing Pakistan to choose through democratic process. Regarding the fear of nuclear war between India and

Pakistan, she advised the 'necessity of pursuing strategic restraint and non-proliferation'. The US supported economic and fiscal reform, and a fair tax system. The educational system needed improvement, because the 'country's public education system is tied to its economic, social and political development'. In 2001 the US government provided $2.5 million to assist the Pakistan government to improve the system.

In regard to Kashmir, she repeated has government's well-known position that dialogue with India was the key to working out the solution. 'Restraint on all sides will facilitate prospects for any dialogue to produce positive results.' Finally she discussed the issue of sanctions. Sanctions triggered by Pakistan's military coup would remain in place 'until the President can certify to Congress that a democratically elected government has taken office' in Pakistan.

Clearly, before 9/11 the Bush administration's policy toward South Asia was to continue to tilt toward India, and downgrade its relations with Pakistan.

NOTES

1. Bill Clinton, *My Life* (New York: Alfred A. Knopf, 2004), pp. 900-3.
2. Clinton, *My Life* p. 103.
3. T.N. Srinivasan, 'Economic Reforms and Global Integration', in *The India-China Relationship: What the United States Needs to Know*, eds. Francine R. Frankel, Harry Harding (New York: Columbia University Press, 2004), p. 256.
4. Jan S. Prybyla, 'Is China a Model of Economic Success?' in *The Role of the United States, Russia and China in the New World Order*, ed. Hafeez Malik (London: Macmillan, 1997), p. 315.
5. Roger Cohen, 'What the World Wants from America', *The New York Times*, 11 January 2005.
6. Jonathan Watts, 'China Shifts from Receiving to Giving Foreign Aid as Economic Boom Continues', *The Guardian*, 15 December 2004.
7. *Dawn* (Karachi), 12 May 2001.
8. Jane Parlez, 'China Emerges as Rival to US in Asian Trade', *The New York Times*, 27 June 2004.
9. Clinton, *My Life* pp.768, 879.
10. James Dao, 'New Pentagon Report Sees Rapid Buildup by China', *The New York Times*, 13 July 2002.

11. Grigory Nekhoroshev, 'Russia, China and Central Asian Countries Continue to Forge Closer Relations', *Nezavisimaya Gazeta*, 6 July 2000.
12. Steve Coll, *Ghost Wars* (New York: The Penguin Press, 2004), pp. 410, 628.
13. Clinton, *My Life* p. 799.
14. Taliban officers' talks with this author.
15. Clinton, op. cit., p. 799.
16. Coll, op. cit., p. 444; Clinton, op. cit., pp. 797-9, 865-6.
17. Bose, op. cit., p. 103.
18. Ibid., p. 107.
19. Ibid.
20. Paul A. Pillar, *Terrorism and US Foreign Policy* (Washington DC: Brookings Institution Press, 2001), p. 182.
21. Clinton, *My Life*, p. 799.
22. L.M. Singhvi et al., *The Indian Diaspora* (New Delhi: Non-resident Indians and Persons of Indian Origin Division, Ministry of External Affairs, Government of India, 27 August 2001).
23. 'About Indian Americans', *US Indian Political Action Committee (USINPAC)*, <www.usinpac.com>; also Amit Gupta, *The Indian Diaspora's Political Efforts* (Bombay: ORF, Occasional Paper, September, 2004), pp. 3-4.
24. Sharon M. Lee, 'Asian Americans: Diverse and Growing', *Population Bulletin 53* (June 1998); also see an exceptionally informative article by Robert Hathaway, 'Unfinished Passage: India, Indian Americans and the US Congress', *The Washington Quarterly* (Spring 2001), p. 23.
25. Singhvi, op. cit., p. 169.
26. Hathaway, op. cit., p. 24.
27. Brajesh Mishra, National Security Advisor of India, at the American Jewish Committee Annual Dinner, 8 May 2003, see <http://meadev.nic. in/speeches/bm-nsa-ad.htm>.
28. Gupta, op. cit., p. 10.
29. Subhash Kapila, 'India-Israel Relations: The Imperatives for Enhanced Strategic Cooperation', *South Asia Analysis Group* Paper No. 131 (8 January 2000) <http://www.saag.org>.
30. John Lancaster, 'Israel and India Draw Closer', *The Washington Post*, 11 September 2003.
31. Ibid.
32. *The News*, 11 September 2003.
33. Ibid.
34. Clinton, *My Life* p. 902.
35. Ibid., p. 903.
36. Bill Broadway, *Washington Post*, 17 September 2000.

37. Jay Hancock, 'Vajpayee's Visit Marks Changing Relationship with US, India', *Baltimore Sun*, 14 September 2000; John Lancaster, 'Indian Leader Urges Close US Ties', *Washington Post*, 15 September 2000.
38. Pamela Constable, 'Pakistani Losing War of Images', *Washington Post*, 16 September 2000.
39. Elaine Sciolino, 'Opinion is Softening on Divided Continent', *New York Times*, 20 February 2005.
40. Ibid.
41. BBC News, 24 May 2001.
42. *The New York Times*, 23 February 2005.
43. Ibid.
44. Thom Shanker and David E. Sanger, 'US Lawmakers Warn Europe on Arms Sales to China', *The New York Times*, 2 March 2005.
45. *The News*, 2 March 2005.
46. Senate Committee on Foreign Relations, *Where are US-China Relations Headed?* 107th Congress, 1st Session, 2001, S. Hrg. 107-45, p 5.
47. *The New York Times*, 27 August 2001.
48. *The Guardian*, 22 January 2001.
49. Melfang Lee, 'Officials from Washington and Taipei Condemn Beijing's Anti-Separatist Law', *Taiwan Journal* (18 February 2005). For the full text and explanation of the Anti-secession Law, see *China View* (16 March 2005).
50. Yusukuni Enoki, 'The Japan-India New Partnership', *The Journal of the United Service Institution of India* (July-September 2004), p. 329.
51. Pamela Constable, 'Missile Defence Plan is Unifying US, India: Americans Hint at Possibly Lifting Sanctions', *Washington Post*, 20 May 2001; 'Friends and Allies: India May be Part of the New Order', *The Statesman*, 15 May 2001.
52. Ambassador Robert D. Blackwill, 'The Future of US-Indian Relations', text of his speech of 17 July 2003 in New Delhi.
53. 'Bush Proposals Aimed at Rogue States: Armitage', *The Hindu*, 12 May 2001.
54. Ibid.
55. 'Friends and Allies: India...' *The Statesman*, 15 May 2001; 'Bush Administration to Intensify Ties with India: Armitage -US Not to Get in the Middle of the Kashmir Dispute', *The Hindu*, 18 June 2001.

6

Diplomatic Calm before the Storm

By the end of 1996 Afghanistan's chessboard of struggle for power was thoroughly dominated by the Taliban. They controlled 90 per cent of the territory, and for a short period of time in May 1997, the famous Uzbek city of Mazar-i Sharif had also fallen to them. Within the city's domain the two well-known Uzbek warlords, Abdur Rashid Dostum and his rival Ata Muhammad, were engaged in a feud. Ata Muhammad joined forces with the Taliban, and drove Dostum out. He expected the Taliban to reward his efforts with a share of the power. Instead, they sidelined him and brought in hundreds of young fighters from Kabul to enforce their decrees. Unwisely Taliban leaders tried to disarm the local militias. In consequence the Uzbek leaders and their Hazara allies turned on the Taliban, killing hundreds of them.

This thoughtless and uncompromising policy of establishing a monolithic rule on multi-ethnic Afghanistan solidified the Northern Alliance, which brought together Dostum and Ata Muhammad, Gulbuddin Hekmatyar, Hazaras, and Tajik stalwarts Ahmad Shah Massoud and Burhan-ud-Din Rabbani. The Northern Alliance and their commanders in the field were supported by India, Iran, Russia, and the Central Asian states that lie between Afghanistan and Russia, especially Tajikistan, Uzbekistan, and Turkmenistan who share borders with Afghanistan. All of them feared the spread of Taliban-type militant Islam if northern Afghanistan, settled by their kinsmen, fell under the Taliban's control.

The Taliban had obtained diplomatic recognition from Saudi Arabia, the United Arab Emirates, and Pakistan. The US had serious concerns about the Taliban regime; however, it stood aloof diplomatically until 11 September 2001 as did Iran. The US treated the terrorist attacks on its embassies in Tanzania and Kenya, and the attack on the USS *Cole* in the Port of Aden as individual criminal acts. Their solution, the US diplomacy believed, could be found through the UN's punitive resolutions, and then through negotiation with the Taliban. The major events of US diplomacy related to Afghanistan can be summed up to include: 1) the UN Security Council resolutions imposing sanctions on Afghanistan; 2) US support to the international effort for reconciliation in Afghanistan, which would persuade the Taliban to share power with the Northern Alliance; 3) US support to the UN to prevent the Taliban's vandalism against the Buddha's statue in Bamiyan, in central Afghanistan and 4) Washington's demand that the Taliban extradite Osama bin Laden (who was described as most-wanted terrorist) to the US.

UN RESOLUTIONS: IMPOSING SANCTIONS ON AFGHANISTAN

The Clinton administration achieved the adoption of UN Security Council Resolution 1267 on 15 October 1999. This was the first UN resolution imposing sanctions on the Taliban regime. The resolution banned Afghan Ariana Airlines flights outside Afghanistan, and directed UN member states to freeze all Taliban assets. On 19 December 1999 the Security Council passed Resolution 1333, a follow-up to Resolution 1267. Resolution 1333 called for a worldwide ban on the provision of arms and military advice to the Taliban, a reduction of Taliban diplomatic representation abroad (directed particularly at Pakistan), and prohibited foreign travel by senior Taliban officials.

Lastly before 9/11, the UN Security Council adopted Resolution 1363 on 30 July 2001 providing for the stationing of monitors in Pakistan to ensure that no weapons or military advice was being provided to the Taliban. In may be pointed out that in the aftermath of the Taliban's overthrow from power, these provisions were narrowed to focus on Osama bin Laden's Al Qaeda network and not the Taliban. This was directed in UN Security Council Resolution 1390 of 17 January 2002. In May 2002 the US media reported that prior to the 9/11 attacks the Bush Administration was considering a plan to 'destabilize' the Taliban regime; in reality the US maintained dialogue with the Taliban.

As part of its compliance with UN Security Council Resolution 1333, in February 2001 the US State Department ordered the closing of a Taliban representative office in New York. However, the Taliban's representative, Mulla Abdul Hakim Mujahid, continued to operate informally. In fact, Bush Administration officials received Taliban envoy Rahmatullah Hashem in March 2001 to discuss bilateral issues and three State Department officials visited Afghanistan in April 2001. Officially the purpose of the Afghanistan visit was stated to be for an assessment of humanitarian needs, but in reality the objective was to achieve the extradition of Osama bin Laden.

Like the Executive Branch, the US Congress became highly critical of the Taliban regime well before the 9/11 tragedy. The Senate passed a resolution on 24 September 1996 by a unanimous vote that the settlement of the Afghan civil war should be a top US priority. A similar resolution passed the House of Representatives on 28 April 1998.

US SUPPORT FOR RECONCILIATION AMONG THE WARRING PARTIES IN AFGHANISTAN

In 1998-9 some efforts were made to bring peace to Afghanistan by implementing a power-sharing plan between the Taliban and the Northern Alliance. Surprisingly the US and Iran agreed to participate in this international endeavour for peace. Relations between Iran and Pakistan at this time were strained over Pakistan's support of the Taliban. In 1998 several envoys from the EU, China, Uzbekistan, Turkey, Iran and other leading Muslim states visited Pakistan to urge Prime Minister Nawaz

Sharif to pressure the Taliban to conduct serious negotiations to establish a government of major Afghan groups.[1]

This approach was in line with the creation of the US's 'Six Plus Two' group, a confabulating concert of Afghanistan and its neighbours, Pakistan, Iran, Uzbekistan, Turkmenistan, and Tajikistan, with the addition of the US and Russia. The US pressed the UN Secretary-General Kofi Annan to convene the 'Six Plus Two' ministerial session on the sidelines of the General Assembly session starting in September 1998. Tension between Iran and the Taliban was high. In August, when the Taliban overran Mazar-i Sharif, their troops attacked the Consul General and killed several Iranian diplomats and captured several civilians. There were speculations that this massacre was a case of revenge killing. Prior to this incident there were reports that 'thousands of Taliban had been killed' in Shibergan and that 'the local wells were packed with dead bodies.'

Nawaz Sharif was alarmed by these developments. He sent his Minister of Foreign Affairs Sartaj Aziz to Tehran with his personal letter addressed to President Khatami, who refused to see Aziz. The letter was delivered to First Vice President Hassan Habibi. Very indignantly Iran's Foreign Minister Kamal Kharazi told Aziz: 'As you can see the relations between the two countries [Iran and Pakistan] are deteriorating, and there is significant pressure on the Iranian authorities to resort to military means to avenge the crime.' Kharazi then added that: 'Iranians felt their national interest had been harmed in Afghanistan.'[2] Outraged by the killing of Iranian diplomats, the Iranian public uncharacteristically started to harass the Afghan refugees in Iran. Some were so badly beaten in Isfahan that they died from their injuries. About 1.5 million Afghan refugees, who fled from the civil war after Soviet intervention in 1979, still lived in Iran.

However, the regime's official newspaper, *Jomhuri Islami* (10 September 1998) condemned this harassment of fellow Muslims. Former President Akbar Hashemi Rafsanjani called on his countrymen 'not to take out their anger against the Taliban on the Afghan' refugees.[3] Nevertheless Iran started to deploy

200,000 troops along the border of Afghanistan, threatening military action. It sought Russia's help to deal with the Taliban. As his government's representative, Iranian Majlis' Speaker Ali-Akbar Nateq-Nuri told the visiting speaker of the Russian Duma, Gennady Seleznev, that: 'the Taliban are an irrational and rigid-minded group which kills, plunders and destroys the country with foreign backing'. Clearly this was a more than obvious reference to Pakistan's support of the Taliban. He then added: 'The sad thing is that all this takes place in the name of Islam. The Taliban have no understanding of Islam.'[4]

Actually Russia even in 1997–8 was providing military aid to the Northern Alliance, especially to Ahmad Shah Massoud. By 2001 Russia publicly urged western powers to share with Russia 'the burden of providing comprehensive support to the anti-Taliban coalition.' Even before Kabul fell to the Taliban in 1996 Russian generals went to the Afghan capital and had extensive parleys with Afghanistan's Tajik provisional President, Burhan-ud-Din Rabbani and his Minister of Defence Massoud. Before Moscow could deliver weapons to the Northern Alliance the Taliban moved swiftly to cut off the main supply routes to Afghanistan from the central Asian republics and Iran. Military supplies for Massoud's forces had to take a roundabout route through Kyrgystan and Tajikistan's Gorno-Badakhshan Autonomous Region.[5]

Actually the 'Six Plus Two' formula was stacked against the Taliban. With the exception of Pakistan no other state had diplomatic relations with the Taliban. Each one maintained an antagonistic policy towards the Taliban regime.

On 21 September 1998 the UN convened the 'Six Plus Two' meeting in New York. Valiantly Sartaj Aziz presented the Taliban's case:

1. The Taliban posed no threat to any of its Afghan neighbours and wanted cordial relations with all.
2. The Taliban offered amnesty to all those who would give up fighting.

3. The Taliban recognized the right of all minorities to participate in Afghanistan's administration. (Aziz pointed out that their interim government included four ministers at the centre and eleven governors of provinces, belonging to non-Pashtun minorities.)
4. The 'Six Plus Two' states must help the Taliban in their effort to form a multi-ethnic government.
5. Afghanistan needed assistance to fight the twin menaces of drug trafficking and terrorism.
6. Afghanistan needed strong support for socio-economic development.

The 'Six Plus Two' dialogue, however, focused on two issues which concerned the US and Iran. Its resolution urged the Taliban to 'cease providing haven to international terrorists residing on its soil', an unmistakable reference to Osama bin Laden. The resolution asked the United Nations to investigate the reports of mass killings and mass graves in Afghanistan, and urged the Taliban to fully respect international law and human rights, guarantee the rights of women, and prevent the production and trafficking of narcotics. The Six Plus Two resolution also called for the release of all non-combatants captured by all forces, especially the Iranians, and urged the Taliban to expedite the return of three Iranian diplomats in Afghanistan, cooperate fully with an investigation into the killing of Iranian diplomats, and bring the guilty individuals to justice.

Pakistan and Afghanistan's tensions with Iran subsided as the Majlis in Tehran met behind closed doors, and a new conciliatory policy toward Afghanistan was announced by Deputy Foreign Minister Mohammad Javad Zarif. He said that Iran would seek a diplomatic solution to its problems with the Taliban and placed no time limit on the endeavours.[6]

The power-sharing issue, Osama's presence in Afghanistan, and the Taliban's war continued well into 2001. However, in September 1999 China sent a five-member team of diplomats for talks with the Taliban. This visit was significant as China had not had any formal contact with the Taliban since closing its embassy in Kabul eight years earlier. But no change occurred in the Taliban's policy on the most sensitive issues of war and peace.

THE TALIBAN'S VANDALISM

Mulla Umar needed international understanding in order for his regime to be viable. Yet he did everything possible within his means to antagonize world public opinion and earn the reputation of a barbarian. He issued a decree on 26 February 2001 based on the verdict of Islamic scholars and the decision of the Supreme Court of the Islamic Emirate of Afghanistan, ordering the destruction of the Buddhas of Bamiyan and all other pre-Islamic figures, including those in Kabul's National Museum, on the grounds that they were idolatrous.

Above a valley inhabited mainly by the Shia Hazaras in Bamiyan, the twin sandstone Buddha statues, poised at 175 and 125 feet high respectively, had stood majestically for 1,500 years. Reflecting the art of Gandhara, of which relics still exist from Bamiyan to Chitral and Swat in Pakistan, these twin Buddhas displayed the exquisite blending of second-century Greek Hellenistic art with an Indian spirit. It took the Taliban twenty days to destroy the relics of the bygone civilization. The larger of the two ancient statues, which was carved into the side of a cliff—the tallest Buddha known in the world—was completely destroyed initially by artillery fire, and then finally by explosives. After enduring its bombardment, the smaller Buddha's only intact fragment, an elbow, remained adhering to the cliff.

In addition to this grotesque vandalism, the Taliban also destroyed paintings on the walls of nearby caves, once used by monks inside the Buddhist monasteries. They were built when Afghanistan was a centre of the Buddhist civilization which had spread outwards from northern India several centuries before the arrival of Islam in this region.

Surprised by the international condemnation that this vandalism provoked, Mulla Umar made another outrageous statement: 'All we are breaking are stones.' A Taliban envoy then touring the US, Sayyid Rahmatullah Hashemi, offered a macabre explanation: 'The decision to destroy the statues was taken when UNESCO and EU delegates offered money to protect the figures, but not to help the Afghan people. When your children are dying in front of you, then you don't care about a piece of art.'[7] But the ordinary people around the world did care, and condemned the Taliban's actions. In Paris, the UNESCO director, Koichiro Matsuura sadly announced that the Buddhas of Bamiyan could not be restored as they were reduced to sandy rubble. UNESCO's special envoy to Pakistan and Afghanistan stated in March 2001 that the Taliban had received 'financial proposals to buy the statues, offers to build a wall in front of the statues in order to hide them, or to take them apart.'[8] The Maha Bodhi Society, a private Sri Lankan Buddhist organization, offered to build a scaled-down replica of the Buddhas in Colombo. It sought detailed drawings from the archaeological experts in Pakistan and India to complete the project.[9]

Infuriated by the destruction of the statues, the European states retaliated in a not so subtle manner against the Taliban by inviting Ahmad Shah Massoud to address the EU Parliament in Strasbourg. Like music to European ears, Massoud sweet-talked about the rights of women and democratic elections.[10] In frustration the Taliban announced: 'To invite him personally for this meeting is a tyranny against the Afghan people. Europe is fanning the flames of war.'[11] In another gesture of 'inspired diplomacy' in May the Taliban issued another decree, compelling Hindu citizens of Afghanistan to wear distinct labels to identify themselves from the Muslim majority.

Despite the Taliban's unpopularity in the US the Bush administration attempted a policy of engagement. There was a flicker of hope that it might succeed in modifying their behaviour. In March 2001 the US shipped 30,000 tons of wheat to the Afghans 'to show sympathy and admiration'. Incidentally, this was the first installment of the 75,200 tons of wheat for Afghanistan promised.[12] In May Secretary of State Colin Powell announced that in 2001 the US intended to increase its aid to Afghanistan by $43 million.[13] Actually this policy of limited engagement with the Taliban continued until August 2001. In September the dynamics radically changed.

DEMANDS FOR OSAMA'S EXTRADITION OR EXPULSION

The Clinton and Bush administrations, officials met with the Taliban envoys more than twenty times. Their discussions over Osama's extradition remained inconclusive. Washington offered a reward of $5 million for information leading to Osama's arrest and conviction for acts of terrorism. In February 1999 the US Assistant Secretary of State, Karl Inderfurth, handed over in Pakistan to the Taliban envoy Mulla Abdul Jalil his government's letter in Pakistan, which proposed that the Taliban hand over Osama bin Laden to the US or Saudi Arabia, or they expel him. Where he should be expelled to was not explained. The Taliban's spokesman in Kabul, Abdul Haye, called the US demand for Osama's expulsion or extradition irrational. 'Any move on these lines against Osama', he added, 'will cause a lot of resentment and a chaotic situation among the Afghans and the whole Muslim world.' However he offered a guarantee to the US that 'we will control his political and military activities.'[14] The Taliban's unacknowledged representative Mulla Abdul Hakim Mujahid was called into the State Department for a meeting with Inderfurth, where he stated that Osama had left the Taliban-controlled territory. Very quickly his statement was contradicted by a key Afghan opposition group who asserted that Osama was still in Afghanistan.[15] The Taliban leader Mulla Umar then announced that 'Osama has disappeared, and the government of Afghanistan did not know his whereabouts.' However, *The New York Times* (4 March 1999) stated in a front page report that the Taliban had taken harsh action against Osama after a fight had broken out between Taliban officials and Osama's bodyguards some weeks previously. After this fight Osama was expelled from Kandahar, and was transported to isolation in the Afghan countryside, and stripped of his satellite telephones.

Now the Taliban took an 'aggressive' attitude and asked the US to submit evidence of Osama's crimes of terror, because in cases where extradition is requested, evidence is provided. Meanwhile the Federal District Court in New York had handed down an indictment of Osama's culpability. The US government asserted that Osama must be brought to justice, and the Taliban must stop harbouring well-known terrorists like him.

In pursuit of this policy the CIA sent, in the autumn of 1997, its fifth mission to the Panjsher Valley to enlist Ahmad Shah Massoud's support to capture Osama. His whereabouts had become a daily mystery for the US government: he is in Afghanistan; no, he is not. The CIA believed that Osama's movements were deliberately mystified to mislead the US quest. As an earnest the CIA paid 'a few hundred thousand dollars' to Massoud. Despite the fact of Osama being the common enemy of the US and Massoud, the US was not prepared to fight Massoud's larger war for power against the Taliban. It had 'declared a policy of strict neutrality in that war.' The National Security Council under Clinton had approved written guidance to authorize intelligence cooperation with Massoud, while making it clear that the CIA could provide no assistance that would 'fundamentally alter the Afghan battlefield'.

Massoud, on the contrary, wanted a strategic partnership. He tried to convince the CIA operatives that it would serve no useful purpose to eliminate only Osama and a handful of his senior associates. In the larger scheme of the terror structure Al Qaeda needed to be studied, and its relations with the Taliban needed to be examined. The roles of the United Arab Emirates, Saudi Arabia, and Pakistan must be examined. Al Qaeda could operate without Osama as it operated as an organization in more than sixty countries. The CIA agreed with Massoud's assessment, but told him that US policy at this point in time was focused on capturing Osama and his chief associates for criminal trial in New York.

On 12 October 1999 General Musharraf toppled the elected but inept Prime Minister of Pakistan, Nawaz Sharif. Three days later the American Ambassador William Milam handed him a letter from President Clinton chastising the general for taking power by illegal means, and urged him to establish a road map for restoring democracy. Simultaneously, however, Clinton wanted Musharraf's help in apprehending Osama. Musharraf advised Clinton to 'engage with the Taliban, seek their moderation, and to win the hearts and minds of the Afghans.'[16] The US by this time was convinced that very solid links had developed between Pakistani intelligence (ISI), Osama bin Laden, the Taliban and other *jihadi* organizations operating from Afghanistan and Pakistan. This grand alliance included Pakistan's regional objective, bleeding Indian forces in Kashmir and helping the Taliban defeat the Northern Alliance, where Massoud was the charismatic and shining star. The Clinton administration feared that Pakistan's incursions in Kashmir might provoke a nuclear war with India. Pakistan's army and the political leadership at that time had calculated that the benefits they received in their support of the Taliban and Afghanistan-based *jihadi* organizations, trained at the Osama bases, far outstripped the costs, including the antagonistic US policy under Clinton, which was tilting in the direction of India anyhow.

Now the US attempted to recruit the Director General of Pakistan's ISI, General Mahmud, into partnership. The way they handled him, after he arrived in Washington in April 2000, alienated General Mahmud. Thomas Pickering, President Clinton's 'diplomatic intimidator', and an under secretary of state, gave the general a dressing down talk: 'The Taliban were harboring terrorists who killed Americans. People who do that are our enemies, and people who support those people will be treated as our enemies.' He added that Washington might extend support to Massoud, if the Taliban did not do something about Osama.

Subsequently the humiliated Pakistani general visited Mulla Umar at Kandahar, and passed the American pressure to the Taliban's amir. He added that the US might coordinate its actions against the Taliban with Russia. Nothing short of Osama's extradition would satisfy the US. When Musharraf met Mulla Umar's envoy in May 1999 he did not threaten economic punishment, nor did he demand that Osama be extradited. He proposed that Mulla Umar might revive the idea of establishing an Islamic Court, which would try Osama in Afghanistan. The Clinton Administration had rejected this proposal.[17] By December 1999 Musharraf attempted to explore a common ground in Iran or Afghanistan, but he 'signalled no change' in Pakistan's backing for the Taliban. Also he brushed aside allegations that Pakistan continued to arm the Taliban as Iran was supporting the Northern Alliance. 'We don't have the resources…financial or military, especially now, to pass on to Afghanistan.' He asserted that the Taliban controlled 90 per cent of the territory – '27 districts out of 31,' then added: 'within this reality one has to devolve a broad-based [coalition] government'.[18] Musharraf then stated publicly that he had completed a review of Pakistan's policy toward Afghanistan, and had decided to carry on Pakistan's existing policy. When President Clinton's term ended, no change had occurred in the Taliban policy of support to Osama or in Pakistan's steadfast friendship for the Taliban.

George W. Bush succeeded Clinton in 2001; uninitiated in foreign policy Bush did not even know the name of Pakistan's military ruler, General Pervez Musharraf. Bush's closest foreign policy advisers were not experts of South Asian politics. He relied heavily on his National Security Advisor Condoleeza Rice – a Soviet specialist, Vice President Richard Cheney, and the powerful Secretary of Defence Donald H. Rumsfeld who had no special knowledge of India-Pakistan affairs. Secretary of State Colin Powell and his Deputy Richard Armitage had experience in South Asia. However, during the 2000 election campaign Bush had raised huge financial contributions from the Indian-American community. Everyone around Bush advised him to continue Clinton's tilt toward India.

Musharraf wrote a letter to Bush, outlining common ground between Pakistan and the US, and asking for closer ties. The US response held out the prospect of improved relations – after the Osama problem was resolved. The impasse between the two governments continued, while the Americans believed that Pakistani intelligence could do much more to help track Osama's location and destroy his network of terrorist camps. The US government invited the head of the ISI, Lieutenant General Mahmud Ahmed, to Washington in September 2001.

THE TALIBANIZATION OF PAKISTANI SOCIETY

In 1999 Nawaz Sharif visited the federally-administered tribal area on the borders of Afghanistan. He lavishly complimented the Taliban for implementing the Sharia laws in their country, and expressed the hope to do so in Pakistan. Nationally, this was the official inauguration of the Taliban's brand of Islam in Pakistan. Historically this trend of Islamization was started by a secular Muslim nationalist leader, Liaquat Ali Khan, the first prime minister of Pakistan. Khan presented the Objectives Resolution to Pakistan's National Assembly in 1949. The draft was actually prepared with substantial contributions from Maulana Shabbir Ahmad Usmani and Mufti Muhammad Shafi, two former faculty members of Deoband's Darul Ulum.[19] The resolution set forth that the state shall enable the Muslims to order their lives according to the teachings and requirements of Islam, as enunciated in the Qur'an and the *Sunna*. One of Khan's zealous military successors, General Zia-ul-Haq, acting in his capacity as the supreme ruler of Pakistan in 1985, inserted the Objectives Resolution as the Preamble of the 1973 Constitution. Since then Pakistan's polity continued to be on the slippery slope of Talibanization.

The advent of Pakistan caused a serious rift in the denominational ranks of the uluma (religious scholars). Their organized parties did not support the creation of Pakistan. Notably among them were the Jamiat-ul Ulama-i Hind, Jamaat-i Islami of Maulana Maududi, and some well-known scholars of Darul Ulum Deoband seminary. They feared that a smaller Muslim state would 'jail' Islam in a limited territory, and the vast space of India would be closed to their missionary endeavours. Moreover they were concerned about the security of the Muslim minority in India after the partition of India. After the creation of Pakistan some of them settled in the new state. Formerly affiliated with the Deoband Madrassa, Maulana Shabir Ahmad Usmani, Mufti Muhammad Shafi, and their associates created the Jamiatul Ulama-i Islam (JUI) and those attached to the Barelvi school of thought established their own party – Jamiatul Ulama-i Pakistan (JUP). Both the JUI and the JUP have been partners off and on in the governments of Pakistan. They claim success in shaping the Islam-oriented policies of the government. As the Pakistani government neglected education, these religious parties and other more sectarian violent parties established Sunni and Shia madrasas, which attracted the children of the impoverished masses.

By 2000 Pakistan had almost 8,000 madrasas all over the country, but the majority of them were located in Balochistan, NWFP and the Punjab. During the war in Afghanistan against the Soviet Union students from Afghanistan, Kashmir, Bosnia, Tajikistan, Uzbekistan, Algeria, Chechnya, the Philippines, and the Uighurs from the Xinjiang province of China were attracted to these madrasas.[20] It is this pan-Islamic group of young students who enthusiastically fought for the Taliban; some of them went on to volunteer to join the ranks of Al Qaeda. These warriors in the cause of Islam also fought in Kashmir against the Indian forces. Between 1994 and 1999, an estimated 80,000 to 100,000 Pakistanis were trained in Afghanistan and fought there. An alliance developed between the Taliban and the JUI, which began to impact on the Muslim populations of Central Asia.

By 1989 the Taliban-oriented Islamic parties has begun to assert themselves in the Pakistani provinces of Balochistan and the NWFP. As vigilantes they banned television viewing, imposed sharia punishments (stoning and amputation of hands), assassinated Pakistani Shiites, and forced women to wear burqas which concealed them from head to toe. Subsequently this Talibanization started to creep from the Pashtun areas to the flatlands of the Punjab and Sindh. In July 1999, when the Taliban's offensive against the Northern Alliance was launched, 6,000 to 8,000 Pakistani militants joined the vanguard. Most of these volunteers were non-Pashtun Pakistanis. Also, the Taliban continued to support the two extremist JUI splinter groups, the Sipah-Sahaba Pakistan (SSP) and the Lashkar-i Jhangvi (LIJ). Both groups have killed hundreds of Pakistani Shiites. It was alleged by the Nawaz Sharif government that two unsuccessful attempts were made to assassinate the prime minister.[21]

Sharif reacted by cracking down on these two extremist groups in the Punjab. In order to escape, their leaders took refuge in Afghanistan. Despite the Pakistani government's request to extradite them, the Taliban refused to oblige. Their standard answer was: 'we don't know where they are'. Yet the Taliban continued to have Pakistani ISI and Ministry of Defence support. Why? There are three compelling reasons for Pakistan's support of the Taliban:

1. The Pakistan Army believed that a dependent and Taliban-dominated Afghanistan would be its 'strategic depth', especially during Pakistan's ongoing conflict with India over Kashmir

2. A friendly Afghanistan would not raise the issue of Pashtunistan, claiming Pakistan's vast territories of the NWFP and the tribal belt.

3. An alliance of the Taliban with the Deobandi-oriented groups in Pakistan and bin Laden's terrorist network gave major support to Kashmiri insurgents resisting India's control over its part of Kashmir. If Pakistan were to withdraw its support of the Taliban, it would fundamentally weaken its policy toward the solution of the Kashmir dispute with India. However, the critics of Pakistan's

Kashmir policy asserted that the Islamization of the Kashmir struggle was undermining the indigenous struggle for self-determination, and Pakistan's endeavours to win international mediation of the dispute. Moreover the Kashmiris' aspirations for independence were losing world sympathy 'as more and more Pakistani and Arab volunteers join the fight and turn it into a Taliban *jihad*.'

When looking at the Afghan scene from the US perspective a few complex situations become obvious. The withdrawal of the Soviet Union from Afghanistan in 1989 and the collapse of the USSR in 1991 marked the start of US unipolar predominance, yet the US had never articulated a strategic framework for the vast areas of South and Central Asia, where Afghanistan plays the pivotal role. The anti-Soviet struggle had transformed itself into an ethnic conflict. Religiously zealous Pashtuns were now struggling to re-establish their preponderance in the Afghan polity under the Taliban movement. Into this ethnic civil war, neighbours stepped in to protect what they perceived as their national interest. Pakistan and Saudi Arabia supported the Taliban with weapons and 'acceptable' advisement. Uzbekistan and Russia had their protégés in Abdur Rashid Dostum (Uzbek) and Ahmad Shah Massoud (Tajik). Naively, the UN envoy to Afghanistan Lakhdar Brahimi believed if only the neighbours would stop sending weapons to the combatants, they would be compelled by the circumstances to negotiate a settlement peacefully. He believed that it could be done if the US pressured Pakistan and Saudi Arabia to back off from the situation.

Pakistan was determined to support the Taliban until it ultimately achieved success. The Taliban and the Pakistani ISI believed that it would take twelve months to finish off the Massoud resistance. They felt the power-sharing plans fancifully articulated by Brahimi were designed only to deny the Taliban the fruits of their victory. They looked upon Massoud as the last minor hurdle to power. Osama bin Laden and the Taliban hatched a plan to get rid of him. On 9 September 2001, they sent two

members of their organizations as 'Arab journalists' to interview
Massoud in order to 'project a positive image of him to the Arab
world'. One of the 'journalists' read out several questions to
Massoud while the other set up a camera—at chest level.
Massoud listened to the questions, most of them concerned
Osama bin Laden. Steve Coll of the *Washington Post* described
the scene that then ensued as follows: 'The explosion ripped the
cameraman's body apart. It smashed the room's windows, seared
the walls in flame, and tore Massoud's chest with shrapnel. He
collapsed unconscious'.[22] Massoud was gone for ever. The
Taliban celebrated the event in the hope that their total control
over Afghanistan would be established in the near future.

Two days later Al Qaeda operatives attacked the US. This
titanic strike changed the world political dynamic radically. The
US was now poised to reshuffle the strategic deck.

NOTES

1. *The Nation*, 16 April 1998.
2. *Dawn*, 18 September 1998.
3. *Dawn*, 18 September 1998.
4. *Dawn*, 22 September 1998.
5. Yury Golotyuk, 'Made in the USSR', *Vremya Novostei*, 28 September 2001, p. 1.
6. *Dawn*, 23 September 1998.
7. *The New York Times*, 14 March 2001.
8. The *New York Times,* 14 March 2001.
9. *Dawn*, 28 March 2001.
10. Michael Griffin, *Reaping the Whirlwind: Afghanistan, Al Qaeda and the Holy War* (London: Pluto Press, 2003), p. 239.
11. Griffin, *Reaping the Whirlwind,* p. 239, *Dawn*, 13 April 2001.
12. *Dawn*, 23 March 2001.
13. Griffin, *Reaping the Whirlwind*, p. 239.
14. *Dawn*, 11 February 1999.
15. *Dawn*, 19 February 1999.
16. Ibid., p. 481.
17. Coll, op. cit., p. 510.
18. *Dawn*, 8 December 1999.
19. See, Maulana Muhammad Zubair Ashraf Usmani, 'Ta`mir-i Pakistan Awr Hifaz-i Islam Key A`iymi Jaddo Jahed Mein Darul Ulam Ka Kirdar', *Jang: Darul ulam Karachi Kay 50 Sal* (Karachi, 15 February 2000), p. 13.

20. A.H. Nayyar, 'Madrasah Education Frozen in Time', in *Education and the State: Fifty Years of Pakistan*, ed. Pervez Hoodbhoy (Karachi: Oxford University Press, 1998), p. 241
21. Ahmad Rashid, 'Talibanization?' *The Nation*, 17 November 1999.
22. Coll, op. cit., p. 575.

7

Policy Change in Pakistan
Regime Change in Afghanistan

On the morning of 11 September 2001 in Manhattan, the crystal clear sky and the crispness in the air promised to produce a picture-perfect early autumn day—a promise that disappeared unfulfilled at 8.45 a.m. when a hijacked Boeing 767, American Airlines Flight 11, crashed into the north tower of the World Trade Center. The broadcast over American television screens grew even more ominous at 9.03 a.m. when yet another Boeing 767, United Airlines flight 175, tore through the south tower— both towers were now burning. Precisely forty minutes later a third hijacked plane, American Airlines Flight 77, in what we now know was a scientifically planned attack, crashed into the Pentagon—the very citadel of American military power—killing sixty-four people aboard the plane and 125 people inside the building. Among the dead was Lieutenant General Timothy Maude, a 34-year Army veteran. According to one engineering report, the jet pierced through 310 feet of concrete in less than a second.

On that fateful day, just when it seemed that the horror could escalate no further, the passengers aboard a fourth and final hijacked plane learned of the World Trade Center and Pentagon plane crashes via their cell phones. One passenger, Todd Beamer, managed to contact the FBI on the phone. When it became clear that Flight 93 was part of this master terrorist plan and not en route to a safe landing anywhere, Beamer was heard by an FBI operator to say the words permanently ingrained in the memories of Americans, 'Let's roll'. He along with other passengers stormed the cockpit and fought the hijackers, resulting in the plane crashing in Shanksville, Pennsylvania, hundreds of miles short of Al Qaeda's intended target—the White House—killing forty-four passengers, the crew, and the hijackers. This was in addition to the nearly 2,800 people who lost their lives in the World Trade Center.

The attacks on American soil were the worst since Pearl Harbour. They were the first on the continental US since the War of 1812, when the British burned down the White House. Four days after the attack on the World Trade Center, President Bush visited the smouldering ruins. Shocked at the sight of the devastation, he climbed to the top of the rubble, put his arms around a firefighter, and shouted through a bullhorn: 'America today is on bended knee in prayer for the people whose lives were lost here, for the workers who work here, for the families that mourn.' The crowd shouted back: 'We can't hear you.' Bush roared back: 'I can hear you. The rest of the world hears you. And the people who knocked these buildings down will hear all of us soon.' The crowd shouted its approval, and in unison began to chant: 'USA! USA! USA!' A few days later on 20 September 2001 Bush addressed a joint session of Congress. To applause he said: 'Tonight we are a country awakened to danger and called to defend freedom. Our grief has turned to anger, and anger to resolution. Whether we bring our enemies to justice or justice to our enemies, justice will be done.'

In these two appearances Bush impressively performed the role of a leader; he calmed the frayed nerves of a grief-stricken nation. His ratings in public opinion polls soared. His presidency changed fundamentally, finding its purpose and sense of strategic direction. Arguably, it can be said that these performances 'won' him the second-term election in advance. There is, however, a scholarly divergent view that maintains that Bush's strategic direction or 'world view that drove it existed long before jet planes plowed into the Twin Towers and the Pentagon.' 11 September only provided 'the rationale and opportunity' to implement the strategic vision. This strategic architecture was based upon three beliefs: 1) To protect US security in this dangerous world America should 'shed the constraints imposed by friends, allies and international institutions. 2) The US should use its power to change the status quo in the world. 3) The US should not be reluctant to use its military superiority to 'produce change in rogue states'.[1]

When Bush addressed the Joint Session of Congress on 20 September 2001, he pledged a multi-front campaign against terrorism, and made the following demands of the Taliban:

1) Deliver all Al Qaeda leaders and members harboured in Afghanistan to the appropriate US authorities.
2) Immediately and permanently close every terrorist training camp in Afghanistan.
3) Provide the United States with full access to training camps, so that their elimination is verified.
4) Release all foreign nationals, including US citizens.
5) Protect foreign journalists, diplomats, and aid workers.[2]

In addition to these demands, Bush held Al Qaeda responsible for the bombing of the American embassies in Tanzania and Kenya and the USS *Cole* in Yemen. Also, he pointed out that Al Qaeda maintained terrorist organizations in sixty countries. He vowed to carry the war against every terrorist group of global reach until all are 'found, stopped and defeated'. He suggested that the Al Qaeda terrorists 'hijacked Islam itself' and blasphemed the name of Allah. Then he added that only this radical network of terrorists was the enemy of the United States—not the Muslim people. Finally, he delivered a barely veiled threat to Pakistan: 'Every nation, in every region, now has a decision to make. Either you are with us, or you are with the terrorists.'[3]

On 14 September 2001 the US Congress in a joint resolution authorized the President to use force against two targets: nations, organizations or persons responsible for the attacks of 11 September and states, organizations or persons 'who harbored' the terrorists responsible for the attacks. When on 7 October 2001 the US Ambassador to the UN, John D. Negroponte, announced in a letter to the UN Security Council that the US together with other states had launched military strikes against Afghanistan, he added that 'we may find that our self-defence requires further actions with respect to other organizations and other states.' Many Arab and Muslim leaders around the world believed the term 'self-defence' was being used to justify the US taking military action in other Muslim states, including Iraq, Iran and Syria. A few days after the 11 September attacks, Indian Prime Minister Atal Bihari Vajpayee wrote a letter to President Bush stating that India would extend 'whatever support the United States wanted, including military bases, in its global war against terrorism.'[4] India soon went public with its offer of full operational military support.

The new relationship that evolved between the US and Pakistan must be studied against this political landscape. Bush looked upon the military regime of General Pervez Musharraf with disdain. The US believed Pakistan to be dead set in its policy of support of the Taliban and Al Qaeda. In 1999 the CIA had started a covert operation to train Pakistani commandos from the ISI to enter Afghanistan and capture Osama bin Laden. When Musharraf came to power, he terminated the operation.[5]

Fortunately, we have a fairly detailed account of the blunt diplomatic dialogue between the US government and the Pakistani emissaries. A reliably accurate picture can be drawn as to how the US exercised power to compel Pakistan to radically alter its policy toward Afghanistan and Al Qaeda. In a meeting with CIA Director George Tenet and Associate Deputy Director for Operations James Pavitt, Pakistan's ISI Director General Mahmud Ahmad described Mullah Muhammad Umar as 'religious, a man of humanitarian instincts, not a man of violence, but one who had suffered greatly under the Afghan warlords.' Abruptly Pavitt said: 'Stop. Spare me. Does Mulla Umar want the United States to unleash its force against the Taliban? Do you want that to happen? Why would Mulla Umar want that to happen? Will you go ask him?' Sufficiently cowed, poor Mahmud kept his mouth shut.

When Mahmud visited the State Department a barrel-chested weightlifter and well-known diplomat, Deputy Secretary of State Richard Armitage, confronted him and stated that what the US wanted from Pakistan would 'force deep introspection'. He then added: 'Pakistan faces a stark choice; either it is with us or it is not. This is a black and white choice with no gray.' Deeply intimidated, the ISI chief began to play humble and stated that Pakistan 'had faced tough choices in the past, but Pakistan was not a big or mighty power'. In an effort to lessen Mahmud's obvious anxiety Armitage cut in: 'Pakistan is an important country.' Mahmud started to talk about the past. Armitage again cut in: 'The future begins today. Pass the word to General Musharraf—with us or against us.' Then Armitage invited Mahmud to visit Secretary of State Colin Powell.

General Mahmud called his boss, General Musharraf and conveyed to him Washington's mood. In an interview with the *60 Minutes* news programme of CBS, which was nationally televised on 25 September 2006, President Musharraf stated that Armitage threatened Pakistan when he said to General Mahmud: 'Be prepared to be bombed. Be prepared to be bombed back to the Stone Age.'[6] (Incidentally, Armitage denied that he ever made this threatening statement.) Be that as it may, when Mahmud went to the State Department he was presented with a list of seven demands:

1. Stop Al Qaeda at your border, intercept arms shipments through Pakistan and end all logistical support to bin Laden.
2. Blanket overflight and landing rights.
3. Access to Pakistan, naval bases, air bases, and borders.
4. Immediate intelligence and immigration information.
5. Condemn the 11 September attacks and crush all domestic support for terrorism against the US, its friends or allies.
6. Cut off all shipments of fuel to the Taliban and stop Pakistani volunteers from going into Afghanistan to join them.

7. Should the evidence strongly implicate Osama bin Laden and the Al Qaeda network in Afghanistan, and should Afghanistan and the Taliban continue to harbour him and the network, Pakistan would break diplomatic relations with the Taliban government and support for the Taliban and assist the US in the aforementioned ways to destroy Osama bin Laden and his Al Qaeda network.[7]

In handing General Mahmud a single sheet of paper containing these seven conditions, Armitage told him: 'These conditions are not negotiable.'[8] Pakistan must accept all seven. General Mahmud briefed his superior, General Pervez Musharraf, and conveyed to him the urgency of his decision. In Islamabad, Musharraf immediately called his army corps commanders and chiefs of the air force and navy. 'You are with us or against us' was a very powerful ultimatum; however, its acceptance clearly meant that Pakistan would have to abandon its well-entrenched policy of support for the Taliban, and Osama's Al Qaeda network that effectively helped sustain the insurgency in Kashmir. In addition to the repudiation of its well-established policy, Pakistan would be called upon to stand by the US to destroy its former allies and brothers in arms.

However, if Pakistan were to decide to stay its course, the corps commanders realized that the US would turn to India and some Central Asian republics for aid in the accomplishment of its objectives in Afghanistan. In addition, it was clear that a lack of full cooperation on Pakistan's part under the US's current vindictive mood would lead to its punishment in Kashmir, and the destruction of its nuclear assets, possibly by the Indian military. These were indeed weighty considerations and the junta had no room to bargain.

A day after giving General Mahmud Ahmad a dressing down, Secretary of State Colin Powell (a retired Chairman of the Joint Chiefs of Staff) called Musharraf. Known for his delicacy in diplomatic discourse, Powell said: 'We need someone on our flank; fighting with us...the American people would not understand if Pakistan was not in this fight with the United States.' Meekly Musharraf replied that 'Pakistan would support the United States with each of the seven actions.' Powell had expected assurances of cooperation but not a total unconditional acceptance of the ultimatum. He was pleasantly surprised, as were President Bush and the members of the National Security Council when Powell read out to them loudly and clearly the seven demands that had been presented to and accepted by General Musharraf. Bush then exclaimed: 'It looks like you got it all...it was the State Department at its best, no stripe-pants formality.'[9] At that same National Security Council meeting, Bush issued an order to Secretary of Defence Donald Rumsfeld: 'Tell the Afghans to round up Al Qaeda...we're going to hurt them bad, so that everyone in the world sees, don't deal with bin Laden. I don't want to put a million dollar missile on a five dollar tent.'

At noon on 14 September 2001 President Bush attended a memorial service at the National Cathedral along with many prominent Americans, including former presidents, George H.W. Bush, Bill Clinton, and Jimmy Carter. Bush delivered a war speech in the house of worship. 'This conflict was begun on the timing and terms of others. It will end in a way, and at an hour of our choosing.' After the conclusion of his speech, the congregation stood and sang the 'The Battle Hymn of the Republic.' Composed by Julia Ward Howe, and published in 1862 in *The Atlantic Monthly*, the poem has become a well-loved American patriotic anthem. It is the best-known Civil War song of the Union Army, which rouses crusading fervour:

Mine eyes have seen the glory of the coming of the Lord:
He is trampling out the vintage where the grapes of wrath are stored;
He hath loosed the lightening of His terrible swift sword:
    His truth is marching on.
I have seen him in the watch-fires of a hundred circling camps,
They have builded Him an altar in the evening dews and damps;
I can read His righteous sentence by the dim and flaring lamps:
    His day is marching on.
I have read a fiery gospel writ in burnished rows of steel:

'As ye deal with my contemners, so with you my grace shall deal;
Let the hero, born of woman, crush the serpent with his heel,
    Since God is marching on.'
He has sounded forth the trumpet that shall never call retreat;
He is sifting out the hearts of men before His judgment seat:
Oh, be swift, my soul to answer Him! Be jubilant, my feet!
    Our God is marching on.
In the beauties of the lilies Christ was born across the sea,
With a glory in his bosom that transfigures you and me:
As he died to make men holy, let us die to make men free,
    While God is marching on.

What Bush thought of the enemy is well reflected in a comment that he made to Congressional leaders. 'The enemy is not only a particular group,' he reasoned, but also 'a frame of mind' that fosters hate. They hate Christianity. They hate Judaism. They hate everything that is not them.' He added that 'other nations would have to choose.'[10] A wise Democrat, Senate Majority Leader Thomas A. Daschle advised the President to be careful in his rhetoric. A saner view prevailed, which cautioned that the key themes of the war should be: 1) this is not a war against Islam; 2) this is not a war against the Afghan people; 3) the war is Afghanis versus Arabs—not some westerners versus Afghanis. The Arabs who had come to Afghanistan to train in Osama's camps were the foreigners and the real invaders. The American war efforts were directed against them; and 4) this war was for the freedom of Afghanistan. These ideas became the principal themes of US's rhetoric about the war against the Taliban.

PREPARATION FOR WAR

US and British forces attacked Taliban military targets throughout Afghanistan with bomber and cruise missiles on 7 October 2001. During the intervening twenty-five day period between the 11 September attacks and the retaliation against the Taliban, the US undertook a hectic agenda of diplomatic activities to secure military facilities or bases in neighbouring countries. On 1

October the US announced that twenty-seven countries had granted overflight and landing rights to US forces, and 29,000 military personnel had been deployed overseas. Nineteen countries agreed to freeze suspected Taliban and Al Qaeda assets—$6 million was frozen in bank accounts. The Gulf Cooperation Council (GCC) states froze all assets of persons and groups believed to be in collusion with Osama bin Laden. More than 150 people in twenty-five countries were arrested or detained. US aircraft carrier, USS *Kitty Hawk* left Japan for the Persian Gulf to serve as a mobile base for the ground troops.

Uzbekistan offered to allow US forces to conduct humanitarian and combat search and rescue missions from its military bases. As a consequence, a reinforced battalion from the 10th Mountain Division arrived in Uzbekistan the next day.[11] Uzbekistan and Turkmenistan agreed to open their borders to UN relief supplies bound for Afghanistan. Later, Tajikistan joined Uzbekistan in offering its airbases for operations in Afghanistan. Azerbaijan and Armenia were the next to come on board and offer US the use of their territories for operations. The US held a particular interest in the bases of Azerbaijan as they could be used for resupply operations and serve as a backup to the Uzbek and Pakistani bases.

In solidarity, NATO granted unlimited access to member states' airspace, ports, airbases, and refuelling facilities. In addition, NATO offered to replace US peacekeeping forces in the Balkans if necessary. The encirclement of Afghanistan by the US military was almost complete. President Bush and his Chinese counterpart Jiang Zemin met in Shanghai and agreed to work together to combat terrorism, especially in Afghanistan. In a gesture of cooperation with the US even Iran agreed to allow refugee camps to be set up in a 'no-man's land' on its borders with Afghanistan.

In the US government there was a consensus that Pakistan was the linchpin for military action against Afghanistan and the destruction of the Al Qaeda network. As soon as President Musharraf unconditionally accepted the seven demands set forth in the US's ultimatum the relationship between Pakistan and the US began to improve exponentially. 'Democracy' as an irritant between the two states virtually disappeared. On 27 October Bush signed a bill into law that provided him with the authority to waive the US sanctions imposed on Pakistan after General Musharraf seized power in 1999. In return, Musharraf quietly offered to allow US forces the usage of airbases in western Pakistan. In an act of reciprocity, the State Department announced on 29 October that President Bush would meet with General Musharraf at the UN General Assembly on 10 November and offer more than $1 billion in economic aid.

The US placed a hefty burden upon Musharraf's shoulders. It wanted bin Laden 'dead or alive', and expected Musharraf to use his influence with the Taliban in order to achieve that objective. Accompanied by military officers, ISI Chief General Mahmud Ahmad traveled to Kandahar on 17 September to persuade Mulla Umar to give up Osama bin Laden. Mulla Umar called a large *shura* (council) of 600 ulema to debate the US demands and issue a fatwa. Umar made his case: 'Our Islamic state is the true Islamic system in the world. For this reason the enemies of our country look at us as a thorn in their eye, and seek different excuses to finish it off. Osama is one of these.'[12]

Mulla Umar was never known for his diplomacy or ability to compromise. However, the ulema's collective decree was a judgment of practical wisdom demonstrating that the conservative ulema could be good diplomats. It stated: '...the High Council of the honorable ulema recommends to the Islamic Emirate of Afghanistan to persuade bin Laden to leave Afghanistan whenever possible...and to choose another place for himself.'[13] Osama duly disappeared. Pakistan dispatched a second delegation to Kandahar that consisted of ten Pakistani ulema well-known for their Deobandi linkages. Again General Mahmud, whose sympathy for the Taliban was now widely recognized, led the delegation. During the flight to Kandahar, General Mahmud reportedly communicated the need to support Mulla Umar to the ulema. 'America should give up its stubbornness', Mulla Umar told the Pakistani delegation, 'and only then can Afghanistan negotiate.'[14] Upon the delegation's return to Islamabad, it publicly endorsed Mulla Umar's decision not to hand over Osama to the US.[15]

While US diplomacy failed with Mulla Umar, it succeeded in isolating Afghanistan. In the last week of September 2001, Saudi Arabia broke off diplomatic relations, and shortly after the United Arab Emirates did the same. Pakistan continued to maintain a channel of communication with Afghanistan right up to the start of US military action, when the Afghan Ambassador in Islamabad was arrested and, against all diplomatic traditions, handed over to the US.

WAR

Much to the chagrin of India, which had offered its military facilities US for use against Afghanistan, the US relied on Pakistan. However, the geo-political landscape presented a complex picture. US strategy was, at the initial stage, to enlist the willing cooperation of the Northern Alliance, and then move on to control Mazar-i Sharif, and Kandahar. By 7 October US and British forces attacked thirty Taliban and Al Qaeda targets, which included airfields, air defence systems, Al Qaeda terrorist training camps, and troop concentrations facing Northern Alliance forces. In three days and nights US forces had achieved air superiority over Afghanistan. In addition to other land and sea bases, the US Air Force utilized air bases at Pasni and Jacobabad in Pakistan. On 10 October the US announced that the Northern Alliance had 'agreed not to attack Taliban forces outside Kabul until an interim government had been established for Afghanistan.'[16] This policy clearly reflected US thinking that minority ethnic communities, especially the Tajiks, Uzbeks, and Hazaras, should not be allowed to establish their pre-eminence in the post-war power-sharing. This view was further strengthened when a few days later on 16 October Secretary of State Colin Powell on his visit to Pakistan announced a new element of this policy, which was clearly supported by Pakistan. It stated that: 'there was a role for moderate elements of the Taliban in a post-war Afghan government,' and urged Afghan opposition groups to hasten their efforts to form an interim government. This roused the Northern Alliance's ire. Their Foreign Minister, Abdullah Abdullah rejected any Taliban role in the post-war government.[17]

The US war strategy of working closely with the Northern Alliance encouraged this defiance. Special forces were already on the ground, operating with the Northern Alliance and in some parts of southern Afghanistan. A special operations soldier is a superman. He is part of a small mobile unit sometimes accompanied by air support. Special units make up some 46,000 of 2.7 million uniformed military personnel. They include the army's Green Berets and Rangers, air force Special Operations and even a group that does not exist officially – the army's Delta Force. Some of them are specialists in medicine (almost junior doctors), in engineering (construction and demolition), in communications, and intelligence gathering. They are also experts at high-altitude jumping – can jump out of an airplane and land where they want to be, disguising themselves or digging a hole and living in it and blending into their surroundings. They were already teaching the Northern Alliance some of the tricks of their trade.

By 27 September a CIA Special Operative known only as Gary had given $1 million in cash to Abdullah and Muhammad Fahim, Commander of the Northern Alliance Forces, explaining that they could do with the money as they pleased. Fahim offered 10,000 fighters. In addition to buying the support of the Northern Alliance, the CIA bought off warlords or sub-commanders in the north and in the Pashtun belt in the south for as little as $50,000. Some sub-commanders took $10,000 to $20,000 in cash. The CIA operatives spent $70 million bribing the anti-Taliban forces.[18] But this figure does not cover payments into secret bank accounts around the world for senior Pashtun tribal leaders, who later turned on Mulla Umar and the Taliban. In a sense the US won the war with a cheque-book, and the air force.

In overthrowing the Taliban regime in 102 days the US had committed 110 CIA operatives and 316 Special Forces super soldiers, and used massive air power. After the Taliban's defeat, the US and Britain were able to introduce significant ground forces into Afghanistan. By June 2002 twenty nations had deployed more than 16,000 troops to the Central Command's area of responsibility. Coalition partners contributed 7,000 troops to the US operations and the International Assistance Security Force (ISAF) in Kabul – 'making up more than half of the 14,000 non-Afghan forces in Afghanistan'. Among the coalition countries were nine Muslim states, which made small but strategically significant military contributions.[19]

Supported by the exceptionally heavy bombardment of the US Air Force guided by Special Forces personnel, the Northern Alliance infantry had advanced to capture Konduz, Herat and Bamiyan by 12 November. In other words, Afghanistan was cut in two—the non-Pashtun areas were controlled by the Northern Alliance, and the control of the Pashtun belt in the south was in a precarious situation. Kabul was mostly vacated, and thousands of Taliban and Al Qaeda fighters had fled to the Pakistan border of the tribal autonomous areas, and to the Tora Bora caves. While the Special Forces and the bombers made it exceptionally difficult for the Taliban and Al Qaeda to hold on to territory and the capital city of Kabul, the Northern Alliance forces advanced toward Kabul and entered it. This was contrary to the understanding that existed between the US and Pakistan. Fahim and Abdullah explained that they had advanced on the capital in order to preserve peace and law and order and to prevent an ethnic blood-bath in the city. Clearly the political objective was to establish a commanding position for the Uzbeks and especially the Tajiks of the Northern Alliance in the formation of the interim government and a new republican constitution.

A few brief comments about the Taliban's rout may be in order. Socially, the Taliban, being primarily a Pashtun movement, had made itself unpopular with the non-Pashtun ethnic communities. The imposition of draconian punishments, widespread unemployment, their moral police's repressive actions, and endless military campaigns had also taken a heavy toll on the Pashtun population. The Taliban and Al Qaeda were supposed to have a force of up to 125,000, but according to an American specialist's estimate, 'only 25,000 were serious fighters'.[20] The Taliban had no air force; their anti-aircraft guns and shoulder-fired missiles were obsolete. This enabled the US to establish supremacy in the air. The Taliban and Al Qaeda could not disperse or retreat without exposing themselves to US air attacks. Convoys and ground forces could not move or stay and survive. They suffered casualties in the thousands. Last but not least, the Taliban were greatly dependent on Pakistan's military aid and advice. This was no longer available. Lacking in moderation, Mulla Umar stuck to his 'sublime principles', and let his regime be destroyed.

Mulla Umar escaped with his life, so did Osama bin Laden. The Taliban and Al Qaeda were by no means finished. They retreated, hid in caves, took refuge with the remote tribal chieftains in Pakistan's tribal belt. Only a few Al Qaeda operatives were captured. At the Tora Bora caves the US failed to commit ground troops and instead relied upon Afghan allies to hunt for the Al Qaeda fighters. Also US Centre Command Centcom insisted upon controlling the operations from its headquarters in Florida, enabling Al Qaeda operatives including bin Laden to escape. This decision, according to one of America's critics, exposed the 'culture of caution and milkiness that lay at the heart of CENTCOM'.[21] US forces also relied upon 61,600 Pakistani troops to scour the border for fugitives from Tora Bora. Sympathetic to the Taliban and Al Qaeda, they arrested no more than 300 fugitives.[22] US forces offered villages $4,000 for each Al Qaeda fighter captured alive—especially in Shertankel where US forces blocked possible Al Qaeda escape routes over the 10,000–12,000 ft. passes through the Shah-i Kot mountains. Despite the high reward offered for each capture, as many as 600

Al Qaeda and Taliban fighters—Chechens, Arabs, and Pakistanis—with their itinerant families were deliberately allowed to escape. In some operations in the Shah-i Kot Mountains, Afghans defected from the American side in the heat of battle to rejoin the Taliban. The US claimed that the battle for Shah-i Kot was an 'unqualified success' despite the widespread apprehension that fighters had escaped intact across the border into Miranshah, Waziristan.

Groups associated with Al Qaeda continued to operate in Pakistan, regardless of General Musharraf's claim that Osama might have died in the US bombardment. On 21 February 2002, a militant group called the National Movement for the Restoration of Pakistani Sovereignty released a videotape of the execution of the *Wall Street Journal* reporter Daniel Pearl, who had been kidnapped in Karachi on 23 January while investigating links between the ISI and militant Kashmiri groups. Less than a month later a US diplomat's wife and daughter died in a grenade attack on a church—just a few yards away from the US Embassy in Islamabad. The attack was made on the day General Tommy Franks was due to arrive in Islamabad. It gave General Franks an excuse to press General Musharraf to authorize 'hot pursuit' operations by US forces against the Taliban and Al Qaeda fighters in the tribal areas of Pakistan. Musharraf had no choice but to approve the request on 27 March 2002.[23] Joint US-Pakistan military operations in the tribal area, especially Waziristan, became a familiar routine.

The US military campaign against the Taliban and Al Qaeda began on 20 October 2001 and came to an end on 1 May 2003, when the US asserted that from that time on its forces would concentrate on the stabilization of Afghanistan. The US undertook the following measures in this effort:

1) Extending the writ of Hamid Karzai's central government, which was widely viewed as weak and unable to control many regional leaders, generally known as warlords.

2) Setting up regional enclaves to create secure conditions for reconstruction.

3) Disarming independent militias maintained by the warlords.

The military defeat of the Taliban had returned Afghanistan to the *status quo* which had prevailed before their rise to power. Eight principal warlords exercised control over different parts of the country. In the north Uzbek warlord Abdur Rashid Dostum was back in control in Mazar-i Sharif; (2) his former ally, Ata Muhammad contesting his power. In the west Ismail Khan was in command of Herat. In the north-east Doud Khan established firm control. In the centre Karim Khalili was in power in Hazara. In the south on the Pakistani frontier Bacha Khan Zadran asserted his authority. Also on the Pakistan border, Hazrat Ali had sidelined Haji Abdul Qadir, once head of the Eastern Shura in Nangarhar province, and Gul Agha Shirazi controlled Kandahar with 20,000 fighters. The whereabouts of the notorious soldier of fortune Gulbuddin Hekmatyar, once a Pakistani favourite, were at this point unknown. Actually he was in Iran and soon returned. After November 2002, Kabul came under the power of Hamid Karzai and General Fahim and the International Security Assistance Force (ISAF).[24]

In the stabilization programme the first step was taken in the form of a conference of major Afghanistan ethnic leaders. The UN issued an invitation to almost all Afghan factions, notably the Northern Alliance and the former Afghan king, Mohammad Zahir Shah, to meet in Bonn. Obviously the Taliban were ignored. On 5 December 2001 the factions signed an agreement to establish a thirty-member interim administration to govern until the holding in June 2002 of a *loya jirga* to be inaugurated by Zahir Shah. The *loya jirga* would then choose a new government to run Afghanistan for the next two years until a new constitution was drafted and elections held. Also, it established a 111-member parliament. The new government was to operate under the constitution of 1964 until a new constitution was adopted.

The Bonn Agreement also provided an international peace keeping force to maintain security, at least in Kabul. The Northern Alliance forces were to withdraw from Kabul. The agreement's provisions were endorsed by UN Security Council Resolution 1385 (6 December 2001), and the international peace keeping force was authorized by Security Council Resolution 1386, adopted on 20 December 2001. At the Bonn conference Hamid Karzai, a Pashtun, was elected chairman of an interim administration, which governed from 2 December 2001 until 2002 when the *loya jirga* was convened. Karzai presided over a cabinet consisting of thirty positions, seventeen held by the Northern Alliance. General Fahim became Minister of Defence, Younis Qanooni the Minister of the Interior, and the Ministry of Foreign Affairs was occupied by Abdullah Abdullah. All were Tajiks except Abdullah, who was half Tajik and half Pashtun. Clearly the first Karzai government was dominated by the Tajiks.

Karzai was a 'stranger' in this crowd of Northern Alliance Tajiks. A young charismatic junior khan of the Popolzai tribe of Kandahar, he had spent much of the anti-Soviet war in the US, where his family had invested in several Afghan restaurants. In 1994 he was deputy foreign minister in President Burhan-ud-Din Rabbani's government. Then his sympathies switched to the then-embryonic movement of the Taliban.[25] As an interim chief executive of Afghanistan, Karzai often appeared to be less a head of state than a mayor of Kabul. The struggle for power continued as Rabbani attempted to form an alliance of warlords which included Pashtuns of a militantly Islamic orientation, including Abdul Rab Rasool Sayyaf and Gulbuddin Hekmatyar, a warlord considered responsible for killing 50,000 civilians during rocket attacks on Kabul in the 1990s.

Karzai had to dispel the impression that he was a client of the US or a captive of the Northern Alliance. Much of his eventual leverage resided in the $4.5 billion in foreign aid pledged over the next five years to help rebuild Afghanistan. Also, the US announced the first training phase, to last two and a half months, to prepare three ground combat battalions, each with 600 troops, and two border battalions, each with 300 troops. More than 150 Special Forces troops were assigned at this initial stage to train the new Afghan army to consist of 70,000 troops. Within the city limits of Kabul 4,500 troops from Britain, Italy, Germany, and other western countries were deployed to provide security in the capital.[26]

By September 2003 at least 7,000 Afghan recruits had completed the military training. A battalion of this Afghan National Army (ANA) launched a sweep in south-eastern Afghanistan against the Taliban and performed rather well. Throughout 2003 there was some concern that Defence Minister General Fahim, who bestowed the title of Field Marshal on himself, opposed the formation of a national army as a potential threat to his power base. Fahim favored Tajiks for recruitment in the ANA, causing the Pashtuns to leave the national army.[27] This problem, however, was alleviated to some degree with more involvement by US Special Forces.[28]

In late September 2003 Karzai announced Defence Ministry reforms that approved the replacement of about five senior Tajik officials with officials of Pashtun, Uzbek and Hazara ethnicity. To what extent this reform measure restored ethnic balance to the structure of the ANA remains unclear.

The Bonn Agreement of 5 December 2001 had also laid out a timetable for further steps toward establishing a new government, constitution, and, ultimately, elections. The emergency loya jirga of June 2002 was held in Kabul to accomplish these objectives. The tent to which 1,600 delegates were invited for eleven days of deliberations was donated by Germany. Equipped with air-conditioning and erected on the grounds of Kabul Polytechnic Institute, it measured 230 by 130 feet. There was no building big enough and undamaged by the war which could have accommodated so many delegates. This loya jirga brought together former Taliban, former royalists, former communists, and former Mujahideen fighters. Professing his commitment to the rule of law, Dostum submitted a proposal for a federal constitution, with King Zahir Shah as the head of state. This subtle proposal was a viable bulwark against the Tajiks who 'controlled' Karzai.

Karzai was elected President of Afghanistan with 1,295 votes out of 1,575 in 'an orchestrated election sealed behind closed doors'.[29] The US, which helped put him in power at Bonn, now openly backed his candidacy for president. His influential opponents had been won over to withdraw in his favour. Old and feeble, King Zahir Shah publicly ruled out any position for himself, but accepted the title of Baba-i Afghans. Clinging still to his defunct position as the President of Afghanistan, Burhan-ud-Din Rabbani meekly endorsed Karzai, and so did 'Field Marshall' Defence Minister Muhammad Qasim Fahim. Always a gentleman and sensitive to the ethnic pride of northern non-Pashtun Afghans, Karzai delivered his acceptance speech in Pashto and also partly in Dari. He paid homage to the Islamic guerillas who fought against the Soviet occupation, and then against the Taliban and Al Qaeda, and remembered the slain leaders of some of these groups, such as the Tajik leader Ahmad Shah Massoud, the Hazara leader Mazari, and Pashtun leader Abdul Haq. Also he complimented Iran and Pakistan for the help they had given to Afghanistan's millions of refugees over the last twenty-three years of war.

After Karzai's election heated debate ensued in the *loya jirga* over the role of Islam in the constitution. A formula was adopted, which was later incorporated into the constitution as Article Three: 'no law can be contrary to the sacred religion of Islam, and the values of this constitution.' A more contentious issue was the composition and powers of a new Shura-i Milli (National Assembly), which was a matter of great concern to those in the *loya jirga*, who sought to establish checks and balances over executive authority. This issue, however, remained unresolved by the time the *jirga* had run its course.

Karzai appointed a cabinet of four vice-presidents, four special advisers, and twenty-eight ministers. Through a constitutional commission, government drafted a new constitution, which was released in early November 2003, and adopted amendments by a constitutional *loya jirga* on 4 January 2004. Under the new constitution, a presidential general election was held on 9 October 2004, and Karzai was elected once again. Afghans turned out in large numbers to vote. The event was relatively peaceful, but was marred by fifteen candidates declaring the election illegitimate because of what they said was widespread cheating, fraud, and violence. The Taliban failed to disrupt the election, and were considerably weakened. The single most important factor in the success of the election may have been average Afghans who were exhausted by decades of war. Probably they tipped off the authorities about possible Taliban attacks, and used the elections to elect an acceptable Pashtun leader.

Some other factors, in addition to this psychological phenomenon, explained the success of this election. In addition to aggressive American-led security efforts in Afghanistan, the Bush Administration poured $1.76 billion into reconstruction funds for the country during 2004. After blocking the expansion of an international peacekeeping force in 2002, the US now supported it. In 2004 the Pentagon nearly doubled its forces in Afghanistan from 11,000 to 20,000, deploying small military reconstruction units across the country and marines to scour dangerous southern areas. The US also trained thousands of Afghan soldiers, police officers, and civil servants.

Last but not least, Pakistan played a supportive role in reining in the Taliban after President Bush met with General Musharraf at the UN General Assembly session in New York on 21 September 2004. Very specifically Bush had asked Musharraf not to allow Taliban infiltration into Afghanistan. However, the Taliban spokesman offered his own explanation: 'we refrained from election day attacks because we didn't want to hurt civilians.'[30]

FOREIGN MILITARY PRESENCE IN AFGHANISTAN

Basically the Afghan central government has functioned with the security assistance of foreign forces, especially those of the US. The UN Security Council had authorized the creation of the International Security Assistance Force (ISAF), and by the summer of 2002 it had 5,000 troops from nineteen countries. Initially the ISAF was to provide security in Kabul; in October 2003 the UN expanded its functions to include all of Afghanistan. NATO took over the command of the ISAF. However, the ISAF operated separately from 'Operation Enduring Freedom' (OEF), the US-led military operations focused on destroying the remnants of the Taliban and Al Qaeda. With 11,500 troops participating, OEF was the most lethal force in Afghanistan.

By spring 2003 the Taliban had started to reassert themselves, and the security situation deteriorated throughout Afghanistan. Now American troops started to provide humanitarian assistance, and took on some road and school construction projects. The US initiated a programme to deploy Provincial Reconstruction Teams (PRT) near major cities throughout Afghanistan. The PRTs were designed to provide assistance in rebuilding local infrastructure and local security, but not to perform police duties. In 200 of eight PRTs, which were operational, one was under NATO command and comprised 240 personnel, two were 100-person teams commanded by the United Kingdom and New Zealand, and the remainder were thirty-person US teams commanded by a senior US officer. The PRTs, according to specialists, were 'the centerpiece of the international community's strategy for establishing areas outside Kabul, and enabling the central government to extend its reach.'[31] Some observers have questioned their impact. In some provinces the central government relied on the presence of the PRTs to remove troublesome local warlords, while not challenging the more powerful ones. (There was another US military operation, which was conducted covertly in cooperation with Pakistan in the tribal areas and Pakistan's provinces to hunt for the Al Qaeda militants.)

For nation-building programmes some NATO members and US-allied states—Italy, Germany, and Japan assumed specific responsibilities as the lead nations. There was no functioning judicial system. 'To a great extent, the written law in Afghanistan is not applied—or even widely known, including by judges and lawyers.'[32] In 2003, the US spent about $13 million on rule of law activities other than police, including support for judicial reforms. This amount was insufficient relative to the needs of the Afghan judicial system. The field was left to the 'lead nation', Italy, which was generally known to be focused on implementing its own projects, rather than coordinating broader efforts for the judicial system. They decided to extend the judicial system to areas of Afghanistan where courts were not functioning.

Germany was the 'lead nation' for training and equipping the Afghan police. The Afghan police suffered from lack of uniforms, equipment, and transportation, and received little or no pay. Germany committed $70 million toward restructuring the police academy in Kabul. By November 2003 the academy had 1,000 officer cadets and 500 non-commissioned officers. They were composed of 60 per cent Pashtuns, 30 per cent Tajik and Uzbeks, and 10 per cent others. Germany also assumed responsibility for training an Afghan border patrol. In 2003 the US also established a police assistance programme to provide in-service training for police currently serving in Kabul.

Japan took on as 'lead nation' a very tough job: to help deal with the warlord problem—to disarm, demobilize, and reintegrate 'as many as 100,000 soldiers and militia members'.[33] While this problem existed throughout Afghanistan, it was particularly serious in the north, where the Northern Alliance leaders (real warlords) had entered into an alliance to topple the Taliban regime. The US wanted to have its proverbial cake, and eat it too. It wanted the Northern Alliance to continue to fight the Taliban and the Al Qaeda militants and regularly provided them with money and military support. Yet it expected them not to be a major impediment to Afghanistan's national unity. Encouraged by their own ambitions and US support, the warlords refused to disband their private armies, and routinely engaged in armed clashes over control of territory and transportation routes. To control the local population they used intimidation tactics and often violence. The most senior and well-known warlords served as provincial governors, but refused to accept direction from Karzai's central government in Kabul.

Japan's UN-mandated programme was initiated in October 2003 and started in the Kunduz and Paktia provinces. Two months later 2,000 former Northern Alliance soldiers surrendered their weapons in Kabul, and agreed to participate in a job-training programme to prepare for civilian life. This transformation was possible only in Kabul, where the US and allied forces' presence was very heavy. By March 2004 Karzai had extended the influence of his government across the country. He replaced sixteen governors (head warlords), either by moving them around and bringing them over to Kabul or by actually firing them.[34] In other words the plan of demilitarization, demobilization, and reintegration had achieved some success.

A comprehensive study conducted by the World Bank, the government of Afghanistan, and the Asian Development Bank concluded that around $27-28 billion over seven to ten years would be needed to enable Afghanistan to 'stand on its own feet.'[35] These funds can be available to Afghanistan if the United States remained committed to the security and economic development of Afghanistan.

OVERT AND COVERT MILITARY OPERATIONS OF PAKISTAN AND THE UNITED STATES

The third dimension of security operations against the Taliban and the Al Qaeda militants was focused on Pakistan and its tribal belt, especially the autonomous areas of North and South Waziristan. In Pakistan CIA officers worked closely with US Special Forces in the hunt for Osama bin Laden and other senior Al Qaeda members. Both services worked very closely with

Pakistan's main intelligence service, the ISI. Their efforts remained hidden, enabling Pakistan to deny participation. In a 25 May 2005 appearance on CNN, Stephen J. Hadley, US National Security Advisor to President Bush, refused to comment on these cooperative operations. 'The relationships we have are very sensitive', Hadley said. 'They are a matter of domestic politics to these countries, and it would not help our effort against terror to be talking publicly about these relationships.'[36]

This collaborative program enabled Pakistan to capture a high-ranking Al Qaeda leader, Abu Faraj al-Libbi on 2 May 2005 in Mardan. The CIA had played a major role in gathering the intelligence that led to al-Libbi's arrest, while Pakistan described it as being a purely Pakistani operation.[37] On 7 May 2005 a remotely controlled CIA aircraft struck Haitham al-Yemeni, an important Al Qaeda operator, in North Waziristan. The missile was fired by a Predator aircraft operated from a base hundreds of miles from the target. A US government official confirmed that Yemeni was killed by a Predator. On 14 May 2005 Pakistan's information minister contradicted this statement, saying, 'No such incident occurred on the soil of Pakistan.'[38] Despite these formal denials, General Musharraf had been praised by US officials for his government's close cooperation with the US in counterterrorism efforts. The Bush administration understood that Musharraf faced powerful anti-American sentiment within the Pakistani population, and it was his political need not to acknowledge the presence of the CIA and US Special Forces in Pakistan.

The Pakistani public is familiar with the subtleties of secret diplomacy. Pakistan's first field marshal and martial law President, General Muhammad Ayub Khan, signed an agreement in February 1957 with the US to allow an airbase near Peshawar for U-2 flights over the Soviet Union. The base remained off limits to all Pakistanis. However, the US assured Pakistan that, if the U-2 flights were exposed, 'the United States would declare it had waged the incursions without [Pakistani] approval.'[39]

US–PAKISTAN OPERATIONS IN WAZIRISTAN

A secret war started in Waziristan in May 2002. Officially there were no foreign troops in Pakistan other than a few logistical-support personnel. However, on 30 April 2002 US forces launched an operation code-named Mountain Lion, using unspecified members of elite British, Australian, and US 101st Airborne troopers to seek out Taliban and Al Qaeda hideouts. US officials did not say where the forces were searching. However, subsequently it was confirmed that US Army Rangers and Delta operatives were inside Pakistan in the tribal areas. The plan called for the US and allied forces to enter Waziristan from Afghanistan and the Pakistani Army units to operate from their side of the border to mount a pincer operation. There were 1,200 American and British soldiers in the tribal belt.[40]

An impression existed that the Pakistani government did not welcome US military operations on its soil, but it soon ran out of excuses. In March 2002 US communication interceptions led to the capture of Abu Zubaydah, one of Osama's top lieutenants, at a safe house in the Pakistani city of Faisalabad, hundreds of miles from the tribal areas. Armed FBI and CIA agents accompanied elite Pakistani police on the operation, and captured fifty Al Qaeda fugitives in addition to Zubaydah. After suffering this embarrassment, General Musharraf decided he had no choice but to allow cooperative operations with the US.

North and South Waziristan are parts of Pakistan's seven autonomous tribal areas that border NWFP. The others are Khyber, Kurram, Orakzai, Mohmand, and Bajaur. Of all the Pashtun tribes the Wazirs are known as the most conservative and irascible. They passionately oppose any outsider who might attempt to penetrate their land. No foreign imperial invader has ever been able to control the Wazirs completely. Both the British government and Pakistan woefully neglected the economic development of the areas. However, Pakistan has given the population of all tribes parliamentary representation in the federal and provincial assemblies.

In the late nineteenth century the British debated two policies for the tribal areas. The earlier, known as masterly inactivity, was supported by Lord Lawrence during his tenure as Viceroy of India. Under this the British abstained from all trans-frontier politics and left the tribes strictly alone as long as they did not cause any trouble for the British government. After Lawrence, Sir Robert Sandeman advocated the forward policy, which was widely practised by the British frontier administration. The forward policy modified the masterly inactivity orientation by stipulating a system of controlling all the political affairs of the trans-border tribes while leaving their internal policy to the tribal chiefs, who were 'guided' by the political officers.

The tribal chiefs, however, were left free to maintain the tribal social, cultural, and religious traditions. Also, allowances were made to the tribes; in return, however, they guaranteed the security of the British posts on the highways, and assumed responsibility for any misdemeanours on the part of other members of their tribes. Tribal levies were organized under young officers of the British Army, who gave them military training and discipline. The pay of these soldiers became a substantial economic source to the tribes.

Through several decades of relations between the British and the tribes a pattern of interaction developed, which became the hallmark of the forward policy. First, the unruly sections of the tribes carried on raids on the frontier villages under direct British control, as was their custom since time immemorial. Sometimes the raiders were captured and met their fate. More often they escaped and, in accordance with the system of collective tribal responsibility, a fine was imposed on the tribe to which the raiders belonged. These fines went on accumulating, and the tribes ran up an account with the government for its misdeeds.

The second stage began when the government's patience was exhausted. The tribal chiefs were called in and an ultimatum delivered: the tribes must deliver to the government's control the raiders, and pay a pre-determined fine. If the tribes failed to satisfy these demands, then they must be prepared to confront an expedition of superior military force. The third stage was reached when the tribes failed to meet the government's demands, and the punitive expedition was launched. The expeditionary force invariably penetrated the hilly tribal villages, burned some of the culprit's houses, confiscated some weapons, fought some rearguard actions, and then returned. Subsequently, the tribe was now neat and clean, and ready to run up a new account—new raids, new defiance, new expeditions and punitive actions.[41]

After the Taliban's defeat and Al Qaeda's destruction their remnants found asylum in the tribal areas, where the US and Pakistan followed in the footsteps of the forward policy with much the same results. Among the tribes, the Wazirs were sympathetic to the Taliban rule, and admired the type of 'Islamic Emirate' they had established in Afghanistan.

US–PAKISTAN EXPEDITIONS IN THE GUISE OF THE FORWARD POLICY

Until 2002 the tribal areas were effectively off-limits to Pakistani troops, which had been withdrawn by Quaid-i Azam Jinnah in 1948. Pakistan's policy commingled elements of the forward policy with that of masterly inactivity. Consequently, tribal elders became unchallenged rulers of the tribes, especially in Waziristan. This situation radically changed after the Taliban were routed. The US military command claimed that a large number of fighters had found refuge in Pakistan's tribal areas and exercised a tremendous amount of pressure on the Musharraf government to start military operations in Waziristan, which borders Afghanistan's provinces of Khost, Paktia, and Paktika.

A three-dimensional policy was adopted: repeat the forward policy process to capture the Taliban and Al Qaeda elements in North and South Waziristan; if that yielded no results then undertake military expeditions; and last but not least, undertake massive developmental projects (with help US) to win the hearts and the minds of the tough Waziris. First the development projects: North Waziristan was allocated Rs. 564 million during the fiscal 2004-5 to bring the most neglected parts up to the level of the more developed parts of the area. A population of 361,246 persons spread over an area of 4,707 sq. km. had been ignored in development plans during the past six decades. Under construction in 2005 were 18 projects in education, totalling Rs. 102,285 million, 12 in the health sector, 10 in communication, 7 in irrigation, 6 in livestock, 5 each in forestry and agriculture, and 4 projects dedicated to new industries and technical education. For the irrigation project alone Rs. 149 million were allocated. Construction began on a four-year college for women.[42]

In tandem with these development plans, military operations were also conducted to capture the Taliban and Al Qaeda operatives. The military operations, and especially the US participation, were most unpopular in Pakistan. The leaders of religious political parties—Jama't-i-Islami and Jamiat ulama-i Islam—were banned from the tribal areas. These parties were in power in NWFP, and Maulana Fazl-ur- Rahman, a stalwart of the Jamiat ulama-i Islam, was the recognized leader of the opposition in the lower house of the National Assembly.

In 2002 Pakistan initiated the first phase of its operations in North Waziristan. Jirgas were held with the tribal chiefs, when mutual obligations were assumed. The government pledged that it would undertake the development of the infrastructure of Waziristan. The chiefs in exchange gave 'a guarantee' of cooperation in allowing the soldiers to check the infiltration of the militants from across the border of Afghanistan. The chiefs also agreed to impose a fine of Rs. 5 million on any tribal members found 'guilty' of providing shelter to any Al Qaeda militant and to bulldoze the house of that member.

Supervised by the American commandos, at least seven unsuccessful raids were conducted in Miranshah by the Pakistan Army units. In South Waziristan forty-eight military raids were conducted, and some focused on Azam Warsak, a border town on the Durand Line that separates Afghanistan from Pakistan, where more than 160 Afghanis were arrested; some were released after screening. At least two militant training camps were smashed, and an extensive network communication system was destroyed. The militants had created an elaborate system of governance, including a budget office, departments of finance, and an elaborate propaganda-generating media centre. Housed in an eight-foot deep cellar, the militants' secretariat possessed a plethora of electronic gadgets – computers, cameras and other communications equipment. This system was managed entirely by foreign militants.[43]

The US forces started to pay $200 monthly to guards from the Wazir tribes, who were supposed to have influence on either side of the border.[44] By January 2003 Pakistan had arrested 400 Al Qaeda suspects. In May 2005 it was successful in the Bajaur tribal area, when 150 Mohmand tribal chiefs reached a fresh agreement on denying shelter to Al Qaeda members or other suspected terrorists. Any tribe member found guilty of harbouring foreign terrorists would be liable to pay a fine of Rs. 5 million, and would be expelled along with his family from the area. Those actions would be taken in accordance with tribal customs and established traditions. Almost one month before the signing of this agreement, Pakistan's security forces arrested more than a dozen suspects in Bajaur.[45]

In 2005 US officials pushed for Pakistan to move on North Waziristan. Military operations in South Waziristan in 2004 destroyed two militant training camps – more than 300 foreign fighters and Pakistani tribesmen were killed or captured, but more were thought to have fled into the North Waziristan mountains. In these operations approximately 200 members of the Pakistani military forces were lost. As a result they conducted military operations in 2005 with targets based upon specific intelligence, rather than the broad sweeps that had proved so costly for them in 2004.

The US commander in Afghanistan, Lt. General David W. Barno, disclosed Pakistan's secret when he publicly acknowledged that US forces were training Pakistani forces in night-flying and airborne assault tactics to combat Al Qaeda militants and tribal fighters. General Barno stated that he had visited the Special Services Group headquarters in Cherat, near Peshawar, and watched a display by the American-trained Pakistani units in their new Bell 4 helicopters. General Barno made these comments as the Pakistani army was preparing to hunt Al Qaeda militants in North Waziristan. However, Pakistan's Army contradicted General Barno's statement, saying that 'There were no American military trainees at Cherat', and that he 'had probably been referring to joint military exercises between the two countries.'[46] Clearly, Pakistan's chief military spokesman did not think that the American general knew the difference between joint exercises and American Special Forces headquarters for training Pakistani troops at Cherat.

Before he departed from Afghanistan in May 2005, General Barno's assessment of the Taliban/Al Qaeda's military capability included the following salient points: 1) The Taliban would suffer a major schism within the ranks of their senior commanders. Some would give up insurgency, and join a reconciliation programme. A small hardcore group would continue to fight. 2) Part of that core, loyal to the former Taliban commander Jalaluddin Haqqani, would continue to attack across the border in Afghanistan. These elements operated at the behest of Al Qaeda, and were financed by Al Qaeda to conduct operations from Pakistan's tribal areas to disrupt development in Afghanistan. Also they operated from both sides of the border. 3) The fighters had shown an ability to adapt and shift to new areas, using winter to regroup, reorganize, and re-equip. 4) The insurgents' coordinated attacks along the border on 22 March 2005, when Afghan president Hamid Karzai visited Pakistan, indicated that they were capable of a large operation. 5) Lastly General Barno observed that 'there's clearly a flow of funding that comes through the Al Qaeda network.' He added: 'It probably ebbs and flows a bit, but there's funding out there.'[47] 'Out there' clearly referred to Pakistan, and the larger Muslim world.

TRIBE MOTIVATION: GREED FOR MONEY OR RELIGIOUS ZEAL

Pakistan's military contended that the tribes' motivation to support and to lay down their lives for the Al Qaeda militants did not stem from religious zeal, but rather from greed for money. Only a small fraction was inspired by religious sentiment. To buttress this argument, the Peshawar corps commander, the man who supervised military expeditions in Waziristan, highlighted the financial support system for recruitment. Each fighter was paid a stipend, which enabled the Al Qaeda soldier to 'live reasonably well'. Even a very modest pension was paid, at least in some cases. As an example, the confessional statement of an Algerian Al Qaeda veteran revealed that some members receive between $60-$90 US dollars every three to four months. Being married to the local Pashtun girls, many decided to settle down in Waziristan.

In some cases Al Qaeda loaned substantial sums of money to the tribes. In South Waziristan the Pakistani Army initiated dialogues with the tribes, and was informed that they had taken huge loans from Al Qaeda and were honour bound to offer its militants 'shelter' or 'employment'. Also, on one known occasion, the Pakistan Army paid Rs 32 million to some of the most-wanted Wazir fighters, who signed peace agreements. The money was supposed to be used to repay the Al Qaeda loans in full. For the same reason three well-known tribal warriors were paid Rs 15 million. In June 2004 an arrested Taliban leader said that he had distributed over Rs 100 million in Afghanistan in order to disrupt the presidential election of Hamid Karzai.[48]

If money alone keeps the insurgency alive in Afghanistan, and keeps the tribal areas in turmoil, then it should not be difficult for the US money and Pakistani Army to defeat it in short order. But this is not expected. All reasonable indicators point to the continuation of the conflict for several more years, and the tribal areas of Pakistan will remain destabilized.

Surely, money is the source of life; financial incentives as well as religious motivations encourage recruitment. Anti-American sentiment, which continues to grow in intensity in the Muslim states, galvanizes religiously oriented wealthy Muslims to express their resentment and to remain committed to the 'Islamic Cause'. Donations collected through zakat (Islamic mandatory charity) and general collections from the mosques can be funnelled, directly or indirectly, to the Al Qaeda network through the *hawala* system, bypassing the normal mode of transferring funds to foreign countries. The banking laws which were introduced after the 11 September tragedy have decreased the volume of foreign remittances through banks, but have failed to make a dent in the traditionally well-established *hawala* system. Money and volunteers are likely to pour into Afghanistan for an indefinite future.

NOTES

1. Ivo H. Daalder and James M. Lindsay, *America Unbound: The Bush Revolution in Foreign Policy* (Washington DC: The Brooking s Institution Press, 2003), pp. 13-14.
2. *The New York Times*, 21 September 2001.
3. President Bush's speech to the Joint Session of Congress, 20 September 2001; *The New York Times*, 21 September 2001.
4. C. Raja Mohan, *Crossing the Rubicon: The Shaping of India's New Foreign Policy* (London: Palgrave Macmillan, 2003), p. XI.
5. Bob Woodward, *Bush at War* (New York: Simon and Schuster, 2002), p. 5.
6. 'Pakistan Tells of US Threat after 9/11, CBS Reports', *The New York Times*, 22 September 2006; 'US Threatened to Bomb Pakistan after 9/11: Musharraf Says He Acted Responsibly', *Dawn*, 22 September 2006; see also, Pervez Musharraf, *In the Line of Fire: A Memoir* (New York: Simon & Shuster, 2006).
7. Woodward, *Bush at War* pp. 47, 58-59.
8. Ibid., p. 59.
9. Ibid., p. 61.
10. Ibid., p. 45.
11. *The Washington Post*, 7 October 2001; 14 October 2001.
12. *The New York Times*, 20 September 2001.
13. *The New York Times*, 21 September 2001.
14. *The Daily Telegraph*, 29 September 2001.
15. *Time*, 29 April 2002.

16. US Department of State, *The United States and Global Coalition Against Terrorism* (Washington DC, September 2001 – December 2003), p. 12.

17. Ibid., p. 13.

18. Woodward, op. cit., p. 317; George Friedman, *America's Secret War* (NY: Doubleday, 2004), p. 163.

19. Anthony H. Cordesman, *The Lessons of Afghanistan* (Washington DC: Center for Strategic and International Studies, 2002), pp. 82-99.

20. Cordesman, *Lessons of Afghanistan*, p. 15.

21. Michael Griffin, *Reaping the Whirlwind* (London: Pluto Press, 2003), p. 337.

22. Ibid., p. 338.

23. *The Washington Times*, 27 March 2002.

24. For the emergence of the warlords, see Barnett R. Rubin, *The Fragmentation of Afghanistan* (New Haven: Yale University Press, 1995), pp. 233-240.

25. Griffin, op. cit., p. 293.

26. Dexter Filkins, 'Charm and the West Keep Karzai in Power, For Now', *The New York Times*, 26 March 2002.

27. Kenneth Katzman, *Afghanistan: Current Issues and US Policy* (Washington, DC Congressional Research Service, 2004); see also, David Rohde, 'Training an Afghan Army that Can Shoot Straight', *The New York Times*, 6 June 2002.

28. Carlotta Gall, 'In a Remote Corner, an Afghan Army Evolves from Fantasy to Slightly Ragged Reality', *The New York Times*, 25 January 2003.

29. Carlotta Gall, 'Afghan Leader Urges Unity to Build a New Parliament', *The New York Times*, 16 June 2002.

30. Carlotta Gall and David Rohde, 'Assessing the Afghanistan Elections', *The New York Times*, 20 October 2004.

31. 'Unfinished Business in Afghanistan: Warlordism, Reconstruction and Ethnic Harmony', US Institute of Peace, Special Report 105 (Washington, DC, April 2003), p. 4.

32. Ibid., p. 5.

33. Ibid., p. 15.

34. 'Scene Setter on the International Conference on Afghanistan, March 31 – April 1', US Department of State (Washington DC, 26 March 2001), p. 3.

35. Ibid., p. 4.

36. Douglas Jehl, 'Remotely Controlled Craft Part of US-Pakistan Drive Against Al Qaeda, Ex-Officials Say', *The New York Times*, 16 May 2005.

37. Ibid.

38. 'Al Qaeda Leader's Death is Denied', *The New York Times*, 15 May 2005.

39. Michael R. Beschloss, *May Day: Eisenhower, Khrushchev and the U-2 Affair* (New York: Harper Row, 1986), p. 145; See also Hafeez Malik, *Soviet-Pakistan Relations and Post-Soviet Dynamics* (London: Macmillan, 1994), pp. 168-9.
40. Rod Nordland and Scot Johnson, 'Pakistan: Secret Hunt, Elusive Prey', *Newsweek*, 13 May 2002.
41. For details on the forward policy see, T.L. Pennell, *Among the Wild Tribes of the Afghan Frontier* (London: Steeley and Co., 1909), pp. 55-67; Sir Olaf Caroe, *The Pathans* (London: Macmillan and Co., 1958), pp. 391-400; David Dichter, *The Northwest Frontier of West Pakistan* (Oxford: Clarendon Press, 1969), pp. 155-70.
42. Javed Aziz Khan, 'Rs. 564 Million Uplift Schemes NWA to Bring Neglected Agency at Par with Developed Parts', *The News*, 8 April 2005.
43. Owais Tohid, 'Greed for Money...Not Religious Motivation...', *Newsline* (Karachi), 2 April 2005, pp. 53-55.
44. Meikaél Khan, 'Resentment Simmers Among the Tribals', *The News*, 2 June 2002.
45. 'Accord in Bajaur to Crush Terrorists', *Dawn*, 31 May 2005.
46. Carlotta Gall, 'US Training Pakistani Units Fighting Al Qaeda', *New York Times*, 27 April 2005.
47. Ibid.
48. Massoud Ansari, 'Newsbeat', *Newsline* (Karachi), May 2005, p. 50.

8

Consolidation of Power

Since the tragedy of 11 September relations between Pakistan and Afghanistan have become so symbiotic that at times the two neighbours appear to be twins tied at the hip. However, an analysis of Pakistan's security situation and economic development also requires an examination of its relationship with India—a relationship growing under the umbrella of the US. In the not too distant future Pakistan will impinge upon the grand architectural design of the US, especially in its strategic policy toward China that appears to have the features of the policy of containment which was so successfully applied to the Soviet Union.

I

Backed by the US, Hamid Karzai consolidated his position fairly quickly after assuming power in December 2001. The monarchy in Afghanistan was replaced by ethnic and tribal aristocracy, which would be democratic, if possible. The new system would be protected by a national army 70,000-strong, and the indefinite presence of US power. This US umbrella of power indeed extends from Kabul to Islamabad.

Afghanistan confronted several problems of nation building: legitimizing the presidential authority, warlordism, reconstruction, ethnic reconciliation, and establishing security. These tasks have been pursued under the patronage of the US with varying degrees of success since the Taliban's ouster from power.

Hamid Karzai, the first democratically elected president in Afghanistan's history, was inaugurated on 7 December 2004. Seventy per cent of the registered voters, nearly 8.1 million Afghan citizens participated in the presidential election held on 9 October. Forty per cent of those who voted were women. Karzai received more than 50 per cent of the votes against a field of seventeen candidates. However, critics have charged that the constitution and the presidential election were the results of deals made between Karzai and his US backers.[1] Nevertheless, it must be recognized that the constitution is not without positive qualities. It grants equal rights and duties under the law for men and women. It provides for the election of at least two women from every province to the *wolesi jirga* (House of the People).

To complete the electoral aspects of the Bonn process, elections were held for the bicameral legislature in December 2005. Seventy political parties applied for accreditation; thirty-three were rejected. However, no explanation was offered. Elections were held without the parties' participation and 2,707 parliament candidates (328 female and 2,379 male) were all independent, voter turnout (60 per cent) was highest in Turkmen, Uzbek, and Tajik provinces in the north, and lowest (30 per cent) in the some of the Pashtun provinces of south-eastern Afghanistan, where insurgency was still strong. A quarter of the seats (sixty-eight) in the 249-seat lower house or w*olesi jirga* are reserved for women and ten seats are reserved for the *kuchi* (nomadic) community whose candidates hold their seats in the *wolesi jirga* for five years. There is no maximum for the number of seats for these two groups. The 102 members of the *meshrano jirga* (the upper house or Senate) are directly elected by thirty-five provincial councils. The total number of candidates for the provincial councils was 3,025. The demographic picture of the elected members contained the ethnic map of Afghanistan, and reflected almost perfectly the circulation of the elites. Nine important and internationally recognized leaders, representing old regimes and ethnicities, were elected: 1) Tajiks (Yunus Qanum, Burhan-ud-Din Rabbani and 'Field Marshal' Mohammad

Qasim Fahim); 2) Pashtun (Adbul Rasul Sayyaf and Sebghatullah Mujaddidi); 3) Hazara (Haji Mohammad Mohaqaq and Ramazan Bashardost); and 4) Taliban (Mohammad Islam Mohammadi, one of four Taliban members, including a former Taliban commander Abdul Salaam Rockety—who gained his last name from his skill in shooting down Russian warplanes with shoulder-fired American-supplied missiles. The warlords or people associated with them were estimated to make up two-thirds of the new legislature. In addition to a mix of former jihadi leaders one could even see former communists.[2]

Meeting after a thiry-year hiatus, the new Afghan legislators lacked even elementary knowledge of the workings of western-styled democracy. The UN sponsored a week-long orientation to educate the new legislators on the fundamental procedures required for the operation of a parliamentary system. Constitutional and governmental experts in addition to members of foreign parliaments participated. They emphasized the necessity of compromise – a hard lesson to learn and practise.

For the first time an Afghan constitution allows the use of Shia jurisprudence in matters of personal law, especially cases involving only Shias. The fully-developed liberal democracy envisaged in the constitution has not come to fruition. Like the constitution of 1931, a hodgepodge of unworkable elements, the US-sponsored constitution does not suit the Afghan 'national' character and its current status of social development. The renowned and very perceptive anthropologist, Louis Dupree, who spent most of his life working and teaching in Afghanistan, described the Afghan social system as 'tribal, authoritarian, patrilineal and patriarchal'.[3] Since Dupree's 1980 description, and for that matter since 1931, Afghanistan's social structure has not changed so radically that it can now be considered primed for the complete absorption of 'western democracy'—the goal of US policy. Even though the international community recognizes the Karzai government, and it holds a seat in the UN General Assembly, which was denied to the Taliban regime, the destruction of the Afghan political system took twenty-five years; it cannot possibly be rebuilt overnight.

II

The Bonn Agreement had laid out as the eventual goal the establishment of a multi-ethnic and fully representative government for Afghanistan. Also it included protection for human rights, services for citizens, and a modern judicial system. In addition to these attributes of a democratic system, the people of Afghanistan expected their state centre to be strong, which would control the ethnic diversity of the state. In reality Afghanistan has never existed as a centralized state ruled from Kabul. Against this background the phenomenon of warlordism must be examined. During the long period of political instability and the 'absence' of central authority, regional ethnic leaders came to enjoy substantial autonomy. Some of them combined both administrative and military roles, and maintained a modicum of social peace and justice. Immediately after the US takeover, the Karzai government appointed (in fact accepted) provincial or regional governors from factional groups dominant in their areas. These governors owed their positions to their existing military control; their appointments did not confer any power to them. In fact some of them were very popular with the people.

The most notable warlords were Ismail Khan in Herat, Abdul Rashid Dostum and Ata Muhammad in the Uzbek region, and Karim Khalili in Hazara. The self-appointed Field Marshal Muhammad Qasim Fahim had inherited Ahmad Shah Massoud's position as a commander of the Tajik militia, and had established his control over the Ministry of Defence immediately after the fall of Kabul. He continued to treat the ministry as the fiefdom of his Tajik clan. Ninety out of 100 generals appointed by Fahim in 2002 were from his Panjshiri group. The *loya jirga* of Kabul (July 2002) accepted the position of Fahim as Defence Minister, and Dostum as his deputy. Younis Qanooni, another Tajik from the Panjshir Valley, became the Minister of the Interior.

The legendary Ismail Khan had established a statelet in Herat. The location of Herat provided his greatest source of strength. For centuries the city has been a crossroads of international trade and its closeness to Iran has enabled it to adopt the Persian language and culture. Iran has consequently looked upon it as within its sphere of influence. Iran committed $560 million in aid to Afghanistan at the Tokyo Donors Conference. 'Much of that monetary assistance is spent on Herat.'[4] Like Iran, the US valued his help and provided him with support.

The powerful existence of the warlords was directly linked to Afghanistan's existence as a unified state. One view maintains that US policy was the main obstacle. In the remote and difficult areas of Afghanistan the warlords could have helped the US maintain security and fight Al Qaeda.[5] When Secretary of Defence Donald Rumsfeld visited Kabul in May 2003, Karzai presented him a plan to take out certain key warlords. 'Rumsfeld declined to offer US assistance.'[6] Another view maintained that warlords were not going to disappear in the foreseeable future. A distinction could be made between those who were unreformed and militaristic and those who were willing to view the future of Afghanistan through a political rather than a military lens – in other words, those who were willing to make a transition from warlord to political ward leader. In this view the US and its military forces could also deal with ethnic leaders, rather than exclusively with Kabul. The argument made an historical point: The deepening of ethnic identity and regional autonomy rendered Afghanistan incapable of ever achieving the type of central government it had before 1978.

Karzai appeared to be of two minds on the best approach to deal with the warlords – fight or co-opt. In 2003 he attempted to co-opt the two well-known warlords Abdul Rashid Dostum and Ata Muhammad. There were repeated outbreaks of factional fighting between soldiers loyal to their two regional leaders. Supported by the UN, Karzai attempted to disarm private militias. Under his deal the armed fighters loyal to Dostum and Ata Muhammad were merged under a single neutral commander appointed by Karzai. The deal was an optimistic attempt to end this continued infighting as Karzai's government began a major disarmament plan. This programme aimed to disarm up to 100,000 private militiamen across the country, either helping them to return to civilian life or integrating them into a new national army.

Karzai launched a campaign against Fahim, his Minister of Defence, Ismail Khan of Herat, and Gul Agha of Kandahar, while he appointed Ata Muhammad governor of the province of Balkh; Hazrat Ali of Jalalabad was named the chief of police in Nangarhar province, and Khan Muhammad was appointed to the same position in Kandahar. In a bold stroke he stripped Ismail Khan of his military command in Herat, but temporized, and retained him as its governor. By another decree Karzai removed Gul Agha as governor of Kandahar, and appointed him the Minister of Urban Affairs in Kabul. He then shook up the Ministry of Defence, which Fahim was using as his fiefdom, and removed twenty-two senior Tajik officers. In their place he appointed officers who represented the ethnic mix of the population. Finally in July 2004 Karzai dropped Fahim from the position of vice president on his presidential ticket. In September 2004 he dismissed Ismail Khan from his post as governor of Herat, and appointed him to the harmless position of Minister of Mines and Industry in Kabul.[7]

Did this reshuffling and reappointing of the warlords mean that Karzai created a centralized government in Afghanistan? This was far from the reality. Karzai was 'often viewed as a token Pashtun and front man for the Panjsheri [Northern Alliance] and American interests.'[8] Although this image changed, the fact that the 15,000 American, Coalition and NATO troops based in Afghanistan supported the Karzai government also ensured that the warlords act on their best behaviour. Moreover the warlords were US allies when the Taliban were routed, and benefited economically from their alliance with the US. They could not challenge the US with impunity. Karzai succeeded in reducing the stigma of being a front for the Northern Alliance, but his dependence upon the US for political survival remained visible.

III

National reconstruction remained a daunting task, complicated even further by insufficient security to fend off the surviving Taliban forces and the emerging Gulbaddin Hikmatyar forces.

Over twenty-five years of conflict, Afghanistan experienced Soviet occupation, jihadi insurgency, civil war, Taliban rule and Operation Enduring Freedom from the US, which left the country a wasteland. When I visited Afghanistan in 2000, the country's infrastructure was in ruins. Roads, electrical power plants, hospitals, schools, irrigation, and telecommunication systems were destroyed. The capital Kabul was in shambles; nearly 80 per cent of all public buildings were totally or partially damaged. Moreover Afghanistan's administrative structure had collapsed. The upper and middle classes, which produced professionals of all kinds, had migrated to Pakistan, the US and to some European states.

Truly the Karzai government started from scratch, like Pakistan's federal government in 1947. Establishing and coordinating a mechanism for development was a formidable enterprise. The international aid machinery began to function, and slowly established areas of donor coordination. The humanitarian needs called for immediate attention, especially when Afghan refugees began to pour in from Pakistan and Iran. Pakistan was home to the single largest refugee population anywhere in the world for more than twenty-five years. The UN-conducted census in 2005 revealed that 1,861,412 Afghan refugees lived in NWFP; 783,545 in Balochistan; 136,780 in Sindh; 207,754 in Punjab; 44,637 in Islamabad; and 13,097 in

Azad Kashmir.[9] By April 2002 when the UN began to assist repatriation, more than 300,000 Afghans left Pakistan and migrated home. UN refugee officials estimated that as many as 1.2 million could return in 2002 from Pakistan and Iran, and in three years or longer most of the 5-6 million Afghan refugees would come home. Some will never return, having settled into relatively prosperous lives, particularly in Peshawar, Islamabad Lahore Karachi and Iranian cities where some of them have established successful businesses. Others also married into Pakistani and Iranian families.

Major industrial nations pledged $45 billion in development aid for Afghanistan. However, the UN member states have been very slow to respond to an appeal for $271 million for the repatriation programme. The former Dutch Prime Minister, Ruud Lubbers, who directed the refugee agency, made an interesting assessment about the refugees' political orientation. He said that their successful rehabilitation would 'improve the chances that Afghanistan would resist a slide back into political extremism.'[10] This assessment ignored the fact that many of refugee camps in Pakistan served as incubators for conservative or anti-western Islam. Also many of the refugee children were educated in the madrasas of NWFP, who produced Taliban soldiers and leaders.

The UN Commissioner for Refugees (UNHCR) stated in June 2005 that the current rate of repatriation was similar to that of 2003, when 104,092 Afghans had gone home by the end of May, but behind the pace in 2004 when 141,660 returned home during the same period. The total number of refugees repatriated was 343,074 in 2003 and 383,598 in 2004. The pace of repatriation was likely to pick up in the summer of 2005 because the Pakistani government announced that Afghan refugee camps in North Waziristan would close by the end of June. Other Afghan refugee camps in the Tribal Areas would be closed also, where more than 70,000 refugees lived.[11]

The rehabilitation of millions of refugees was a formidable task; however, in 2002-3 the Northern Alliance added more to the woes of the Karzai government. The years of hyperinflation rendered Afghanistan's currency worthless. In 2000 an Afghani was worth no more than 1/400 of a cent. After the overthrow of the Taliban, the Afghan Central Bank made an appearance. It spent more than 1$ million of its meagre reserves to buy Afghanis to stem the currency's collapse. At this stage the members of the Northern Alliance, who did most of the fighting in collaboration with the US, unloaded huge amounts of Afghanis that they had printed for themselves during the period of internal conflict. The northern warlords became wealthy as they cashed in their wads of Afghanis for dollars, and the Afghani took a further plunge and became worthless. Between 1992 and 1996 a Russian-Swiss company, Appleline Ltd., served as the money printer for the government of Burhan-ud-Din Rabbani, who presided over Afghanistan as it convulsed in civil war. Then the Taliban entered Kabul in September 1996 and Rabbani fled to the north. Even though he was a fugitive and without a capital, he insisted that he was still the president, and that his fighters, known as the Northern Alliance were the country's real government.

Through the five years of Taliban rule, the Northern Alliance retained control of the country's money. While the Taliban could persuade no one to print money for their government, the Northern Alliance printed trillions of notes, financing their war efforts against the Taliban, and rendering the currency virtually worthless.

According to one account, Appleline Ltd. printed 7 trillion Afghanis for the Northern Alliance, or approximately $175 million at the currency exchange rate from 1996-2001. In the process the value of the Afghani evaporated. A decade before, one dollar bought about 1,200 Afghanis. In May 2002 it bought about 37,000. Appleline Ltd. printed $8 million worth of Afghanis for the Northern Alliance leaders early in December 2001. Hamid Karzai, the interim leader, took power on December 22. Rabbani confirmed this transaction in a press interview, but claimed not to know exactly where the money might have gone.

The scandal over the printing of the Afghanis was only one of the many problems that faced the Karzai government. During Afghanistan's civil war in the 1990s, many warlords ordered up their own currencies, all of them from foreign countries. Three of them, in addition to the main currency and Pakistani rupee notes, circulated widely. Their values differed greatly, and the routine exchange of money was often a source of confusion, and sometimes violent argument.

The only solution was to tear them all up and start all over again. That is exactly what the Karzai government did with the full backing of the US. In October 2002, 27 billion newly printed Afghanis were introduced into the economy. They took out of circulation about 15 trillion old ones.

IV

After the swift collapse of the Taliban the US Department of Defence came to believe in a new form of warfare: massive bombing guided by small cadres of Special Operations troops on the ground, and the use of proxy forces (like the Northern Alliance) to do the actual fighting. This strategy reduced the possibility of American casualties to the absolute minimum. The ultimate weapon was the Predator drone, an unmanned spy plane fitted with a Hellfire missile that could be fired by remote control, eliminating any chance of harm befalling an American, because there was nobody onboard. However, this neat and efficient warfare failed to capture or kill Osama bin Laden, Mulla Umar, and the Taliban and Al Qaeda leadership. American policy since the Taliban's overthrow was to offer strong political and economic support to the Karzai government, which took office in late December 2001 with a mandate to guide Afghanistan through the first six months of a 30 month transition to elections. The US also played a role in establishing the British-led 17-nation multinational force that helped provide security for the Karzai government in Kabul but 4,000 US ground troops remained apart from that effort, focused on the pursuit of the Taliban and Al Qaeda.

In southern Afghanistan the US forces initiated in early 2002 the practice of dropping leaflets aimed at encouraging Al Qaeda and Taliban fighters to surrender.[12] The time-consuming surrender negotiations involving two or more anti-Taliban groups, enabled the leaders to escape or buy their way to freedom. Sometimes the protracted negotiations involved the Taliban with their own tribesmen, who had to protect a fellow tribesman and let him 'escape' to freedom. In some instances the Taliban and Al Qaeda leaders used 'their dollars, rupees [Pakistani], cars and weapons' to fund their way to freedom. In Washington, Donald Rumsfeld, Secretary of Defence, acknowledged that American military officials had little control over the surrender negotiations. But he added that anti-Taliban leaders had given assurances that they would not allow the Al Qaeda or Taliban leaders to escape.[13]

No wonder that two years after their defeat the Taliban re-emerged. Their security threat to the Karzai government was initially concentrated along Afghanistan's south-eastern border with Pakistan. They staged attacks, and attempted to regain political influence in Pashtun areas. Similarly, Al Qaeda's training camps in Afghanistan were destroyed, and a substantial proportion of its cadre were eliminated, but it regained the capacity to conduct military operations. The US maintained that Al Qaeda operatives staged cross-border raids on American bases from sanctuaries in Pakistan's tribal areas throughout 2004-05. A new menacing force of the renegade militia commander and former prime minister-designate Gulbuddin Hikmayar operated in the northern border provinces of Kunar and Nuristan, where he declared his own jihad against the US.[14]

In July 2005 Afghanistan's defence minister offered his assessment of the security situation in his country: 'Taliban members have joined forces with insurgents loyal to other anti-American commanders of Al Qaeda, and have redoubled their efforts in recent months to attack Americans and government forces in Afghanistan.'[15] In the first week of July American and Afghan forces faced some of the worst violence they had encountered in three and a half years of conflict in Afghanistan. The issue of the US military presence emerged at the forefront of public debate. It is difficult indeed to manage any 'honest' election in peacetime; it becomes doubly difficult under the violent conditions which prevailed in southern Afghanistan. However, elections would deliver a parliament divided on ethnic lines with a strong element of jihadi leaders and Islamists.

Aware of this handicap, Karzai called a national consultation conference of 1,000 'representatives' from the provinces, which met in Kabul on 8 May 2005. He won broad support (no votes) for the continued presence of foreign troops, especially American, after the parliamentary elections, which were scheduled to be held on 18 September 2005. There was no Status of Forces agreement to regulate the presence of 17,000 American troops in Afghanistan. At the UN-sponsored conference in Bonn in 2001 the timetable covered the presence of international bodies and American troops until the elections. Karzai wanted a long-term strategic partnership with the US that extended beyond the presence of American military bases in Afghanistan to ensure a continued US commitment to Afghanistan's security and economic development.

Despite the fact that the Kabul conference brought together hand-picked 'representatives', serious reservations and disagreements over Karzai's stated position were expressed by some of them. They recognized that Afghanistan would need foreign troops and large-scale international aid for some time. But they also told him frankly that 1) he should delay any decision on the long-term presence of foreign troops or permanent bases in Afghanistan until a parliament was elected, that this general conference was not a meeting where they could decide these issues, and that they should wait for the parliament. The delegates also called for an end to unilateral American combat operations, saying that the US should cooperate in all operations with the Afghan government and its forces. Lastly the delegates endorsed an American plan to bring Afghan detainees from Guantanamo Bay, Cuba to prisons in Afghanistan.[16]

In 2005 the US announced its plan to reduce the overall number of American troops in Afghanistan from 19,000 to about 16,500. Despite this planned reduction the US still retained the largest number of foreign soldiers in Afghanistan, and continued to have control of its eastern sector along the mountainous border with Pakistan. Moreover, it had been successfully training Afghan battalions and increased the number of battalions from eighteen to forty in 2004. Twenty-four of these were considered combat units. Confidence grew in the Afghan Army to take on the Taliban, who typically fought in groups of fifteen to twenty men, but could rally as many as sixty. The US military commanders believed that 'the Taliban still receive training and assistance from operatives of Al Qaeda in Pakistan.'[17] The reduction in American troops was compensated by the proposed deployment of NATO troops by March 2006. Some American allies, including Germany and France, had opposed expanding NATO's role to include counter-insurgency missions. But the Canadians seemed to be agreeable in playing this role. Clearly, they believed that 'this is not a peacekeeping mission', and that 'an active insurgency is underway in Afghanistan, especially in the east.'[18]

V

GOOD NEIGHBOURLY 'WAR' WITH PAKISTAN

After the Taliban's forceful resurgence in 2005, the Karzai government started to blame Pakistan for its security problems. In June President Karzai openly accused Pakistan of interfering in Afghanistan's internal affairs. Before a session of the ulema's *shura* in Kabul he castigated Pakistan for 'backing anti-government elements in his country'. He added, that 'Pakistan had threatened the Taliban that members of their families would be handed over to the US if they did not fight against Afghanistan.'[19] Simultaneously, the US military announced that increasing numbers of foreign militants were entering Afghanistan to help the Taliban insurgents. In Washington, the State Department's spokesman stated that the Afghan police had informed the US authorities that they had foiled an assassination attempt on US Ambassador Khalilzad's life, and had detained a number of individuals who were plotting to assassinate him. Yet the State Department refused to verify the facts as reported by the Afghans.[20] The Afghanistan-born US Ambassador Khalilzad jumped into this fray by publicly speculating that there was a good chance that the fugitive leader of the ousted Taliban regime, Mulla Mohammad Umar, was hiding in Pakistan. In an interview to an Afghan television station Khalilzad stated that a Pakistani television station had interviewed a senior Taliban commander, Mulla Akhtar Usmani. If a television station could get in touch with senior Taliban leaders, then why was it that 'the intelligence service of the country, which has nuclear bombs and a lot of security and military forces could not find them.' Then he repeated a call for Pakistan to do more to track down Taliban leaders. Pakistan described his statement as 'irresponsible'.[21]

The war of words between the allies erupted on the Waziristan front. In April 2005 the commander of the US forces in Afghanistan, Lieutenant General David Barno, stated that the Taliban and Al Qaeda terrorists were infiltrating into Afghanistan through Pakistan. Barno made his statement during a meeting of the Tripartite Commission of the US, Afghanistan and Pakistan held in Islamabad on 18 April. However, on 27 April, Barno, in an interview repeated his accusations: 'The Americans have been training Pakistanis in night flying and airborne assault tactics to combat foreign and local fighters in the tribal areas of Pakistan.'[22] A Pakistani military spokesman contradicted Barno's statement, saying that 'Barno had probably been referring to joint military exercises between the two countries'. Barno also made some predictions which proved to be fairly accurate. He said: 'The

Taliban and Al Qaeda can launch their big offensive from North Waziristan in nine months.' However, the Pakistani army started operations in South Waziristan in January 2003. Actually the army was called upon to launch its operations after Pakistan was alerted by the US to the presence of the Taliban and Al Qaeda elements in Waziristan.

Pakistan's army announced in January 2005 that out of the 6,000 foreign terrorists, 600 had already been captured and 150 killed. The corps commander of the army admitted that during the operations 200 Pakistani army personnel had been killed by the militants. In view of the heavy losses the military campaign was suspended, and attempts were made to seek peace pacts with the local tribes. In 2004 the first accord was signed at Shakai with Waziri fighter, Nek Muhammad. He reneged and was killed by an American guided laser missile. In February 2005 the second agreement was signed at Sararogha with Baitullah Mahsud, the chieftain of the Mahsud tribe. The deal was mediated by Maulana Fazlur Rehman, leader of the opposition in the National Assembly and a major figure in the Jamiat ulama-i Islam of Pakistan.

The two peace accords made no mention of the Pakistan Army's previous condition that the tribal militants must produce foreigners hiding in Waziristan, and ensure their registration. The army's insistence on this condition had led to the collapse of the Shakai agreement in April 2004 signed between the Peshawar Corps Commander, and Nek Muhammad's militant group. The failure to produce the foreign militants hiding in the area had triggered a new round of fighting that led up to Nek's death on 19 June 2004.[23]

In the spring of 2005 the Taliban's resurgence became very aggressive, and so was the Al Qaeda movement. The Karzai government believed that the Taliban fighters had joined forces with insurgents loyal to other anti-American commanders and with members of Al Qaeda. Most of these fighters were, according to Kabul, Pakistanis, Arabs, and from the Central Asian republics. The insurgents appeared to have money, better weapons, and more advanced technology in 2005. They possessed remote-control bombs, high explosives and even shoulder-held anti-aircraft missiles, one of which was used against the Chinook helicopter that crashed on 28 June. The MH-47 helicopter was carrying fifteen to twenty people, including a team of Navy Seal commandos. This year (2005) 38 members of the American military died in Afghanistan, in 2004, 52 American soldiers died.

Also, anti-American protests erupted as students in Kabul demonstrated against, what they perceived to be permanent US military bases in Afghanistan. However, the general consensus among US observers was that the prevailing instability and low-intensity conflict did not add up to a national uprising. This consensus also stated that the Taliban movement remained restricted to a narrow core of believers, and that a larger number were motivated by money not ideology.[24] This may very well prove to be wishful thinking. However, as a precaution the US announced on 10 July 2005 that it had sent 700-800 additional troops to Afghanistan. Surprisingly, at this point in time a vast and difficult mountainous country like Afghanistan was 'controlled' by 17,600 American troops and 2,100 from US allied countries.[25]

About the hideout of Mulla Umar, the Taliban leader, an unpleasant war of words raged between Pakistan and the Afghan and American leaders. US Ambassador Khalilzad alleged that 'he was in Pakistan.' Pakistan called the allegations 'baseless', and filed a protest against the ambassador 'through diplomatic channels.' Karzai moved this war of words to a higher level in a speech to a *shura* of *ulema* in Kabul, he stating: 'Pakistan was backing the anti-government elements in Afghanistan'.[26] US military commanders had made specific accusations against Pakistan one month before Karzai's speech. Colonel Gary Cheek, the commander of 4,000 US troops in eastern Afghanistan provinces bordering mainly on Pakistan, stated: 'My base, where I live, is in Khost province, and I will say absolutely, there are insurgents coming across the border from Pakistan attacking Khost, then returning back into Pakistan [the tribal areas].'[27]

Since early spring 2005 the frequency of the Taliban incursions, even into Kabul, had become unsettling for the Karzai government. As a wise strategy it had announced amnesty for most of the Taliban, and won over some of the former Taliban-supporting ulema and fighters. The highest level Taliban commander to accept the Karzai government's amnesty of May 2005 was Abdul Waheed Baghrani, the Rais-da-Baghran (Chief of Baghran), the 100-mile long mountainous valley of northern Helmand. He had fought the Soviet occupation for ten years and joined the Taliban in the early days of the movement. He justified the switching of his loyalty to the Karzai government in religious terms: 'We have an Islamic country and sharia law, and we should accept the rule of the government.' Also, he stated that Osama bin Laden and Mulla Umar had taken refuge in Pakistan. He could not protect them, because Mulla Umar would never have trusted his life to a tribe other than his own. Osama was on the run, but he would be caught one day 'because he was not among his own people, and as a result, risked betrayal.'[28]

As against Baghrani' support, Karzai suffered some losses. An eminent cleric, Maulavi Abdullah Fayaz, was assassinated in Kandahar a week after organizing a grand council of 500 ulema that declared that the Taliban leader, Mulla Umar, had been divested of his title, Amir al-Momineen (Commander of the Faithful), and it was unlawful and against the sharia to follow his orders to fight and kill.[29] However, a week later a suicide bomber detonated a powerful bomb during a mourning ceremony in a mosque in Kandahar, killing nineteen people; among them was the Kabul police chief, General Akram Khakrezwal.

US-sponsored development activity also came under the Taliban's attack. A deadly attack on the US contractor Chemonics, in Helmand province killed five people, forcing the company to suspend work on several projects in southern Afghanistan that were providing employment for 14,000 workers. The US military authorities predicted that in addition to attacks on American and

Afghan troops, the Taliban and Al Qaeda militants would attempt to carry out attacks in cities, especially in Kabul, to demonstrate their operational capability.

Surprisingly, the Taliban issued a warning to the Afghan ulema in Pakistan. In Naushera (near Peshawar) *shabnamas* (leaflets or night letters) were distributed in the Afghan refugee camp at Jallozai. During the war against the Soviet Union, the camp was also used by Arab fighters. The leaflets warned the Afghan ulema that they would be killed if they served or supported the Karzai government. The Taliban's message argued that the ulema supporting the Karzai government were more dangerous than the foreign troops occupying Afghanistan. Ulema who collaborate misled the Afghan people and provided justification to Afghans to serve and support the regime in Kabul.[30] A few days later the head of the Religious Council of Helmand province was killed as he left a mosque after morning prayers. Another religious leader allied to the Karzai government, Agha Jan, and his wife were killed in the south-eastern province of Paktika.[31]

Gulbuddin Hekmatyar, former prime minister-designate in the early 1990s, rejected the offer of amnesty by Afghanistan's National Reconciliation Commission, which was headed by Sebghatullah Majadeddi. In May 2005 he issued a statement saying that Afghans considered 'the Karzai regime as a creation of the United States, and would neither accept it nor lend credibility to institutions created by it'. He blamed the US's presence in Afghanistan as the catalytic dynamic of instability, and urged the Afghan people to stop supporting the US and British forces.[32]

In 2005-6 relations between Pakistan and Afghanistan soured, and if this trend continued the relations between the two neighbours would revert to the pre-1978 period. This slide downward would hurt the vital interests of both countries. Pakistan tended to believe that the Karzai government was still dominated by the Northern Alliance of the Tajiks and Uzbeks. As a result the Afghan government continued to repeat 'baseless' accusations against Pakistan. Karzai made more provocative statements than his ministers. In a speech before a youth conference in Kabul on 20 June 2005, he stated that 'after the defeat of the Soviet forces, a more dangerous occupation came from another neighbour',[33] clearly implying Paksitan.

Despite the strained relations, Karzai sent a ten-member delegation, headed by Transportation Minister Inayatullah Qasmi, to Pakistan to receive gifts from the fraternal neighbour. Pakistan handed him the last batch of 23 buses out of the promised gift of 100, in addition to 200 trucks and 45 ambulances. Pakistan had committed $100 million in aid for the reconstruction of Afghanistan, including the reconstruction of the Torkham-Jalalabad road to Kabul. To expand relations between the two countries, Afghanistan proposed to start bus service, from Kandahar to Quetta, and Jalalabad to Peshawar.[34] Afghanistan also proposed the construction of a railroad from Chaman in Balochistan to Spin Baldak in Afghanistan. Pakistan referred these proposals to the Joint Economic Commission for its approval. However, two-way trade amounted to $1 billion.

Repeatedly, Pakistan assured Afghanistan of its policy of non-interference in Afghanistan's internal affairs. To fight the remnants of the Taliban and Al Qaeda, it deployed 70,000 troops on the western borders of Afghanistan. In several military operations, especially in the tribal areas, Pakistan lost 250 soldiers; moreover, 700 Al Qaeda suspects were arrested in joint operations with the US. Finally President Musharraf called upon President Karzai to end this campaign of accusations. The Karzai government in Kabul was beleaguered; as long as insurgents are successful in finding sanctuaries in the tribal areas, Karzai would suspect Pakistan's motives. The US Department of State acknowledged in a bulletin of 28 February 2005 'increased Taliban, Al Qaeda and other anti-government group's activity, particularly in the south and southeast.'[35]

However, it may be noted that despite the lack of security in the country the Karzai government had made significant achievements by 2005. The government made progress in asserting its authority, and Karzai dismissed and appointed new governors to many of the thirty-four provinces. The Supreme Court started to function, although recognition of the rule of law outside of Kabul was very limited. The judiciary was accused of corruption, and being subject to political pressure. The police remained ineffectual. NATO retained control in Kabul, and its UN Security Council mandate was extended to 13 October 2005. The economic growth rate was estimated at 7.5 per cent for 2004-05. However, Afghanistan remained heavily dependent, as in the past, on foreign assistance. About 50 per cent of its operating budget (2004) came from foreign donors. The opium cultivation increased by two-thirds and spread to thirty-two provinces. In fact narcotics became the main factor of economic growth, involving 10 per cent of the 28.5 million population. This development was a serious international problem, especially for Pakistan and the US.

PAKISTAN: 'ENLIGHTENED AUTHORITARIANISM' AND FOREIGN POLICY DYNAMICS

I

US policy toward General Pervez Musharraf changed radically, the way it had changed for General Ziaul Haq after the Soviet invasion of Afghanistan in 1979. For both military rulers of Pakistan, Afghanistan came to their rescue just in time. Bush received Musharraf in the White House on 13 February 2002 and called him 'a leader of great courage and vision'. Musharraf in return pledged to crack down on terrorism practised against India, and to root out Al Qaeda from Afghanistan.[36] He was invited to visit the White House again in September 2004. Bush praised him at every opportunity as a close ally, and cited Pakistan's turnabout as one of the biggest foreign policy achievements of his presidency. On the second visit, Bush did not press Musharraf to give up control of Pakistan's powerful army. He casually mentioned to him that 'it was important to stay on the road' to democratic reform. Musharraf understood what that meant.

However, a week before his visit to Washington, Musharraf's Minister of Information had announced approvingly that he would renege on a public commitment to take off his military uniform and serve as Pakistan's civilian president. In exchange for the enactment of constitutional reforms which gave him sweeping power, Musharraf had promised to resign as army chief by the end of 2004. On 4 September the provincial legislative assembly of Punjab, the largest in population of the four provinces, passed a resolution urging him to stay as the army chief, while NWFP's assembly asked him to retain only one job. The opponents of military rule filed a case against Musharraf in the Supreme Court of Pakistan. Always obedient and accommodating, the Supreme Court dismissed the petitions in April 2005 challenging Musharraf's right to be both army chief and president. It also rejected challenges to the president's power to dismiss parliament, and the prime minister.[37]

Not known for modesty, Musharraf stated in a Washington press interview that giving up military rule might end the 'renaissance' based on the gradually expanding democracy Pakistan enjoyed under his leadership. In a meeting with this author, General Zia had described his rule as destined to usher in as 'Islamic renaissance', which he thought was more democratic than Z. A. Bhutto's 'democracy'. Another important issue, Pakistan's nuclear proliferation, was not overly discussed in the Bush-Musharraf meeting of 22 September 2004. Bush made no effort to persuade Musharraf to let American intelligence officials interview Abdul Qadeer Khan, the former leading scientist of Pakistan's nuclear programme. Actually, Musharraf had quite adroitly agreed to pass on to the US all the details Pakistan gleaned from Dr Khan about the 'secret' nuclear network that he had built and that supplied nuclear technology to Libya, Iran, and North Korea.

Were Dr Khan's nuclear transactions really conducted secretly, and was Pakistan's military totally unaware of them? The Bush

Administration was sceptical. It was pointed out that Pakistan's military aircrafts were used to make some of the shipments to North Korea. The administration decided that pursuing Al Qaeda was a higher priority than details about nuclear proliferation. To achieve this grand objective, the Bush government came to believe that General Musharraf needed 'maximum latitude' to battle Al Qaeda. The fact that twice unsuccessful attempts were made in 2003 to assassinate him, an allowance was made to let him retain the military control.

After Musharraf's two visits to the US, he no longer worried about democracy in Pakistan; his position within Pakistan's establishment and the general public was very substantially strengthened. Simultaneously, the US-Pakistan relationship was strengthened. In June 2004, President Bush officially designated Pakistan a major non-NATO ally of the US. The notion of major non-NATO ally states first surfaced in 1989 with the addition of Section 2350a ('cooperative agreements with allies') to Title 10 of the US code. For several years this status was limited to Israel, Egypt, Australia, Japan, and South Korea. In January 1998, President Bill Clinton designated Argentina as the first Latin American major non-NATO ally. These non-NATO allies do not enjoy the same mutual defence and security guarantee given to members of NATO. However, the status does carry some advantages in the foreign assistance process. Major non-NATO allies are eligible for: priority delivery of excess defence articles; stockpiling of US defence articles; purchase of depleted uranium anti-tank rounds; participation in cooperative research and development programmes.

A big benefit available to some states which had had the status from 31 March 1995 would not be extended to Pakistan. This benefit allows participation in the defence export loan guarantee programme, which backs up private loans for commercial defence exports.[38] Probably as compensation, the State Department pointed out to Pakistan that major non-NATO allies are exempt from suspension of military assistance under the American Services Member's Protection Act.[39] How long and under what conditions this exemption would be maintained was not explained.

To further strengthen relations with Pakistan's military, the US decided to sell nearly two dozen highly prized F-16 fighter jets, which could be used in ground or air attack, and had a maximum range of more than 2,000 miles. The fighters to be sold, costing more than $18.8 million each, would be newer models off the production line than the old variant purchased by Pakistan in the 1980s. In 1990 Pakistan had ordered more, but delivery was blocked when Congress passed legislation to punish Pakistan for its programme to develop nuclear weapons.

The sale of F-16 fighter jets and award of non-NATO ally status to Pakistan fitted into the broad US architectural design of strategic relationships across South Asia. This grand design envisaged drawing both India and Pakistan into the US orbit, and encouraging a dialogue between the South Asian neighbours for a rapprochement, hoping that both countries would work with each other to resolve their dispute over Kashmir peacefully. To balance this arms sale to Pakistan, the US decided to join India in a larger strategic partnership that would emphasize India's role as a 'world power'. This new approach to relations with India crystallized when the Prime Minister of India, Manmohan Singh, visited Washington on 18-21 July 2005.

II

The US and India agreed on four major issues: 1) the sanctity of the LoC in Kashmir must be maintained; 2) the US would encourage India and Pakistan to find a solution for the Kashmir problem; 3) to work toward 'common security objectives', in Bush's words: 'charting new steps in defence relationships through the recently-signed new framework that will help our two nations work toward common security objectives'.[40] A defence pact signed in June 2005 for ten years envisaged joint weapons production and multinational peacekeeping operations;

and 4) the US recognized India as a nuclear weapons state for all practical purposes, but stopped short of declaring it as one.

It is not clear how the US Congress and major nuclear armed nations—Britain, France, China and Russia—go along with this change of status for India. China had offered to sell additional reactors to Pakistan. However, the Bush Administration argued that it was logical for the world to recognize the reality of India's nuclear weapon status, reinforced by its first bomb explosion in 1974, and again in 1998, a time of heightened tensions with Pakistan. Since then India-Pakistan tensions have eased, and the US has taken a new approach to the Nuclear Non-proliferation Treaty, declaring it outdated and in need of re-drafting. How Iran, Egypt, North Korea, Japan, Taiwan, and Brazil would react to it, remains to be observed.

The US agreement to sell nuclear technology to India obliged India to make important non-proliferation commitments, including placing its entire civilian nuclear programme under international monitoring. India didn't, however, commit to putting its weapons under monitoring, nor has it agreed to stop producing plutonium for nuclear weapons. Bush in fact unilaterally shredded the Nuclear Non-Proliferation Treaty to pieces to favour India. Why? The Pentagon has long argued for strengthening India as a counterweight to China. The June 2005 agreements with India are a vital link in the planned design. The US would want Pakistan to fit into the planned architecture.

III

However, India and China have minimized the prospects of a conflict between them, while India also seemed to be determined not to be a US 'poodle'. Yet, at the same time Indian leaders believed that there was 'simply no alternative to building a close alliance with the United States'.[41] Despite this 'alliance,' India's relations with China have improved very substantially, raising them to the status of a 'strategic and cooperative partnership'.

To settle their border disputes India and China agreed in April 2005 on a set of 'guiding principles'. The three- tier agreement included: 1) the principles; 2) a framework for the settlement; and 3) the actual delineation and demarcation of the border. Very shrewdly the Chinese Prime Minister Wen Jiabo linked 'the settlement on the boundary issue with the overall trajectory of bilateral ties between India and China.'[42] Shorn of its diplomatic veneer, the statement was a warning or a word of caution to India that it had better watch out carefully Washington's warm embrace, which would project India as a counterweight to China. China also presented an olive branch to India.

The visiting Chinese Prime Minister Wen Jiabo personally handed over to the Indian Minister of Foreign Affairs Shyam Saran an official Chinese map of the border showing the tiny state of Sikkim as part of India. China had corrected its official Foreign Ministry website and yearbook. The new map officially presented to India eliminated any doubts that India might have had about China's position on Sikkim. China assured India that it was 'happy' to see India become a permanent member of the UN Security Council. It was satisfied that India had facilitated China's association with the South Asian Association for Regional Cooperation (SAARC). China had reciprocated by letting India have an observer status in the Shanghai Cooperation Organization (SCO).[43]

A total of eleven agreements were signed in April 2005, and a report of the Joint Study Group on Trade and Economics was announced. China was poised to become India's largest trade partner within three years, raising the two-way trade from $13.6 billion in 2004-5 to $20 billion in 2008, and $30 billion in 2010. They also agreed to cooperate in the field of energy security and conservation, including the survey and exploration of petroleum and natural gas resources in other countries. They also committed themselves to creating an 'atmosphere of mutual understanding, trust and cooperation in Asia, and the world at large.'

These two great powers of Asia entered upon a new era of peaceful coexistence in April 2005, which they had promised each other at the Bandung Conference in 1955. How India would handle her new strategic partnership with the United States, and conduct her relations with the regional powers, especially Iran, Central Asia, and the Arab states remains to be observed.

IV

Relations between India and Iran have become problematic, especially over the construction of a 2,775 km proposed gas pipeline from Iran to Pakistan to India. The US officially cautioned India in March 2005 against the gas pipeline project with Iran. Actually in February, the Indian cabinet had authorized the Petroleum and Natural Gas Minister to start formal negotiations for this project. In July, after signing far-reaching agreements with the US over the sale of nuclear technology to India, the Indian Prime Minister Manmohan Singh made a statement to *The Washington Post* (21 July 2005) about the pipeline: 'But I am realistic enough to realize that there are many risks, because considering all the uncertainties of the situation there in Iran, I don't know if any international consortium of bankers would probably underwrite this.'[44]

Some Indian observers rightly believed that Singh had deliberately sabotaged the pipeline project as the Bush Administration extracted 'a very heavy price' from Singh for recognizing India as a state with advanced nuclear technology. His statement indicated a major shift in the Indian position. Before his departure for the US he had publicly stated that a discussion on the pipeline belonged to India, Iran, and Pakistan alone, and 'outside parties' had no role in it. India is desperately in need of energy and so is Pakistan. If India were to walk away from the project it would indeed leave an inescapable impression that Singh yielded to American pressures.

Despite the ups and downs in India-Pakistan relations, there has developed an upbeat mood for future prospects. Encouraged by the US, both sides have taken steps to make the peace process 'irreversible'. To reach that plateau they have yet to take several steps to resolve their basic conflict over Kashmir. Musharraf had visited India in April 2005 and agreed to several new arrangements in relations with India. First on Kashmir, India maintained its traditional position that there could be no change in boundaries, while Pakistan stated just as emphatically that the LoC in Kashmir was unacceptable as a border. This was a classic statement of the territorial status quo. The new approach was adopted to 'make the boundaries irrelevant'.

How was this miracle of miracles to be achieved? Let the interaction between people across the LoC accelerate, eliminate the tensions, increase the two-way trade, and allow the people's voice for peace and reconciliation to be finally decisive. This idealistic approach assumed the following concrete steps, agree to: 1) open trade across the LoC by allowing trucks between Srinagar and Muzaffarabad; 2) open the trans-LoC Punch-Rawalpindi route (the old Mughal road); 3) take steps to facilitate the meeting of divided families along the LoC; 4) re-open the consulates in Karachi and Mumbai by the end of 2005; and 5) re-establish the Khokhrapar-Munabao route by 1 January 2006. The Indian Prime Minister Manmohan Singh accepted Musharraf's invitation to Pakistan.

On the debit side, four major problems found not even a tentative solution: 1) Sir Creek; 2) the Siachen Glacier; 3) the Baghliar Dam issue; and 4) the Neelum River (Kishanganga) Dam. The Baghliar Dam issue was raised by Pakistan in 1992, but got nowhere through normal diplomatic negotiations. Finally Pakistan filed petition with the World Bank; its president had helped the two states to conclude the Indus Waters Treaty in September 1960. This treaty had divided the six rivers of the Indus Valley: the three eastern ones (Ravi, Beas, and Sutlej) were permanently allotted to India, and the three western (Indus, Jhelum and Chenab), with the provision of some uses by India in the upper reaches of the Indus Valley, were reserved for the exclusive use of Pakistan. Under the treaty India can use the water of the Chenab River to generate hydroelectricity, but not for irrigation. In violation of this treaty, the Baghliar Dam built by India on the Chenab would siphon off 7,000 cusecs (cubic feet per second) of water from the river, reducing water flows to Pakistan by a corresponding amount. India had also proposed to build a hydroelectric dam on the Neelum River (the Kishanganga), which flows along the LoC, and debouches into the Jhelum River. Pakistan had charged that both dams violate the Indus Waters Treaty.

Manmohan Singh assured a group of visiting Pakistani editors that the design of the controversial Baghliar hydroelectric dam in Kashmir could be changed, if it was found to be violating the Indus Waters Treaty of 1960. However, the World Bank has appointed a Swiss professor, who is a specialist in hydroelectric engineering, to determine the possible violation of the treaty. He delivered his judgment in February 2007, in which he partially upheld some of Pakistan's objections. But did not find fault with the Indian position

In light of these disputes, one wonders if the peace process between India and Pakistan has truly become irreversible.

NOTES

1. Chris Johnson and Jolyon Leslie, *Afghanistan: The Mirage of Peace* (London: Zed Books, 2004), p. 168.
2. For a more detailed picture of the legislature see, 'Afghanistan's New Parliament', *Agence France Presse*, English dispatches, 19, 20 December 2005.
3. Louis Dupree, *Afghanistan* (Princeton: Princeton University Press, 1980), p. 464.
4. For an excellent study of Ismail Khan, see Gulshan Dietl, 'War, Peace and the Warlords: The Case of Ismail Khan in Herat', *Journal of South Asian and Middle Eastern Studies*, Vol. 28, No. 3 (2005), pp. 51-71.
5. Dietl, 'War, Peace and the Warlords', p. 63.
6. Fareed Zakaria, 'The Stakes in Afghanistan,' *Washington Post*, 3 August 2004.
7. Human Rights Watch, *Country Summary* (New York: January 2005), p. 2; Dietl, 'War, Peace and the Warlords', pp. 64-66.
8. Frank G. Wisner II, Nicholas Platt, Marshall M. Bouton, Dennis Kux and Mahnaz Ispahani, *Afghanistan: Are We Losing the Peace?* (New York, NY: Council on Foreign Relations, 2003), p. 12.

9. Muralidhar Reddy, 'Pakistan's Afghan Problem', *The Hindu*, 13 May 2005.

10. John F. Burns, 'Ignoring Risk, Afghan Refugees Rush Home', *The New York Times*, 29 April 2002.

11. Naveed Ahmad, 'Repatriating 400,000 Afghans This Year: UNHCR', *The News*, 2 June 2005.

12. Norimitsu Onishi and James Dao, 'Taliban Leaders May be Escaping', *The New York Times*, 3 January 2002.

13. Ibid.

14. *Special Report: Unfinished Business in Afghanistan*, (Washington DC: US Institute of Peace, April 2003), p. 15.

15. Carlotta Gall and Tom Shanker, 'Commando Saved in Afghanistan', *The New York Times*, 4 July 2005.

16. Carlotta Gall, 'Afghan Delegates Agree on the Need for Foreign Troops', *The New York Times*, 9 May 2005.

17. Eric Schmitt, 'NATO Troops will Relieve American in Fighting the Taliban', *The New York Times*, 31 December 2005.

18. Ibid.

19. 'Karzai Alleges Interference', *Dawn*, 21 June 2005.

20. *Dawn*, 21 June 2005.

21. Muralidhar Reddy, 'US Ambassador's Statement is Irresponsible, Says Pakistan', *The Hindu*, 20 June 2005.

22. Carlotta Gall, 'US Training Pakistani Units Fighting Al Qaeda', *The New York Times*, 27 April 2005.

23. Amir Mir, 'Al Qaeda Camps, Fighters Active in Waziristan: US Pushes Pakistan to Fight', *South Asian Tribune* (Washington DC), 3 May 2005, p. 2.

24. Carlotta Gall, 'Taliban Attack Afghan Officials', *The New York Times*, 19 June 2005; Carlotta Gall, 'Mood of Anxiety Engulfs Afghans as Violence Rises', *The New York Times*, 30 June 2005; also see, David S. Cloud, 'US Helicopter in Afghanistan Down', *The New York Times*, 27 June 2005.

25. Sultan Mohammad and Somini Sengupta, 'Last Commando is Found, Killed in Afghan Firefight', *The New York Times*, 12 July 2005.

26. 'Karzai Alleged Interference', *Dawn*, 21 June 2005.

27. Robert Birsel (Reuters), 'Afghan Rebels Attack from Pakistan', *The Washington Post*, 16 May 2005.

28. Carlotta Gall, 'Surrendered Chieftain Urges Taliban to Accept Amnesty', *The New York Times*, 2 June 2005.

29. Ibid.

30. 'The Taliban Threaten Pro-Karzai Ulama', *The News*, 13 July 2005.

31. Ibid., 17 July 2005.

32. 'Hekmatyar Rejects Amnesty Offer', *The News*, 18 May 2005.

33. Ibid., 30 June 2005.

34. Ibid.
35. US Department of State, *Afghanistan Country Report, 2004* (Washington, DC, 2005), p. 1.
36. David E. Sanger, 'Bush Hails Musharraf and Warns Iraq', *The New York Times*, 14 February 2002.
37. For how obedient and accommodating the High Courts and the Supreme Court are, see former Justice of the Supreme Court, Javid Iqbal's observations in *Javid Iqbal: Encounters with Destiny*, trans. Hafeez Malik,
   - Nasira Iqbal (Karachi: Oxford University Press, 2006), Chapter VIII.
38. 'Major Non-NATO Ally (MNNA) Status', in *Just the Facts* (Washington DC: Center for International Policy, 2003), p. 1.
39. 'Status of Non-NATO Ally Formalized', *Dawn*, 17 June 2004.
40. N. Ravi, 'Manmohan Expresses Satisfaction over Talks', *The Hindu*, 19 July 2005.
41. Somini Sengupta, 'India to Seek Expanded Access to US Nuclear Technology', *The New York Times*, 17 July 2005.
42. Amit Baruah, 'Guiding Principles on Border Issue Finalized', *The Hindu*, 11 April 2005.
43. Amit Baruah, 'Not a Military Alliance, Says Shyman Saran', *The Hindu*, 12 April 2005.
44. *The Washington Post*, 21 July 2005.

Epilogue

(I)

By the eighteenth century, the British, French, Dutch, Spanish and Portuguese had acquired imperial possessions outside Europe. Commerce and trade had become 'the craze of the century' as capitalism increased in these rapidly developing industrial countries. Some visionaries imagined 'a universal trade federation in which the different peoples of the world would swap new technologies and basic scientific and cultural skills as they would their foodstuffs.'[1] However, every British discourse of empire was driven by the belief that the British Empire had always been dedicated to the 'pursuit of liberty'. In other words, the empire was essentially committed to improving the people's condition—the liberty, both political and economic. This 'liberty' became the ideology of the British Empire.

However, freedom and liberty required the accumulation of power, because power is a condition of liberty. Without establishing the power of the British over other people in distant lands, power could not be obtained. Struggle for power and the rivalry for overlordship became inevitable. Consciously or not, President George W. Bush repeated the language of his 'British legacy', when he delivered his inaugural address in January 2005. He said: 'that spreading liberty around the world was the calling of our time,' and that 'the nation's vital interests and our deepest beliefs are now one.'

Alluding to the United States' military presence in distant parts of the world, he added: 'For half a century, America defended our freedom by standing watch on distant borders. After the shipwreck of Communism came years of relative quiet, years of repose, years of Sabbatical—and then there came a day of fire.' How is freedom to be defended? This goal can be accomplished with 'the expansion of freedom in all the world... [and by] ending tyranny in our world.' In a speech of barely 20 minutes, Bush used the words 'free' and 'freedom' more than 25 times.

In addition to freedom/liberty President Bush added 'democracy' to the ideology of American foreign policy; because democratic countries do not fight among themselves. So democracy became an 'ethical' justification for the policy of regime change in recalcitrant states. A sad example was the case of Iraq, where large parts of the country were destroyed and by 2006 more than half a million people were killed, but by definition the Iraqi people were 'forced' to be free. However, President Bush proclaimed that the spreading of democracy 'is the urgent requirement of our nation's security, and the calling of our time...it is the policy of the United States to seek and support the growth of democratic movements and institutions in every nation and culture.'[2]

The expansion of freedom is essentially a policing operation, which negates direct physical control of foreign territories. Both are expensive operations. Actually, the era of formal empire building is now dead. But the informal American *imperium*, (dedicated to extending its economic interests, promoting trade, sustaining international financial institutions like the IMF and the World Bank, protecting its perceived interests and that of its 'friends', especially those who produce oil and those who produce strategically significant raw materials), is in vogue.

In addition to his ideological commitment to freedom, liberty and democracy, President Bush is a dedicatedly religious man. He is, what believers call a born-again Christian. As a political realist, I am inclined to think that in foreign policy-making the personal religious views of responsible political leaders in the United States and elsewhere do not colour their judgment, and that they make decisions strictly in the light of national interests, without causing horrendous damage to other states.

However, President Bush stated on 9 July 2004 that '*I trust God speaks through me, without that I couldn't do my job*'.[3]

Presumably God does not necessarily favour the President(s) of major powers with the benefit of his personal advice, which might destroy small or weak states; nor does God label some states as the 'axis of evil', and some as the holders of universal moral principles without defining the legitimate aims of foreign policy. In other words, God is not expected to be partisan in the struggle for power which envelopes the diplomatic system. For President Bush to pretend to know with certainty (God's word is expected to be certain) what is good and evil in international relations is arrogance of power so unabashedly expressed by him. Bush's war of choice against Iraq that turned out to be a quagmire for US military power and so dreadfully destructive to the fibre of Iraqi society does not speak well of his communication with God.

In a similar manner Bush labelled the Taliban as 'Islamic fascists', and stated that the al-Qaeda movement of Osama bin Laden was endeavouring to establish 'a totalitarian Islamic empire that reaches from Indonesia to Spain.' In response, he called his policy 'this crusade, this war on terrorism [that] is going to take a while.' The term caliphate was repeatedly used by Vice-President Dick Cheney and Secretary of Defence Donald Rumsfeld. They projected the view that al-Qaeda's ultimate goal is the re-establishment of the Caliphate, which would extend throughout the Middle East and threaten legitimate governments in Europe, Africa and Asia.

Appearing before the House Armed Services Committee in September 2005 General John Abizaid, Commander-in-Chief of the Central Command, sounded no less dire: 'They will try to reestablish a caliphate throughout the entire Muslim world...the caliphate's goals would include the destruction of Israel. Just as we had the opportunity to learn what the Nazi's were going to do from Hitler's words in *Mein Kampf*, we need to learn what these people intend to do from their own words.'[4]

No wonder some tend to believe that a war between the Islamic world and western civilization is raging across much of the world. Actually, no such war is underway; these statements are made to exaggerate the magnitude of the threat of the Taliban and al-Qaeda. These threats and dangers to the West in general and the United States in particular are blown up to shore up US public support for the unpopular war in Iraq.

This assessment, however, does not imply that the United States was not attacked by the al-Qaeda terrorists, or that the US was not justified in its threat perception, and indignant reaction. I have in mind a realistic scenario of the Taliban's and al-Qaeda's military capability in comparison to the most formidable military structure of the United States. No matter how zealously espoused intentions there might be, without resources they hardly ever achieve anything.

No powerful state or any movement like the al-Qaeda could possibly challenge the United States in a set-piece battle. They attacked the US in 2001 when it was asleep, and was not on guard to handle a surreptitious attack of this kind on US territory. The Taliban and al-Qaeda do not have any territory under their control, nor can they maintain a military formation. The Taliban's ambitions did not extend beyond Afghanistan, and in this resurgent phase if they regain control of Southern Afghanistan, which is the homeland of the Pashtuns, it would clearly reflect the incompetence of the Karzai government. At the peak of their power the Taliban controlled 90 per cent of Afghanistan and urgently wanted US diplomatic recognition, trade and the lifting of sanctions. Repulsed by their primitive government, the US rejected them.

(II)

Three powerful threat perceptions, different in their intensity, were the catalytic force to reshape US policy toward South Asia, and the Islamic militants: China, and terror, unleashed by Osama bin Laden. The third element, while quite muted at this stage, is likely to form US policy towards the European Union, which has the potential to be a serious challenge to the power of the United States in Europe.

China looms very large on the political horizon of the US establishment. The current policy of the Bush administration calls for building up India's economic and military power to counter-balance that of China. China, however, is more fearful of the US policy of containment than the rising influence of India. To forestall this possibility, since 2001 China has initiated a policy of building a strategic partnership with Russia, the major European powers, and especially India to prevent their participation in any anti-Chinese coalition.

Currently, China has engaged both India and Pakistan to strengthen their relations with China. Hu Jintao, the President of China, visited India for three days from 20–23 November 2006, and then flew to Pakistan for a four-day visit. India and China have endeavoured to put away their mutual suspicions, and increase trade, which doubled during 2005–6. A report by the Confederation of Indian Industry predicted it would reach $30 billion by 2010. A historic trade route at Nathula Pass was reopened earlier in 2006,[5] which had been shut tight during the Sino-Indian War of 1962.

Despite US support to India, the relationship between India and China is not exactly between equal powers—India's strategic thinkers openly stated so recently. With the notable exception of the size of India's software industry, 'and the number of Indian billionaires,' China is far ahead of Indian economic development. India's minister of state for commerce publicly stated in November 2006, that 'we are not in a race [with China],' because 'they have already won the race'.[6]

To shore up relations between India and China, Hu Jintao, President of China agreed to a ten-point strategy that sought to promote civilian nuclear cooperation with India, increase trade to $40 billion by 2010, encourage the two-way investment flows, increase cooperation in science and technology and establish additional consulates–general in each country. Moreover, it was noted that they were cooperating with each other in African countries, being partners in an oil venture in Sudan. India's bilateral trade with African countries shot up to $12 billion in 2005.[7]

Some suspicions of each others' motives have been difficult to dispel. These suspicions are deeply rooted in the territorial disputes which go back to the nineteenth century when British power penetrated into Tibet, which China considered an integral part of China. Tibet shares a 2000 mile border with India, and also with the Himalayan states of Nepal, Sikkim and Bhutan. In the west, Tibet also shares common borders with the Aksai Chin region of Ladakh, also known as Little Tibet. China controls part of it, but India claims it is a part of Ladakh. However, their political status was defined by British power in the nineteenth century. In 1815, Nepal was defeated and made a British protectorate; Darjeeling in the East was annexed to India in 1835, Kashmir and Ladakh were annexed in 1846, Sikkim was made a protectorate in 1861; Bhutan became a protectorate in 1865, and Assam was annexed to India in 1886. India incorporated some of these areas into a new state of Arunachal Pradesh within the Indian union territory in 1972, and part of the state in 1987.

A few days before Hu Jintao's visit to India, the Chinese Ambassador in New Delhi raised the issue of Arunachal Pradesh, and suggested publicly that the territorial dispute should be settled in a 'fair, rational and acceptable' manner. The same statement was made in Beijing. President Hu himself repeated the same statement, adding that the boundary issue should find 'a mutually acceptable' solution.[8]

To settle their territorial dispute both states have made some procedural progress. In 2003 they appointed special representatives to explore the avenues of the boundary issue. In April 2005 both governments signed the 'Agreement on Political Guiding Principles' for settlement of the boundary issue. In their summit meeting in New Delhi in November 2006, they urged the special envoys to speed up their glacial movement for the territorial settlement.

In addition to the territorial issue, China distrusts India's increasing closeness to the United States, increased naval India–USA exercises in the Indian Ocean, and India's open door of reception to Tibetan dissidents. As a gesture of India's distance from China, Indian Prime Minister Manmohan Singh did not receive Hu Jintao at the airport; instead he sent his foreign minister to do the honours. It was noted that in the past he had personally greeted President Bush at the airport, and had done similar honours at the airport to much less powerful states, receiving Saudi King Abdullah, and Nepalese Prime Minister Girija Prasad Koirala. These nuances of protocol are unmistakably indicative of their competitiveness, and the relentless struggle to demonstrate their 'oversized egos'.

Hu Jintao's visit in November 2006 to Islamabad was very cordial and the China–Pakistan relationship was described hyperbolically as an 'all-weather friendship'. President Musharraf decorated the Chinese President with the sash of Nishan-i-Pakistan, the country's highest civilian award. The two countries signed 18 agreements and memoranda of understanding, including a landmark free trade agreement, which is expected to triple bilateral trade to $15 billion within five years. The establishment of a free trade area is expected to reduce the existing trade imbalance, which is currently in favour of China. Also, an accord was signed to develop aircrafts equipped with long-range early warning radars. A joint investment company was established to provide an institutional mechanism for financial support to the private sector for investing in joint ventures.

The issues of public diplomacy were not ignored. President Hu suggested quite wisely that friendship even among the best of friends must be continuously consolidated. In addition to close diplomatic relations, he proposed a people to people relationship involving legislators, political party operatives, leaders of civic organizations, and young people. He invited 500 young people from Pakistan to visit China during the next five years. In other words, the bridges of 'friendship' should be built between the Pakistanis and the Chinese by engaging in the strategic, economic, technological, security and defence fields. Hyperbolic expressions won the day. 'May China and Pakistan enjoy eternal friendship,' exclaimed President Hu Jintao.

Last but not least, President Hu stated that China would continue to help Pakistan in the field of nuclear power, and 'provide assistance in other sectors including hydroelectricity, coal and alternative sources of energy.'[9] However, no agreement was signed for the construction of six new nuclear reactors, as generally expected. This might be a disappointment to Pakistan, especially after another put down, which Pakistan received with the United States' preference for India. Surely Pakistan could not get a similar nuclear agreement as India, because as US Under Secretary of State Nicholas Burns said: 'That's a unique agreement with a unique country.'[10]

Actually, China built a 300 MW reactor in Pakistan at Chashma, and in 2006 built a second 300 MW reactor at the same location under the 'grandfather clause' of the Nuclear Suppliers Group (NSG) Guidelines. Established in 1975, the NSG is comprised of 45 nuclear supplier states, including China, Russia and the United States. Its aim is to prevent nuclear exports for commercial and peaceful purposes from being used to make nuclear weapons. India's explosion of a nuclear device in 1974 reaffirmed the fact that nuclear materials and technologies acquired under the guise of peaceful purposes could be diverted to build weapons. In response to India's actions, the NSG was established. Its members are expected to forego nuclear trade with governments that do not subject themselves to international inspections. China is a member of this group.

The NSG Guidelines consist of two parts: Part I established in 1978 responded to India's diversion of nuclear imports; Part II identifies the dual-use goods that can also be used to develop weapons. The NSG regime is voluntary; its members may ultimately make any export they wish. For instance, Russia transferred nuclear fuel to India in 2001. Pakistan wants China to establish two 1,000 MW reactors alongside the functioning Canadian built KANUPP-1 reactor in Karachi. Pakistan has also asked NSG to grant the same exception, which is at present being considered for India.[11] There is one very interesting but complicating factor in this complex web of nuclear diplomacy. In authorizing nuclear commerce with India, the US Congress has inserted a restrictive condition that the NSG must make an exception to its rigid rules for India—and India alone. Section 105 (9) (b) states that the NSG 'must not permit nuclear commerce with any non-nuclear weapon state other than India that does not have IAEA safeguards on all nuclear facilities,' an obvious reference to Pakistan and Israel.

Theoretically, if China seeks and wins NSG approval for its sale to Pakistan, the US deal with India would be nullified. The NSG operates by consensus, and the United States can block an exemption for Pakistan. China could do the same to India, and create a deadlock. No matter how the issue is resolved the building of new nuclear reactors for Pakistan would take several years; unless of course China and the United States agree not to create this deadlock, and let the deal go through in both countries.

Despite Hu's visit to New Delhi, India's threat perception of China's threatening and expanding power was not substantially ameliorated, while both powers very prudently continued to improve their trade relations. China's claims on parts of Arunachal Pradesh, and Ladakh have always unsettled India's calculations about China's intentions. Recently, China has significantly improved its economic relations with Bangladesh, Nepal, Myanmar, and Sri Lanka, and consolidated its strategic relations with Pakistan. India sees these developments as China's attempts 'to encircle India'.

Feeling uneasy over China's increasing naval presence in the Indian Ocean, India has simultaneously maintained a policy of military cooperation with China. In 2005 the two countries had signed a memorandum of understanding (MoU) on defence cooperation. In light of this MoU the navies of the two countries, starting on 12 April 2007, conducted a series of naval exercises at the Port of Qingdao, the headquarters of the Chinese Navy's North China Sea fleet. India also extended its naval cooperative endeavours to East and South-east Asia. In the March–May 2007 period India scheduled additional exercises with the US and Japanese navies off the coast of Japan. However, their first joint exercise in these series was conducted in the Pacific Ocean on 16 April 2007. These exercises were to be followed by joint exercises with the Russian, Philippine and Vietnamese navies. Indian analysts have argued that these joint naval exercises 'marked the beginning of a new alliance aimed at containing Chinese influence.'[12] Officially, the Indian government sought to play down this speculation.

India, however, felt particularly sensitive about the construction of Pakistan's deep sea port at Gwadar, 100 km from Karachi on the coast of Balochistan. Indeed, China had provided 80 per cent of Gwadar Port's $248 million initial development cost.[13] Another port's construction at Sonmiani in the Lasbela district of Balochistan was announced on 20 March 2007, when General Musharraf and the Chinese minister of communication announced the opening of Pakistan's third port at Gwadar. An instructor at India's Navigation and Direction School at Kochi, Commander Srinivas Maddula, called the Gwadar Project, a 'strategic setback for India'.[14]

To further strengthen Sino-Pakistan relations, the two states signed 15 new agreements on 15 April 2007 in Beijing for building a new airport at Gwadar and an automobile plant, in addition to deepening collaboration in the agro industry, housing and tourism. Sixty-one new projects were identified in which both the public and private sectors from both countries could collaborate.[15]

Clearly, while Pakistan's strategic partnership for the anti-terror campaign under United States' leadership remained intact, its relations with China simultaneously moved into a more intimate collaboration.

However, the serious and imminent threat to the US security architecture still flows from Afghanistan, where the United States has internationalized the anti-Taliban conflict. By launching a pre-emptive war against Iraq in 2003 the Bush administration has got bogged down in a seemingly endless conflict. Economic and military resources, which the US could have utilized in Afghanistan to build an economically stable democratic polity, were squandered in Iraq. Under economic and manpower pressure the Bush Administration reduced financing for Afghanistan in 2005 by 30 per cent, and proposed the withdrawal of up to 3000 American troops. But the resurgent Taliban took an increasing toll on American and NATO troops. Consequently, the planned withdrawal was cancelled. Instead, $14 million in assistance was rushed to Southern Afghanistan (where the Taliban insurgence is focused). The objective was to repair agricultural infrastructure and damaged houses.

The resurgence of the Taliban became a contentious issue between the Karzai government, Pakistan and the United States. Kabul lamented that Pakistan was not doing enough to stop Taliban attacks from Pakistani sanctuaries. Indignantly, Pakistan denied any implied complicity in the Taliban's resurgence. US sources, however, admitted that 'popular support for the Taliban exists inside Afghanistan,' while 'Taliban commanders continued to use parts of Pakistan as a haven to plan attacks in Afghanistan'.[16]

A CIA assessment found that the Karzai government continues to struggle to exert authority beyond Kabul but has failed to do so. The explanation for this failure was the vacuum of authority between village councils and the central government in Kabul. The necessary connecting links between the two do not exist.

The Taliban have attracted support from disaffected Pashtuns, and also coerced others to join them. Some have been hired, and some who are engaged in drug trafficking found it profitable to use the Taliban's networks of smuggling routes, communications and informal financial transactions.[17] The insurgency has become self-sustaining and could continue for 5 to 10 years.

Meanwhile, in November–December 2006 this vacuum of authority was being filled by tribal leaders and NATO forces. The paradigm of this *modus vivendi* was the Waziristan leaders' agreement of peace with the Pakistan government, which was negotiated in November 2006. The target area was Musa Qala in Helmand province, where 5000 British soldiers were deployed as part of an expanding NATO province. They came under repeated attacks from the Taliban and suffered substantial numbers of casualties. The NATO forces called in air-strikes, even on residential areas, which led to huge numbers of civilian deaths.

The tribal leaders approached the governor suggesting that they would ask the Taliban to leave their area and live in peace. Eventually, the governor of Helmand agreed on a 10-point accord with the elders, who pledged to: 1) support the government, and the Afghan flag, 2) keep schools open, 3) allow development and reconstruction, 4) work to ensure the security and stability of the region, 5) limit arming the people who did not belong to the government, 6) agree on a list of local candidates for the posts of district chief and police chief, from which the governor would appoint the officials, 7) choose 60 local people to serve as police officers in the district, and 8) send the first 20 to the provincial capital for training.[18]

What did the Taliban gain in this agreement? They obtained the withdrawal of the British troops from the area without having to risk additional fighting. However, the Taliban's presence remained strong in the province; they neither disbanded nor were they disarmed. They also retained some police functions in Musa Qala. They could arrest thieves and drug addicts and confine them in their jails. People in the area believed that the Taliban managed to establish peace. If this pattern of peace is repeated the presence of NATO forces would become unnecessary, and the Taliban would establish their 'presence peacefully'. This development remains to be seen!

(III)

It is a very strange twist of history that while the US is at the pinnacle of power, and is militarily invincible it feels most threatened by unorganized and weak enemies in Afghanistan, and elsewhere who have openly challenged the US pre-eminence. By attacking the citadels of US economic and military power on 11 September 2001 the al-Qaeda movement of Osama bin Laden proclaimed to fight asymmetrical wars against the United States and its allies. Roger W. Barnett defined asymmetrical warfare as 'organized violence conducted between political units of vastly unequal military capability, where each side practices different methods of fighting and follows different rules of engagement.'[19] Professors Charles W. Kegley and Gregory A. Raymond further explained that 'belligerents in asymmetrical warfare may be states, or they may involve some combination of state and non-state actors.'[20]

When Osama bin Laden declared war against the United States in 1996 he started asymmetrical warfare between the United States and al-Qaeda (or base in Arabic). The big question is: why did he do so? There are several interpretations of his motives in the West in general and the United States in particular, some of which are in variance with the explanations provided by Osama bin Laden. The official position of Osama's war of terror maintained by President Bush offered one straightforward and simple explanation: 'They hate us, and they hate our freedoms which they are determined to destroy', Bush said in his 20 September 2001 address to the US Congress, and in numerous speeches around the country. Lumping the Taliban and al-Qaeda into one basket, Bush perceived them to be 'driven by a dark vision', and determined they must be eliminated.[21]

While the Taliban Movement was initiated to defeat the Mujahideen's government in Kabul and to establish Pashtun rule over all of Afghanistan, al-Qaeda is a transnational Islamic organization designed to fight against US interests in the Middle East and other Muslim countries. Indeed, there was a marriage of convenience between the two, where Osama bin Laden, as a guest in the Afghan sanctuary, had accepted Mulla Omar as the *Amir al-Muminin* (Commander of the Faithful). Bin Laden stated: 'We are committed under God's laws to obey him.' Mulla Omar had been elected to this office at a meeting of the most notable Afghan *ulama* (religious scholars) in Kandahar in March 1996.

The scholarly view is more sophisticated, and more analytical of al-Qaeda operatives' motivations and their convictions than President Bush's pronouncements. Professor Robert A. Pape of the University of Chicago compiled data on the 71 terrorists who killed themselves between 1995 and 2004 in carrying out attacks sponsored by Osama bin Laden's network. He was able to collect the names, nationalities and detailed demographic information on 67 of these bombers. The data provided insights into the underlying causes of al-Qaeda's suicide terrorism, and how the group's strategy evolved since 2001.

Professor Pape's figures led him to demonstrate that al-Qaeda was 'less a product of Islamic fundamentalism than a simple strategic goal: to compel the United States and its western allies to withdraw combat forces from the Arabian Peninsula and other Muslim countries.'[22] Also, he demonstrated that the overwhelming majority of the attackers were citizens of Saudi Arabia and other Gulf States, where the United States had stationed combat troops since 1990. The other terrorists came from 'America's closest allies in the Muslim world—Turkey, Egypt, Pakistan, Indonesia, and Morocco'—rather than from those the State Department considered 'state sponsors of terrorism' like Iran, Iraq, Sudan, and Libya (before Muammar Qadhafi transformed himself from the 'incorrigible and irredeemable perennial dictator' of Libya to a 'responsible' ruler).

An eminent French scholar who is widely admired and read in the United States, Olivier Roy, posited a thesis in his thoroughly researched book, *Globalized Islam*, and in another article with a very provocative title—'Why Do They Hate Us?'—that 'from the beginning, al-Qaeda fighters were global jihadists and their favoured battle grounds have been outside the Middle East: Afghanistan, Bosnia, Chechnya and Kashmir. For them, every conflict is simply a part of the Western encroachment on the Muslim *Ummah* the worldwide community of believers.'[23]

Roy perceived al-Qaeda as a product of Muslims' migration to, and settlement in, Western European countries and the United States. In the history of Islam this has been a unique migratory movement of millions of Muslims to what might be described as Christendom, where the younger generations, instead of assimilating into the European cultures, have become what he has called, 'deterritorialized'. In other words, they have been dissociated from their native cultures, and detached from their religious moorings. Consequently, a youthful generation of Muslims has emerged which is completely transnationalized belonging neither to the East or the West. They belong to a free floating mass of 'universal' *Ummah* (community of believers).

Mary Habeck, an Associate Professor of Strategic Studies at Johns Hopkins University's Paul H. Nitze School of Advanced International Studies in Washington, DC published a very perceptive analysis of jihadist ideology and terror tactics.[24] She reduced the al-Qaeda ideology to 'unusual definitions' of four Islamic terms—*Tawhid* (unity of God), *jihad* (struggle), caliphate (Islamic state), and *da`wa* (a call to turn away from false gods and to the worship of the one true God). The jihadists believe that they are the true Muslims in the world, destined to go to *Janna* (paradise). Also, they believe that hostile unbelievers dominate the world, and are determined to destroy Islam. The war against the unbelievers is justified because Muslims have been attacked, and aggressed against since 1916, when the Sykes-Picot Agreement was secretly signed, which divided the Arab states into areas of mandates for Britain and France. Bin laden frequently refers to this agreement.

Some jihadis maintained a more historical vision of this war, going back to the crusades—military campaigns, which were undertaken by the Christian powers of the West in the eleventh to the thirteenth centuries to conquer Palestine from the Muslims—or even with the creation of man. To them history has been a constant struggle between the 'believers' and the 'unbelievers', 'light' and 'dark', and 'truth' and 'falsehood'. In this style of reasoning all wars between the believers and non-believers have been defensive wars. Eternal war is the only foreign policy they envisioned for the caliphate.

Habeck maintained that jihadists' campaigns are primarily against other Muslims, who are the majority of the victims. Ideologically their message is aimed almost entirely against other Muslims to convince them to join the jihad. Politically, they are attempting to create a caliphate on 'the backs of other Muslims,' forcing them to follow their vision of Shari`a. Actually, most of the people who have been killed by the jihadis—for instance in Iraq—have been Muslims.

For war against the United States, Osama bin Laden sought justification not in the Qur'an but from Ibn Tamiya 'who argued for taking on the *greater unbelief* first.' Supported by the words of Ibn Tamiya, bin Laden called the United States the *greater unbelief*, the bigger enemy. Without US support 'all those lesser enemies or near enemies, whether it's Israel or the Saudi government would collapse.'[25]

In addition to Ibn Tamiya, Habeck included two additional ideological sources for Bin Laden's jihadi movement: 1) Hassan al-Banna (1906–49); and 2) Sayyid Qutb (1906–66), an internationally known leader of the Muslim Brotherhood, which was established by Al-Banna in Egypt.

Al-Banna believed that most of the Muslims had fallen away from true Islam; however, he preferred preaching Islam to win

over other Muslims, reserving violence for those who occupied
Muslim lands. Immediately he started to take on the British
occupation of Egypt's Suez Canal zone. In a debacle of the 1956
War in which Britain and France had entered into a clandestine
alliance with Israel, the United States under President Eisenhower
forced all three occupiers to vacate the Egyptian land.
Subsequently, Al-Banna turned to the use of violence against the
Egyptian government.

Saiyyid Qutb came to the United States in 1948 as a student,
but returned after one year thoroughly disenchanted with
American culture. He joined the Muslim Brotherhood, and
landed in jail, where he wrote a 30-volume commentary on the
Qur'an, which was subsequently condensed into a short
manifesto, *Milestones Along the Way*, in which he emphasized
that the main enemy is liberalism. Democracy and liberalism, he
emphasized, are a fundamental challenge to the Islamic way of
life and the conviction that 'God should be the only law-giver.'
When Sayyid Qutb was executed by the Nasser government in
1966, his brother Muhammad Qutb sought asylum in Saudi
Arabia and became a teacher. Among his students was Osama
bin Laden.

From the al-Qaeda ideology, Habeck's analysis shifted to their
presence in northern Pakistan, where according to an estimate
'they have 22 camps at last count' in 2006. Now they have
signed a peace treaty with the Pakistan government. Habeck
estimated that 'destroying this new Islamic proto-state will be a
problem, since no one wants to invade the difficult terrain of
ungoverned northern Pakistan.'[26]

Insofar as the structure of al-Qaeda is concerned, its picture
is best developed by the Century Foundation's task force, which
was chaired by Richard A. Clarke, who served three presidents
(Bush I, Clinton, and Bush II) as a Special Assistant for Security
and Counterterrorism. The task force saw the al-Qaeda's
operations within the four concentric circles of jihadism.

The Concentric Circles of Jihadism

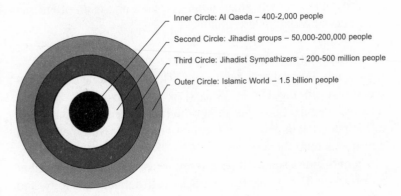

Inner Circle: Al Qaeda – 400-2,000 people

Second Circle: Jihadist groups – 50,000-200,000 people

Third Circle: Jihadist Sympathizers – 200-500 million people

Outer Circle: Islamic World – 1.5 billion people

Source: Richard A. Clarke, et al., *Defeating the Jihadists* (New York: The Century Foundation Press, 2004).

- Within the smallest inner circle are the hardcore operatives of al-Qaeda, who engage in terrorist operations. They pledge their loyalty to the group and its leader. Their number is estimated to be in the hundreds.
- The second circle contains numbers of another dozen or more jihadist groups that are called al-Qaeda related. Many of these individuals are willing to commit terrorist acts personally, and 'some are willing to die in the process as suicide bombers. This second circle probably contains several tens of thousands of people.'
- The third circle consists of those individuals who identify with the jihadist cause or aspects of its ideology. They may provide moral support and some might facilitate logistical or financial activity in support of a jihadist group. This inner circle includes many who want to see their government replaced by a different government, which might be less corrupt, more democratic, or more Islamist. This circle may contain tens of millions or perhaps as many as a few hundred million.
- The outer circle is that of the Muslim World, both in majority Muslim countries, and scattered throughout the

world; they number over one billion people. It is estimated that an extremely small number (about one-tenth of one per cent of Muslims are jihadists).

In contemplating the Muslim world the task force drew a remarkably interesting conclusion: 'There should be clarity that the threat [to the Untied States] is not 'terrorism', or even terrorist organizations, but rather the jihadist terrorists who seek to highjack Islam and use violence to replace governments with non-democratic theocracies.'[27]

From this description it should not be assumed that 'a coherent and tight-knit' organization with a well defined ideology and personnel exists in numerous countries, while it has been stated that al-Qaeda branches exist in 160 countries. A veteran correspondent of the London *Observer*, Jason Burke, investigated the structure of al-Qaeda and maintained that this view would lead 'to misunderstanding not only of its true nature but also the nature of Islamic radicalism.'[28] Al-Qaeda, he believes, 'does not conceive and execute projects globally through well-disciplined cadres, sleepers and activists spread around the world.' Indeed, the hardcore members (in the smallest inner circle) act as links between the leadership and 'the rest of the vast amorphous movement of modern radical Islam, with a myriad of cells, domestic groups, groupuscules and splinters, joining the networks to the hardcore itself.' Sometimes these networks are happy to be brought under Bin Laden's umbrella. Often they are not willing to surrender their autonomy. Indeed, an amorphous structure is al-Qaeda's strength as well as its weakness.

Last but not least, let there now be spotlight on Osama bin Laden, acknowledged leader of al-Qaeda.

Born in Saudi Arabia in 1957, Bin Laden was educated at King Abdul Aziz University in Jeddah where he took courses in Islamic Studies offered by Abdullah Azzam (1941–89) and Sayyid Muhammad Qutb. Azzam was a Muslim Brother from Palestine. Bin Laden reacted very sharply to the American airlift of weapons to Israeli forces in the battlefield in the 1973 War, which guaranteed Israeli superiority in the conflict. Bin Laden didn't complete his education at the university, but joined his father's construction business and earned substantial amounts of money. When the Soviet Union invaded Afghanistan in 1979, he became involved in organizing the flow of Saudi financial aid to the Afghan resistance. At age 23 Bin Laden arrived in Peshawar in 1980 and started to work with Abdullah Azzam. A guest house to receive volunteer Arab fighters was established by him, which was called *Sijill al-Qaeda* (Register of the Base). Later on it came to be known as al-Qaeda or the base.

In 1989 the Soviet troops withdrew from Afghanistan, and the United States not only withdrew funds from the Afghan resistance, it simply lost interest in Afghanistan. Bin Laden returned to Saudi Arabia. A few months later when Saddam Hussein invaded Kuwait, Bin Laden offered to organize a fighting force of Arab Afghans (as they were then called) to defend Saudi Arabia. King Fahad not only rejected his offer, but also invited nearly 500,000 American and other foreign soldiers to protect the country. Their presence was legitimized by a *fatwa* (religious decree) given by Saudi *ulamas*. Those who rejected their *fatwa* were harassed by the Saudi government, including Osama bin Laden, who was kept under house arrest for a short period of time. In 1991 Bin Laden left for Sudan, where he stayed for five years. In 1994 the Saudi government stripped him of his citizenship. In May 1996 he returned to Afghanistan, settling in the Tora Bora caves near the city of Jalalabad. Since 1996 Bin Laden has continued to live in Afghanistan, along with his Egyptian colleague Ayman al-Zawahiri.

In September 1996 the Taliban captured Kabul and in a relatively short period of time established their sway over 90 per cent of Afghanistan's territory. This inaugurated the period of close collaboration between al-Qaeda and the Taliban. In 1998 the simultaneous bombing of American embassies in Kenya and Tanzania followed. In retaliation the Clinton Administration launched a cruise missile attack on one of the bases in Khost, hoping to kill Bin Laden. He escaped death and instantly became world famous. Three years later al-Qaeda activists hijacked four planes in the United States and in suicide missions destroyed the World Trade Center in New York, and damaged parts of the Pentagon in Washington, DC killing nearly 3,000 people, most of them US citizens.[29] Now an open-ended war between the United States, al-Qaeda and the Taliban got underway, which seems to have no terminal point in sight.

Clearly Osama bin Laden never had a thorough study of the Islamic disciplines that the traditional *ulama* (religious scholars) acquire in the *madrassas*. Yet it must be noted that while he issued his pronouncements in Islamic terms, his political ideas and demands were perfectly secular. Bin Laden has never acquired the respectable status of traditional Islamic scholars, but he has gained a tremendous amount of respect and following among the Muslim youth of practically all Arab and Islamic countries, just as he has drawn some devoted followers from the large Muslim diaspora of nearly 26 million Muslims settled in different European states. Practically, what mattered most to his mission was his charisma (which has been very carefully nurtured), and not any pretensions to scholarship.

In 2005, Professor Bruce Lawrence and James Howarth published an English translation of 24 of Bin Laden's *fatwas*. Rendered directly from the Arabic, Bin Laden's pronouncements allow the reader to form an informed opinion of his Islamic learning. He is indeed well-read in the Qur'an, the Prophetic Traditions (*ahadith*), *tafsir*, (exegetical works of the Qur'an), *sira*, (life and conduct of the Prophet Muhammad (PBUH)), and some knowledge of the *Shari`a* (Islamic laws). Indeed, he is well informed about US foreign policy and its objectives, which he has openly rejected. He believes that the United States is fundamentally an enemy of the Arab states, supports Israel at their expense, and plans to occupy the Muslim lands in order to control their major resource—oil—with the help of collaborative Arab regimes.

Among his *fatwa(s)* two were issued (1994–95) from Sudan; four were issued (1996–98) from Afghanistan; five described his views on the nuclear bomb, relations with Mulla Omar, and the tragedy of the 11 September 2001 attacks and cover the period from 1998–2001; six statements are devoted (2001–2) to the affairs of, what he called 'crusader wars', relations with the Americans and the allies of the United States; seven extensive pronouncements dealt with the war in Iraq (2003–4), gave encouragement to the Iraqi resistance, and the fate of Saudi Arabia.

His views on these subjects can be described with utter clarity.

First, he rejected the US official view that 'we despise their way of life'. Calling President Bush 'the Pharaoh of our age', Bin Laden stated that 'we strike them because of their injustice towards us in the Muslim world, especially in Palestine and Iraq, and their occupation of Saudi Arabia.' Nowhere in these *fatwa(s)* does he assume any direct and personal responsibility for organizing the attacks of 11 September. Because of the US 'injustice, arrogance and aggression on the part of the Zionist-American alliance...disaster struck' the United States. 'A group of young believers...attacked the enemy with their own planes in a brave and beautiful operation.'[30]

However, the United States and the international community have held Bin Laden personally responsible for the attacks on the United States and for the declaration of jihad in his *fatwa* of 13 August 1996. The *fatwa* presented the hostilities against the United States as a *defensive war* in as much as it was a response to 'the Judeo-Christian' alliance's onslaught against the Muslims 'in Tajikistan, Burma, Kashmir, Assam, the Philippines, Fatani, Ogaden, Somalia, Eriteria, Chechnya and Bosnia-Herzigovinia.' Bin Laden referred to the killing of Abdullah Azzam and the arrest of Shaikh Ahmad Yassin in Jerusalem in 1989, who was released in 1997.[31] Bin Laden highlighted his own afflictions — his expulsion from Saudi Arabia to Sudan, Pakistan and then Afghanistan. He declared that the Saudi government had lost legitimacy on two grounds:

1. Its suspension of the rulings of Islamic law (*Shari`a*) and its replacement with man-made law and its confrontation with the *ulama* (Islamic scholars), and pious youth.
2. Its inability to protect the land, and for allowing the enemies of God to occupy it for years 'in the form of American crusades'.

Finally, he delivered an appeal to Muslims across the world: 'Your brothers in Saudi Arabia and Palestine are calling for your help, and asking you to share with them in the Jihad against the enemies of God, your enemies the Israelis and Americans.'[32]

In a public statement of 1998, welcoming the establishment of the Islamic Front for Jihad against the Israelis and American crusaders, Bin Laden declared:

> The ruling to kill the Americans and their allies—civilian and military—is an individual duty for every Muslim who can do it in any country in which it is possible to do it, in order to liberate the al-Aqsa mosque and the holy mosque [Makkah] from their grip, and in order for their armies to move out of all the lands, of Islam, defeated and unable to threaten any Muslim.[33]

In commenting on this statement, Professor Stephen Helms stated (and I concur with his judgement) that 'we can say that al-Qaeda's principle aims in its war with the United States are to drive the US forces out of the Gulf, to end US support for Mubarak [of Egypt], and to end US support for Israel. All three aims are perfectly secular...'.[34]

In reality the twenty-four *fatwas* provide political, that is separate explanations for 11 September—to punish 'the unjust and tyrannical America'. Moreover, he does not justify terrorist operations against the United States in order to subordinate 'unbelievers' to the true faith of his interpretations. He has presented his jihad in the form of 'legitimate self-defence.' No matter how it is explained, it remains frighteningly lethal, and invokes an equally lethal response from the United States.

(IV)

The asymmetrical war between the United States and al-Qaeda raging fiercely in Afghanistan, and Iraq has brought untold miseries upon the common man's life, and has pulverized the social fabric of both countries. However, the United States social and political life has also been adversely affected as it has been filled with the fear of terror. In Washington DC, Pennsylvania Avenue, the site of the White House, and Capitol Hill, where the Senate and the House of Representatives are located, are now heavily barricaded and declared off limits to civilian traffic, and so is the Pentagon now isolated. All official buildings have installed metal detectors at their entrance gates, where everyone is searched and screened to detect any hidden weapons. After the 11 September attacks, the Department of Homeland Security was established which is devoted to detecting and combating terrorism. Airports and nuclear installations are secured and remain under constant surveillance, and so is the case for economically significant buildings.

The United States is under siege, and desperately needs allies, like Pakistan, to continue its campaign against terrorism. Pakistan can benefit from its new status of non-NATO ally, but this relationship will not be without cost, as in the future relations between the Untied States and China may become strained and openly competitive. In the past, Pakistan's relations with the United States were strong enough to shift the regional balance of power to Pakistan's advantage, but this advantage would not be available in any crisis with India. To maintain American *imperium*, the United States' strategy toward China, under Republican and Democratic administrations, would call for a policy of containment, where Pakistan, like India, would be expected to oppose China.

Europe is another area where the United States will remain concerned during this century. The European Union could be a serious pole of power to counterbalance the United States. The leading powers of Europe have already started to check US power in subtle ways. France, Germany and Russia jointly opposed the United States from obtaining a UN Security Council Resolution to authorize the invasion of Iraq. Also, the United States (as of October 2007) has not been able to persuade Russia, France and Germany to get tough on Iran's nuclear programme.

In his usual unsubtle way President Bush has remained skeptical of the European Union's progress toward unity. In 2001 Bush startled some visitors to the Oval office with a rhetorical question: 'was the drive toward European unity good for the United States?'[35] As the United States gets bogged down in Iraq, the US would not dream of raising this issue loudly. To Bush's surreptitious delight the European Union's constitution for the enlarged union of 25 states was knocked off course, when France and the Netherlands rejected it in referendums in May and June 2005. So far, 14 countries have fully ratified the constitution, two of them by referendum. The Constitution commits the EU to a common foreign policy, and says it should develop a common defence policy.

The 25-nation European Union weighs in with $11 trillion in economic output, roughly on par with the United States. European currency, the Euro is so strong that it may one day replace the dollar as the principal means of exchange. (The map on the opposite page highlights the comparative strengths and weaknesses of the European Union and the United States.) In the conservative elements in the Bush administration, especially the Department of Defence and the office of Vice-President Dick Cheney, fear remains strong that the new Europe is not always in tune with American *imperium's* objectives. Actually all successive administrations since the 1950s supported European integration in general, 'none was willing to risk the possibility that Europe might become independent of American leadership, and none was able to resist the temptation to use the British as an agent of American influence in Europe.'[36]

Clearly the logic of *imperium* does not encourage the United States to create a formidable rival! Associate Editor of the

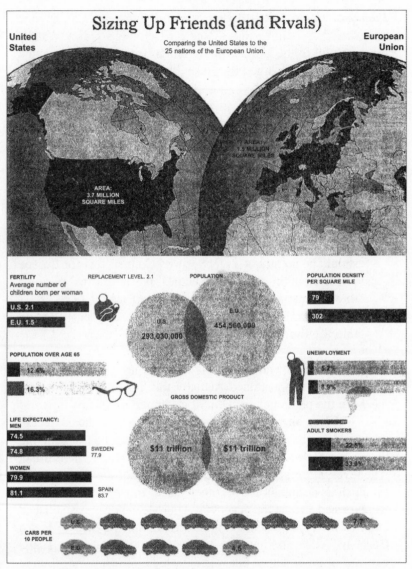

Sizing Up Friends (and Rivals)

United States

European Union

Comparing the United States to the 25 nations of the European Union.

AREA: 1.5 MILLION SQUARE MILES

AREA: 3.7 MILLION SQUARE MILES

FERTILITY
Average number of children born per woman

REPLACEMENT LEVEL. 2.1

U.S. 2.1

E.U. 1.5

POPULATION

U.S. 293,030,000

E.U. 454,560,000

POPULATION DENSITY PER SQUARE MILE

79

302

POPULATION OVER AGE 65

12.4%

16.3%

UNEMPLOYMENT

5.2%

8.9%

LIFE EXPECTANCY: MEN

74.5

74.8   SWEDEN 77.9

WOMEN

79.9

81.1   SPAIN 83.7

GROSS DOMESTIC PRODUCT

$11 trillion

$11 trillion

ADULT SMOKERS

22.5%

33.8%

CARS PER 10 PEOPLE

U.S.   7.7

E.U.   4.6

Sources: The European Union, Eurostat Bureau of Labor Statistics, Centers for Disease Control and Prevention, US Census Bureau; Bill Marsh/*The New York Times*.

Financial Times, Gerard Baker, forcefully argued: 'Can anyone now seriously believe that a single EU foreign policy will be more helpful to the United States than a British or Polish, and a Spanish one.'[37] He urged the Bush administration to:

1. 'Stop spouting' the cold war idea that an integrated Europe is in the best interest of the United States.
2. Strengthen ties with East European countries, and move US troops out of Germany and into Bulgaria and Romania.
3. Temper its enthusiasm for the development of stronger European military capabilities...be careful about a separate European identity within NATO.
4. Oppose any plans to change the membership of multilateral institutions to reflect a single European identity. There should be no talk of a UN Security Council seat for Europe or the creation of a United States–Japan–Europe group of three in international economics to replace the G7.
5. Refrain from doing anything that might help push Britain into the European Union.

While the United States remains a target, its urge for imperial control remains unrestrained. Actually, this 'imperial overstretch'[38] has been the perennial problem of all imperial systems in world history. Since the dawn of the modern age in the sixteenth century there have rarely been instances when one hegemonic power established its sway over the whole world. In Europe, whenever attempts were made by any European power to establish its domination over other states, anti-imperial alliances were formed against the hegemony. (European powers established empires in Asia, Africa, Latin America, and the Middle East.) Germany twice attempted to create a European empire at the expense of other states, but was defeated by the anti-hegemonic alliance.

There is fear in politically educated circles in the Untied States that it may exhaust itself in the process of its 'imperial overstretch'; and then sink to the position of a secondary state like Britain. Precisely for this fearful realization the rise of China is watched so closely. To avoid this debilitating exhaustion some have suggested for the United States the role of an 'offshore balancer'. This strategy proposes that only 'Europe, industrialized Asia, and the Persian Gulf' are of 'strategic importance to the Untied States.' Even in these areas the United States should rely on local actors to maintain the regional balance of power and keep its military presence as small as possible. US military power should be exercised only 'against specific threats to its interests.'[39]

Some have emphasized the threat of Islamic radicalism, and singled out the Islamic world for American long term commitment to democratize it. In their view the intrusion of democratic institutions is the only plausible answer to stem the tide of Islamic terrorism. 'That idea remains the only conceivable one,' according to Charles Krauthammer, 'for ultimately prevailing over the Arab Islamic radicalism that exploded upon us on 9/11.' He added for emphasis: 'Every other is a policy of retreat and defeat that would ultimately bring ruin not only on the US, but the very idea of freedom.'[40]

NOTES

1. Anthony Pagdens, *Lords of All the World: Ideologies of Empire in Spain, Britain and France 1500-1890* (New Haven, CT: Yale University Press, 1995), p. 178.
2. Speech of President George W. Bush, 20 January 2005, *The New York Times*, 21 January 2005.
3. 'Thanks to a Few Religious Extremists...,' *The New York Times*, 17 July 2004. For Bush's 'Messianic idea' of what he thinks God has told him to do see also, Ron Suskind, 'Faith, Certainty and the Presidency of George W. Bush,' *The New York Times Magazine*, 17 October 2004.
4. Elisabeth Bumiller, 'White House Letter: 21st Century Warnings of Threat Rooted in the 7th,' *The New York Times*, 12 December 2005.
5. Pallavi Aiyar, 'Hu's Visit a Chance to Enhance Political Trust,' *The Hindu*, 11 November 2006.
6. Somini Sengupta, 'India and China Become Friendlier Rivals,' *The New York Times*, 21 November 2006. Jairam Ramesh made this statement on 20 November 2006 in New Delhi.

7. Ibid.
8. Amit Baruah, 'Hu Jintao for Stepped Up Talks on Boundary,' *The Hindu*, 23 November 2006.
9. Ihtusham-ul-Haque, 'Free Trade Accord with China: High-Performance Aircraft to be Jointly Produced,' *Dawn*, 26 November 2006.
10. 'US Wants No Nuclear Accord with Pakistan,' *Dawn*, 19 November 2006.
11. *Nucleonics Week*, (Journal of the International Nuclear Industry), 5 October 2006.
12. Pallavi Aiyar, 'India to Conduct Naval Exercises with China,' *The Hindu*, 12 April 2007.
13. Saleem Shahid, 'Gwadar Port Inaugurated: Plan for Second Port in Balochistan at Sonmiani,' *Dawn*, 21 March 2007.
14. For a detailed strategic analysis of the Gwadar Project and its potential setback for the Indian Navy see, Lt. Commander Srinivas Maddula, 'Gwadar Project Strategic Setback for India,' *The Journal of the United Service Institution of India* (New Delhi: July–September 2006), pp. 392, 403.
15. 'Pak, China Sign 15 Cooperation Agreements,' *The News*, 17 April 2007.
16. David Rohde and James Risen, 'CIA Review Highlights Afghan Leaders' Woes,' *The New York Times*, 5 November 2006.
17. Ibid.
18. Carlotta Gall, 'The Taliban Truce in Afghan Region: British and Rebels Leave,' *The New York Times*, 30 November 2006.
19. Roger W. Barnett, *Asymmetrical Warfare: Today's Challenge to the US Military Power* (Washington, DC: Brassey's, 2003), pp. 17-18.
20. Charles W. Kegley, Jr. and Gregory A. Raymond, *After Iraq: The Imperiled American Imperium* (New York: Oxford University Press, 2007), p. 53.
21. Suskind, *Faith, Certainty and the Presidency of George W. Bush*, p. 1.
22. Robert A. Pape, *Dying to Win: The Strategic Logic of Suicide Terrorism*, (New York: Random House, 2005); also see his article, 'Al-Qaeda's Smart Bombs,' *The New York Times*, 9 July 2005.
23. Olivier Roy, *Globalized Islam: The Search for a New Ummah* (New York: Columbia University Press, 2004), and 'Why Do They Hate Us? Not Because of Iraq,' *The New York Times*, 22 July 2005.
24. Mary Habeck, *Knowing the Enemy: Jihadist Ideology and the War on Terror* (New Haven: Yale University Press, 2006).
25. Mary Habeck, *Knowing the Enemy*, (Philadelphia: Foreign Policy Research Institute Bulletin, 17 November 2006), p. 6.
26. Ibid., p. 9.
27. Richard A. Clarke, et al., *Defeating the Jihadists* (New York: The Century Foundation Press, 2004), p. 18.

28. Jason Burke, *Al-Qaeda Casting a Shadow of Terror* (London: I.B. Tauris, 2003), p. 12.

29. For these biographical details see, Bruce Lawrance, ed., and James Howarth, trans., *Message to the World: The Statements of Osama bin Laden* (London: Verso, 2005), pp. XII-XIII.

30. Lawrence and Hawarth, op. cit., p. 193.

31. The quadriplegic Shaikh Yassin Ahmad was the founder of Hamas (Harkat al-Muqawamah al-Islamiyyah) or Islamic Resistance Movement which was established in 1987. Israel's targeted killings of Hamas's top leaders, including Shaikh Yassin (March 2004), and his successor in Gaza, Abdul Aziz Rantisi (April 2004) was a serious blow to Hamas's capabilities.

32. Shaul Mishal and Auraham Sela, *The Palestinian Hamas* (New York: Columbia University Press, 2006).

33. Lawrence and Howarth, op. cit., p. 30.

34. Stephen Helmes, 'Al-Qaeda, 11 September 2001,' in *Making Sense of Suicide Missions*, ed. Diego Gambetta (Oxford: Oxford University Press, 2005), p. 164.

35. Steven R. Weisman, 'Europe United is Good, Isn't It?' *The New York Times*, 20 February 2005.

36. Ronald J. Granieri, 'Allies and Other Strangers: European Integration and the American Empire by Invitation,' *Orbis* (Fall 2006), p. 701.

37. Gerard Baker, 'Against United Europe,' *The Weekly Standard*, 22 September 2003, p. 25.

38. For further explanation of the 'imperial overstretch,' see Paul M. Kennedy, *The Rise and Fall of the Great Powers* (New York: Random House, 1987), p. 515 ff.

39. Stephen M. Walt, 'Taming American Power,' *Foreign Affairs* (September–October 2005), p. 118.

40. Charles Krauthammer, 'Past the Apogee: America Under Pressure,' (Philadelphia: Keynote Address to the Foreign Policy Research Institute, 14 November 2006).

Bibliography

Ackerman, Gary. 'If You Want to be Treated Like India, Be Like India.' *The Hindu*, 6 June 2006.

Ahmad, Ishtiaq. *Gulbaddin Hekmatyar*. Islamabad: Pan Graphic Press, 2004: 89-127.

Ahmad, Naveed. 'Repatriating 400,000 Afghans This Year: UNHCR.' *The News*, 2 June 2005.

_____. 'Hu's Visit a Chance to Enhance Political Trust.' *The Hindu*, 11 November 2006.

_____. 'India to Conduct Naval Exercises with China.' *The Hindu*, 12 April 2007.

_____. 'Made in China—Indian Doctors.' *The Hindu*, 17 May 2006.

_____. 'Extensive Consensus on Defence Cooperation with China.' *The Hindu*, 31 May 2006.

_____. 'A Quick Step Forward in Sino-Indian Ties.' *The Hindu*, 30 May 2006.

Allah, Shah Waliy. *Izalat al Khafa' 'Un Khilafat al-Khalfa'*. Translated into Urdu by Abdul Shakur and Insha Allah, vol. 1, 39. Karachi: Matba'-i-Sa'idiy, n.d.

Amin, Samir. *Beyond US Hegemony? Assessing the Prospects for a Multipolar World*. London: Zed Books, 2006.

Ansari, Massoud. 'Newsbeat.' *Newsline* (Karachi), May 2005.

Ansari, Mufti Muhammad Rida and Baniy Dars-i-Nizami. 'Mullah Nizam-ud-Din Muhammad.' *Ma'arif* (Azamgarh: October 1970).

Art, Robert J. *A Grand Strategy for America*. Ithaca: Cornell University Press, 2003.

Bacevich, Andrew J. *American Empire*. Cambridge: Harvard University Press, 2002.

Baker, Gerard. 'Against United Europe.' *The Weekly Standard*, 22 September 2003.

Barnett, Roger W. *Asymmetrical Warfare: Today's Challenge to the US Military Power*. Washington, DC: Brassey's, 2003.

Baruah, Amit. 'Guiding Principles on Border Issue Finalized.' *The Hindu*, 11 April 2005.

_____. 'Hu Jimtao for Stepped Up Talks on Boundary,' *The Hindu*, 23 November 2006.

_____. 'Not a Military Alliance, Says Shyman Saran,' *The Hindu*, 12 April 2005.

Bello, Walden. *Dilemmas of Domination: The Unmaking of the American Empire*. London: Zed Books, 2005.

Beschloss, Michael R. *May Day: Eisenhower, Khrushchev and the U-2 Affair*. New York: Harper Row, 1986.

Bijian, Zheng. *Speeches of Zheng Bijian: China's Peaceful Rise, 1997–2005* Washington, DC: Brookings, 2005.

Birsel, Robert (Reuters). 'Afghan Rebels Attack from Pakistan.' *The Washington Post*, 16 May 2005.

Blackwill, Ambassador Robert D. 'The Future of US-Indian Relations.' Text of his speech of 17 July 2003 in New Delhi.

Bose, Sumantra. *Roots of Conflict: Paths to Peace*. Cambridge: Harvard University Press, 2003.

Broadway, Bill. *Washington Post*, 17 September 2000.

Brzezinski, Zbigniew. *The Grand Chessboard: American Primacy and its Geostrategic Imperatives*. New York: Basic Books, 1997.

Bumiller, Elisabeth. 'White House Letter: 21st Century Warnings of Threat Rooted in the 7th.' *The New York Times*, 12 December 2005.

Burke, Jason. *Al-Qaeda Casting a Shadow of Terror*. London: I.B. Tauris, 2003.

Burner, David, Virginia Bernhard and Stanley I. Kutler. *Firsthand America: A History of the United States,* Vol. II. New York: Brandywine Press, 4th Edition, 1996.

Burns, John F. 'Ignoring Risk, Afghan Refugees Rush Home.' *The New York Times*, 29 April 2002.

Caroe, Sir Olaf. *The Pathans*. London: Macmillan and Co., 1958.

Carter, Ashton B. 'America's New Partner.' *Foreign Affairs* (July-August, 2006).

Clancy, Tom with General Zinni (Retd.). *Battle Ready*. New York: G.P. Putnam's Sons, 2003.

Clarke, Richard A., et al. *Defeating the Jihadists*. New York: The Century Foundation Press, 2004.

Clinton, Bill. *My Life*. New York: Alfred A. Knopf, 2004.

Cloud, David S. 'US Helicopter in Afghanistan Down.' *The New York Times*, 27 June 2005.

Cohen, Roger. 'What the World Wants from America.' *The New York Times*, 11 January 2005.

Coll, Steve. *Ghost Wars*. New York: The Penguin Press, 2004.

Constable, Pamela. 'Missile Defence Plan is Unifying US, India: Americans Hint at Possibly Lifting Sanctions.' *Washington Post*, 20 May 2001.

————. 'Pakistani Losing War of Images.' *Washington Post*, 16 September 2000.

Cordesman, Anthony H. *The Lessons of Afghanistan*. Washington, DC: Center for Strategic and International Studies, 2002.

Cowell, Alan. '60 Nations Set 5-Year Goals to Aid Afghanistan.' *The New York Times*, 1 February 2006.

Daalder, Ivo H. and James M. Lindsay. *America Unbound: The Bush Revolution in Foreign Policy.*

Daalder, Ivo, Nicole Gnesotto, and Philip Gordon, editors, *Crescent of Crisis: US−European Strategy for the Greater Middle East.* Washington, DC: Brookings Institution Press, 2006.

Dao, James. 'New Pentagon Report Sees Rapid Build-up by China.' *The New York Times*, 13 July 2002.

Dasgupta, Bhushan. *Jammu and Kashmir.* The Hague: Martinus Nijhoff, 1968.

Daudzai, Ayaz. 'Kashmir: Historic Facts Can't Be Altered.' *The Mirror of the World* (Moscow), 14 May 2005.

Dichter, David. *The North-west Frontier of West Pakistan.* Oxford: Clarendon Press, 1969.

Dietl, Gulshan. 'War, Peace and the Warlords: The Case of Ismail Khan in Heart.' *Journal of South Asian and Middle Eastern Studies*, Vol. 28, No. 3, (2005).

Dixit, J.N. *India-Pakistan in War and Peace.* New York: Routledge, 2002.

Djalili, Mohammad Reza, et al, eds. *Tajikistan: The Trails of Independence.* New York: St. Martin's Press, 1997.

Dupree, Louis. *Afghanistan.* Princeton: Princeton University Press, 1980.

Elshtair, Jean Bethke. *Just War Against Terror: The Burden of American Power in a Violent World.* New York: Basic Books, 2003.

Enoki, Yusukuni. 'The Japan-India New Partnership.' *The Journal of the United Service Institution of India* (July-September 2004).

Ferguson, Niall. *The Rise and the Demise of the British World Order and the Lessons for Global Power.* New York: Basic Books, 2003.

Filkins, Dexter. 'Charm and the West Keep Karzai in Power, For Now.' *The New York Times*, 26 March 2002.

Friedman, George. *America's Secret War.* NY: Doubleday, 2004.

Gall, Carlotta. 'Afghan Delegates Agree on the Need for Foreign Troops.' *The New York Times*, 9 May 2005.

_____. 'Afghan Leader Urges Unity to Build a New Parliament.' *The New York Times*, 16 June 2002.

_____. 'In a Remote Corner, an Afghan Army Evolves from Fantasy to Slightly Ragged Reality.' *The New York Times*, 25 January 2003.

_____. 'Mood of Anxiety Engulfs Afghans as Violence Rises.' *The New York Times*, 30 June 2005.

_____. 'Surrendered Chieftain Urges Taliban to Accept Amnesty.' *The New York Times*, 2 June 2005.

_____. 'Taliban Attack Afghan Officials.' *The New York Times*, 19 June 2005.

_____. 'Taliban Rebels Still Menacing Afghan South.' *The New York Times*, 2 March 2006.

_____. 'The Taliban Truce in Afghan Region: British and Rebels Leave.' *The New York Times*, 30 November 2006.

_____. 'US Training Pakistani Units Fighting al-Qaeda,' *New York Times*, 27 April 2005.

_____. 'After Afghan Battle, A Harder Fight for Peace.' *The New York Times*, 3 October 2006.

Gall, Carlotta and David Rohde. 'Assessing the Afghanistan Elections.' *The New York Times*, 20 October 2004.

Gall, Carlotta and Tom Shanker. 'Commando Saved in Afghanistan.' *The New York Times*, 4 July 2005.

Gibbon, Edward. *The Decline and Fall of the Roman Empire*, Vol. I. New York: Modern Library, n.d.

Gilbert, Tony and Pierre Joris. *Global Interference: The Consistent Pattern of American Foreign Policy*. London: Liberation Press, 1981.

Golotyuk, Yury. 'Made in the USSR.' *Vremya Novostei*, 28 September 2001.

Granieri, Ronald J. 'Allies and Other Strangers: European Integration and the American Empire by Invitation.' *Orbis* (Fall 2006).

Grare, Frédéric. 'Pakistan: The Myth of an Islamic Peril.' *Policy Brief No. 45* Washington, DC: Carnegie Endowment for International Peace, (February 2006).

Griffin, Michael. *Reaping the Whirlwind: Afghanistan, Al-Qaeda and the Holy War*. London: Pluto Press, 2003.

Gupta, Amit. *The Indian Diaspora's Political Efforts*. Bombay: ORF, Occasional Paper, September, 2004.

Haass, Richard N. 'What to Do with American Primacy.' *Foreign Affairs,* (September, 1999).

_____. 'Imperial America.' In a paper delivered at the Atlanta Conference, 11 November 2000.

Habeck, Mary. *Knowing the Enemy: Jihadist Ideology and the War on Terror*. New Haven: Yale University Press, 2006.

Hancock, Jay. 'Vajpayee's Visit Marks Changing Relationship with US, India.' *Baltimore Sun*, 14 September 2000.

Haque, Ihtusham-ul. 'Free Trade Accord with China: High-Performance Aircraft to be Jointly Produced.' *Dawn*, 26 November 2006.

Hardt, Michael and Antonio Negri. *Empire*. Cambridge: Harvard University Press, 2000.

Hathaway, Robert. 'Unfinished Passage: India, Indian Americans and the US Congress,' *The Washington Quarterly* (Spring 2001).

Helmes, Stephen. 'Al-Qaeda, September 11, 2001.' In *Making Sense of Suicide Missions*, edited by Diego Gambetta. Oxford: Oxford University Press, 2005.

Hodson, H.V. *The Great Divide*. New York: Oxford University Press, 1997.

Hudson, Michael. *Super Imperialism*. London: Pluto Press, 2003.

Hussain, Syed Talat. 'Lifting of Sanctions Linked to Democracy.' *Dawn*, 3 August 2001.

Ignatieff, Michael. 'The Burden.' *The New York Times Magazine*, 5 January 2003.

Ickenberry, G. John. *Liberal Order and Imperial Ambition: Essays on American Power and World Politics*. Cambridge: Polity Press, 2006.

Jehl, Douglas. 'Remotely Controlled Craft Part of US-Pakistan Drive Against Al-Qaeda, Ex-Officials Say.' *The New York Times*, 16 May 2005.

Journal of Commerce. 'Lag in Disbursements: World Bank Criticized on LCD's Operations.' *Journal of Commerce* (20 February 1973).

Johnson, Chris and Jolyon Leslie. *Afghanistan: The Mirage of Peace*. London: Zed Books, 2004.

Kagan, Robert. *Of Paradise and Power: America and the New World Order*. New York: Knopf, 2003.

Kapila, Subhash. 'India-Israel Relations: The Imperatives for Enhanced Strategic Cooperation.' *South Asia Analysis Group* Paper No. 131 (8 January 2000).

Kaplan, Robert D. 'The Taliban's Silent Partner.' *The New York Times*, 20 July 2006.

Kapur, Ashok. *Pakistan's Nuclear Development*. London: Croom Helm, 1989.

Karimov, Islam. *Uzbekistan: On the Threshold of the Twentieth Century*. New York: St. Martin's Press, 1998.

Katzman, Kenneth. *Afghanistan: Current Issues and US Policy*. Washington, DC Congressional Research Service, 2004.

Kegley, Jr., Charles W. and Gregory A. Raymond. *After Iraq: The Imperiled American Imperium*. New York: Oxford University Press, 2007.

Kennedy, Paul M. *The Rise and Fall of the Great Powers*. New York: Random House, 1987.

Khan, Javed Aziz. 'Rs. 564 Million Uplift Schemes NWA to Bring Neglected Agency at Par with Developed Parts.' *The News*, 8 April 2005.

Khan, Meikaél. 'Resentment Simmers Among the Tribals.' *The News*, 2 June 2002.

Khan, Munir Ahmad. 'Development and Significance of Pakistan's Nuclear Capability.'
In *Pakistan: Founders' Aspirations and Today's Realities*, edited by Hafeez Malik. Karachi: Oxford University Press, 2001.

Khattak, Muhammad Aslam. *A Pathan Odyssey*. Karachi: Oxford University Press, 2004.

Kissinger, Henry. *Does America Need a Foreign Policy*. New York: Simon and Shuster, 2001.

Klugman, Paul. 'The Chinese Connection.' *The New York Times*, 20 May 2005.

Krauthammer, Charles. 'Past the Apogee: America Under Pressure.' In his keynote address to the Foreign Policy Research Institute. Philadelphia: 14 November 2006.

————. *Democratic Realism: An American Foreign Policy for a Unipolar World*. Washington, DC: The American Enterprise Institute, 2004.

Krutkov, Yevgeny. 'Islam Karimov Accuses Russian Intelligence Services.' *Sevodnya* (Moscow), 2 December 1998.

Kuehner, Trudy J. *The New Perspectives on the Genesis of the US* Philadelphia: Foreign Policy Research Institute, September 2004.

Kurlantzick, Joshua. 'China's Charm: Implications of Chinese Soft Power.' *Policy Brief* Washington, DC: Carnegie Endowment, June 2006.

Lamb, Alastair. *Crisis in Kashmir, 1947-1966*. London: Routledge and Kagan Paul, 1966.

Lancaster, John. 'Indian Leader Urges Close US Ties.' *Washington Post*, 15 September 2000.

————. 'Israel and India Draw Closer.' *The Washington Post*, 11 September 2003.

Lawrance, Bruce, editor, and James Howarth, translator. *Message to the World: The Statements of Osama bin Laden*. London: Verso, 2005.

Lee, Melfang. 'Officials from Washington and Taipei Condemn Beijing's Anti-Separatist Law.' *Taiwan Journal* (18 February 2005).

Lee, Sharon M. 'Asian Americans: Diverse and Growing.' *Population Bulletin* 53 (June 1998).

Maddula, Lt. Commander Srinivas 'Gwadar Project Strategic Setback for India.' In *The Journal of the United Service Institution of India*, 392, 403. New Delhi: July- September 2006.

Madelung, Wilferd. *The Succession to Muhammad: A Study of the Early Caliphate*. Cambridge: Cambridge University Press, 1997.

Maisel, L. Sandy and Ira N. Forman, eds. *Jews in American Politics*. NY: Rowman and Littlefield, 2001.

Malik, Hafeez. *Sir Sayyid Ahmad Khan and Muslim Modernization in India and Pakistan*. New York: Columbia University Press, 1980.

————. *Soviet-Pakistan Relations and Post-Soviet Dynamics*. New York: St. Martin's Press; London: Macmillan, 1996.

Malik, Hafeez, ed., *Central Asia: Its Strategic Importance and Future Prospects*. New York: St. Martin's Press, 1994.

Malik, Hafeez and Nasira Iqbal, translators. *Javid Iqbal: Encounters with Destiny*. Karachi: Oxford University Press, 2006.

Mazari, Shireen M. *The Kargil Conflict, 1999* Islamabad: The Institute of Strategic Studies, 2003.

McDougall, Walter A. *Freedom Just Around the Corner: A New American History 1585-1828*. New York: Harper Collins, 2004.

Mead, Walter Russell. *Power, Terror, Peace and War*. New York: Alfred A. Knopf, 2004.

Meyer, Karl E. 'The Invention of Pakistan: How the British Raj Surrendered.' *World Policy Journal* (Spring 2003).

Mir, Amir. 'Al-Qaeda Camps, Fighters Active in Waziristan: US Pushes Pakistan to Fight.' *South Asian Tribune* (Washington, DC), 3 May 2005.

Mishal, Shaul and Auraham Sela. *The Palestinian Hamas.* New York: Columbia University Press, 2006.

Mishra, Brajesh. National Security Advisor of India at the American Jewish Committee Annual Dinner, 8 May 2003.

Mohammad, Sultan and Somini Sengupta. 'Last Commando is Found, Killed in Afghan Firefight.' *The New York Times*, 12 July 2005.

Mohan, C. Raja. *Crossing the Rubicon: The Shaping of India's New Foreign Policy.* London: Palgrave Macmillan, 2003.

Moon, Parker Thomas. *Imperialism and World Politics.* New York: The Macmillan Company, 1937.

Morgenthau, Hans J. *Politics Among Nations.* New York: Alfred A. Knopf, 1963.

Musharraf, Pervez. *In the Line of Fire: A Memoir.* New York: Simon & Shuster, 2006.

Nayyar, A.H. 'Madrasah Education Frozen in Time.' In *Fifty Years of Pakistan: Education and the States*, edited by Pervez Hoodbhoy, 215-250. Karachi: Oxford University Press, 1998.

Nekhoroshev, Grigory. 'Russia, China and Central Asian Countries Continue to Forge Closer Relations.' *Nezavisimaya Gazeta*, 6 July 2000.

Nester, Wilson R. 'The Far East Ménage à Trois.' In the *Roles of the United States, Russia and China in the New World Order*, edited by Hafeez Malik, 83. London: Macmillan Co., 1997.

Noorani, A. G. 'The Truth about the Lahore Summit,' *Frontline* Vol. 19, Issue 4, 16 February–1 March 2002.

Nordland, Rod and Scot Johnson. 'Pakistan: Secret Hunt, Elusive Prey.' *Newsweek*, 13 May 2002.

Novikov, Aleksei. 'Uzbek to Aid in Afghanistan.' *Novaya Yezhednevnaya Gazata* (Moscow), 15 January 1994.

Nucleonics Week. (5 October 2006).

Odom, William E. and Robert Dujarric. *America's Inadvertent Empire.* New Haven: Yale University Press, 2004.

Onishi, Norimitsu and James Dao. 'Taliban Leaders May be Escaping.' *The New York Times*, 3 January 2002.

Pagdens, Anthony. *Lords of All the World: Ideologies of Empire in Spain, Britain and France 1500-1890.* New Haven, CT: Yale University Press, 1995.

Pape, Robert A. 'Al-Qaeda's Smart Bombs.' *The New York Times*, 9 July 2005.

————. *Dying to Win: The Strategic Logic of Suicide Terrorism.* New York: Random House, 2005.

Parlez, Jane. 'China Emerges as Rival to US in Asian Trade.' *The New York Times*, 27 June 2004.

Peace Watch. 'Afghanistan in the Crosshairs.' *Peace Watch* (Washington, DC: US Institute of Peace, April-May, 2006).

Pennell, T.L. *Among the Wild Tribes of the Afghan Frontier*. London: Steeley and Co., 1909.

Pillar, Paul A. *Terrorism and US Foreign Policy*. Washington, DC: Brookings Institution Press, 2001.

Prybyla, Jan S. 'Is China a Model of Economic Success?' In *The Role of the United States, Russia and China in the New World Order*, edited by Hafeez Malik, 315. London: Macmillan, 1997.

Rashid, Ahmad. 'A New Proxy War: Foreign Powers again Feeding Irons to Factions.' In *Far Eastern Economic Review* (1 February 1996).

_____. 'Talibanization?' *The Nation*, 17 November 1999.

Ravi, N. 'Manmohan Expresses Satisfaction over Talks.' *The Hindu*, 19 July 2005.

Reddy, Muralidhar. 'Islamabad Will Not Accept Discriminatory Treatment.' *The Hindu*, 20 March 2006.

_____. 'Pakistan's Afghan Problem.' *The Hindu*, 13 May 2005.

_____. 'US Ambassador's Statement is Irresponsible, Says Pakistan.' *The Hindu*, 20 June 2005.

Riedel, Bruce. *American Diplomacy and the 1999 Kargil Summit at Blair House*. Philadelphia: Policy Paper Series, 2002.

Risen, James. 'Russians are Back in Afghanistan, Aiding Rebels.' *The New York Times*, 27 July 1998.

Rohde, David. 'Training an Afghan Army that Can Shoot Straight.' *The New York Times*, 6 June 2002.

Rohde, David and James Risen. 'CIA Review Highlights Afghan Leaders' Woes.' *The New York Times*, 5 November 2006.

Rourke, John R., Ralph G. Carter, and Mark A. Boyer. *Making American Foreign Policy*. Guilford, CT: Dushkin Publishing Group, 1994.

Roy, Olivier. *Globalized Islam: The Search for a New Ummah*. New York: Columbia University Press, 2004.

Rubin, Barnett R. *The Fragmentation of Afghanistan*. New Haven: Yale University Press, 1995.

Sanger, David. 'Playing the Trade Card,' *The New York Times*, 17 February 1997.

_____. 'Bush Hails Musharraf and Warns Iraq.' *The New York Times*, 14 February 2002.

_____. 'Musharraf Defends Deal Made with Tribal Leaders,' *The New York Times*, 23 September 2006.

Saunders, Phillip C. *China's Global Activism: Strategy, Drivers, and Tools*. Washington, DC: National Defence University, June 2006.

Schmitt, Eric. 'NATO Troops will Relieve American in Fighting the Taliban.' *The New York Times*, 31 December 2005.

Schumpeter, Joseph. *Imperialism and Social Classes: Two Essays*, translated by Heinz Nerden. New York: Meridian Books, The World Publishing Company, 1955.

Schuzman, Franz. 'Afghanistan's Taliban Rebels Blend Islam and Maoism.' *Jinn Magazine* (San Francisco), 30 September 1996.

Sciolino, Elaine. 'Opinion is Softening on Divided Continent.' *New York Times*, 20 February 2005.

Sengupta, Somini. 'India and China Become Friendlier Rivals.' *The New York Times*, 21 November 2006.

―――. 'India to Seek Expanded Access to US Nuclear Technology.' *The New York Times*, 17 July 2005.

Shah, Sajjad Ali, Chief Justice. *An Autobiography: Law Courts in Glass House*. Karachi: Oxford University Press, 2001.

Shahid, Saleem. 'Gwadar Port Inaugurated: Plan for Second Port in Balochistan at Sonmiani.' *Dawn*, 21 March 2007.

Shanker, Thom and David E. Sanger. 'US Lawmakers Warn Europe on Arms Sales to China.' *The New York Times*, 2 March 2005.

Shenkas, Odel. 'Learning from China's Export Boom.' *Business Week*, 19 January 2006.

Shepherd, W. R. 'The Monroe Doctrine Reconsidered.' *Political Science Quarterly* (March 1924).

Smith, Craig S. 'Russia and China Unite in Criticism of US Antimissile Plan.' *The New York Times*, 19 July 2000.

Srinivasan, T.N. 'Economic Reforms and Global Integration.' In *The India-China Relationship: What the United States Needs to Know*, edited by Francine R. Frankel and Harry Harding, 256. New York: Columbia University Press, 2004.

Sullivan III, Michael J. *American Adventurism Abroad*. Westport: Praeger, 2004.

Suskind, Ron. 'Faith, Certainty and the Presidency of George W. Bush.' *The New York Times Magazine*, 17 October 2004.

Tahir-Kheli, Shirin R. *India, Pakistan and the United States*. New York Council on Foreign Relations, 1997.

Talbott, Strobe. *Dialogue, Democracy and Nuclear Weapons in South Asia*. Washington, DC: Department of State, 1999.

Tirard-Collect, Oliver. 'The Taliban in Afghanistan: A French Approach.' *Middle East Studies Bulletin* (1997).

Tohid, Owais. 'Greed for Money…Not Religious Motivation…' *Newsline* (Karachi), 2 April 2005.

Tucker, Robert W. and David C. Hendrickson. *The Imperial Temptation: The New World Order and America's Purpose*. New York: Council of Foreign Relations, 1992.

Usmani, Maulana Muhammad Zubair Ashraf. 'Ta`mir-i Pakistan Awr Hifaz-i-Islam Key A`iymi Jaddo Jahed Mein Darul Ulam Ka Kirdar,' *Jang: Darul ulam Karachi Kay 50 Sal* (Karachi), 15 February 2000.

Walt, Stephen M. 'Taming American Power.' *Foreign Affairs* (September-October 2005).

Wang, Dong. *China's Unequal Treaties*. Lanham, MD: Lexington Books, 2005.

Washington, DC: The Brookings Institution Press, 2003.

Watts, Jonathan. 'China Shifts from Receiving to Giving Foreign Aid as Economic Boom Continues.' *The Guardian*, 15 December 2004.

Weidenbaum, Murray L. 'Why War is Affordable: The Military's Role in the US Economy.' In *American Government 6/07*. Dubuque: The McGraw Hill Co., 2001.

Weiner, Tim. 'Nuclear Anxiety: In Washington, After an Anguished Phone Call, Clinton Analyzes Pakistan.' *The New York Times*, 29 May 1998.

Weisman, Steven R. 'Europe United is Good, Isn't It?' *The New York Times*, 20 February 2005.

Wiseman, Paul. 'Revived Taliban Waging Full-Blown Insurgency.' *USA Today*, 20 June 2006.

Wisner II, Frank G., Nicholas Platt, Marshall M. Bouton, Dennis Kux and Mahnaz Ispahani. *Afghanistan: Are We Losing the Peace?* New York, NY: Council on Foreign Relations, 2003.

Wolpert, Stanley. *Jinnah of Pakistan*. New York: Oxford University Press, 1984.

Woodward, Bob. *Bush at War*. New York: Simon and Schuster, 2002.

Yardley, Jim and Thom Shankar. 'Chinese Navy Buildup Gives Pentagon New Worries.' *The New York Times*, 8 April 2005.

Zakaria, Fareed. 'The Stakes in Afghanistan.' *Washington Post*, 3 August 2004.

Zehra, Nasim. 'Nawaz Sharif and Kargil,' *The News*, 29 July 2004.

————. 'Was There a Deal that Delhi Went Back on?' *The News*, 27 June 1999.

Zubok, Vladislav. 'Tyranny of the Weak.' *World Policy Journal* IX, 2 (Spring 1992).

GOVERNMENT DOCUMENTS

Ministry of External Affairs, Government of India. Singhvi, L.M., et al. *The Indian Diaspora*. New Delhi: Non-resident Indians and Persons of Indian Origin Division, 27 August 2001.

National Assembly. Aziz Ahmad (Minister of State), *Line of Control*, Statement of 11 December 1972. (An unpublished personal copy).

National Defence University. *The Science of Military Strategy*. In Dennis J. Blasko, 'Observations on Military Modernization and International Influence—An Alternative View.' Washington, DC: National Defence University Seminar, June 2006.

Secretary of Defence, *Military Power of the Peoples Republic of China, 2006*. Washington, DC: 2006.

Senate Committee on Foreign Relations, *Where are US-China Relations Headed?* 107th Congress, 1st Session, 2001, S. Hrg. 107-45.

Speech of President George W. Bush to the Joint Session of Congress, 20 September 2001. See *The New York Times*, 21 September 2001.

Speech of President George W. Bush, 20 January 2005. See *The New York Times*, 21 January 2005.

The 9/11 Report.

The Department of State. *US Aid History*. Washington, DC, June 2003.

US Central Intelligence Agency, *The World Fact Book*, 2005.

US Department of Defence. 'Military Power of the People's Republic of China 2006.' Washington, DC: Department of Defence, 2006. Page one of the Executive Summary. Under the rules of the seminar, I am unable to attribute any statement to the speakers, except the written material which was available.

US Department of State. *Afghanistan Country Report on Human Rights Practices for 1992* (Washington, DC: 30 January 1998).

————. 'Scene Setter on the International Conference on Afghanistan, 31 March–1 April.' Washington, DC, 26 March 2001.

————. *Afghanistan Country Report, 2004*. Washington, DC, 2005.

————. *The United States and Global Coalition Against Terrorism*. Washington, DC, September 2001–December 2003.

US Embassy (Islamabad) cable to the Secretary of State, Cable 06863, 'Afghanistan: Demarche to Taliban on New Bin Laden Threat,' 14 September 1998.

US Foreign Relations (Washington, DC: US Government, 1895).

US Foreign Relations (Washington, DC: US Government, 1905).

World Trade Organization. *Understanding the World Trade Organization*. Geneva: Media Relations Division, 2003.

NEWSPAPERS AND MAGAZINES

Agence France Presse (English dispatches). 2005.
China View. 2005.
Dawn. 1998-2006.
Frontier Post. 1993.
The Daily Telegraph. 2001.
The Economist. 2005.
The Guardian. 2001.
The Hindu. 2001.
The Indian Annual Register. 1947.
The Nation. 1993-1998.
The New York Times. 1998-2006.
The News. 2003-2007.
The Statesman. 2001.
The Washington Post. 2001.
The Washington Times 2002.
Time. 2002.
Wall Street Journal. 2006.

ORGANIZATION PUBLICATIONS

Center for International Policy. 'Major Non-NATO Ally (MNNA) Status.' In *Just the Facts*. Washington, DC: Center for International Policy, 2003.
Human Rights Watch. *Country Summary*. New York: January 2005.
US Indian Political Action Committee. 'About Indian Americans.' In *US Indian Political Action Committee (USINPAC)*.
US Institute of Peace, Special Report, *The Taliban and Afghanistan, Implications for Regional Security and Options for International Action*. Washington, DC: November, 1998.
———. 'Unfinished Business in Afghanistan: Warlordism, Reconstruction and Ethnic Harmony.' US Institute of Peace, Special Report 105. Washington, DC, April 2003.
———. *Special Report: Unfinished Business in Afghanistan*. Washington, DC: US Institute of Peace, April 2003.

INTERNET NEWS

BBC News, 24 May 2001.
'The Movement of the Taliban,' an authoritative statement filed by the Taliban on the internet.

Index